D0290673

AMERICAN CRITICISM

AMERICAN CRITICISM IN THE POSTSTRUCTURALIST AGE

Jonathan Culler

J. Hillis Miller

Gayatri Chakravorty Spivak

René Girard

Murray Krieger

Stanley Fish

Wesley Morris

Gerald Graff.

Barbara Herrnstein Smith

edited by Ira Konigsberg

michigan studies in the humanities

Michigan Studies in the Humanities
Horace H. Rackham School of Graduate Studies

On the cover Jiří Kolář's collage "Venus"

ISBN 0-936534-03-6 (pbk.)

CONTENTS

PREFACE

The debate in contemporary critical theory continues to rage with an intensity that is both encouraging and stimulating. As the title of this volume attests, we are now living in a poststructuralist age. No matter how much or how little of poststructuralism remains with us in the future, with all its diversity of approaches and plurality of meanings, this movement has established the issues debated today and the nature of our critical discourse. The papers in this volume, all part of a symposium in critical theory at the University of Michigan, are published here because they offer an overview of many of the theoretical claims now being contested and because they also offer the opportunity to see these theoretical issues applied to literature itself. Even though a number of the authors represented in this volume strongly question many of the concepts of poststructuralism, their essays prove that scholars and critics, as well as teachers and students, are being forced to reinvestigate basic assumptions about their professional beliefs and practices whether they affirm traditional methodologies or move in the direction of the new. The result can only be a more energetic and profound field of literary study.

I wish to acknowledge here the people who helped so significantly in both the Symposium and in the preparation of this volume. Jay Robinson, the chairman of the English Department at the time of the Symposium, was a constant source of support and sound advice. My colleagues Sandor Goodhart and Michael Clark were indispensable in planning and bringing into reality the various professional and social activities that took place throughout the academic year. The publication of the papers delivered at the Symposium would not have occurred without the encouragement of Ladislav Matejka, who constantly offered help and council with patience and friendliness. I also wish to thank Kimberly Devlin for her help in the preparation of the manuscript for this book.

Ira Konigsberg

INTRODUCTION

The papers collected in this volume were all presented as part of a symposium in critical theory that took place at the University of Michigan during the academic year 1979-1980. Since in many ways the literary affairs of the larger academic community were reflected in the reasons for the Symposium and the reactions of both faculty and students at Michigan to the discourse that continued during the entire year, this collection offers an opportunity to examine the general state of both critical theory and literary study in this country.

By the summer of 1979, it had become clear that critical theory was again in fashion at institutions of higher learning, that it was being taught and even forged by some of the leading humanities departments in this country. Critical theory had already infiltrated the University of Michigan, but in a dispersed manner through a few scholars and teachers in disparate departments. The Departments of English, Slavic Languages, Romance Languages, and Linguistics occasionally offered courses that dealt with some of this material from their own particular perspectives, and the Program in Comparative Literature also gave occasional classes in the new critical theory drawing from the faculty of these various departments. A conference in semiotics had already been held at the University the previous spring and had helped develop a desire among a number of the faculty for a more permanent commitment to the field of critical theory in general. The University was responsive to this desire and granted substantial funds to the English Department for a symposium in critical theory to be held at the University during the coming academic year. The Department was to invite some of the top people in the field who would offer a perspective of the major issues in the current critical debate.

The general intellectual community, then, was enthusiastic about developing the field of critical theory at the University. The members of the Department of English predominantly were not. Those very colleagues who most complain about the intellectual community's refusal of respect for literary study found that community beating on their door, opened it a peep, shuttered and ran back inside. Foremost in this negative reaction, I believe, was a pervading suspicion among a number of colleagues and downright anger in others about the field of critical theory itself, about the very notion that there need by such a field. The argument most often expressed was that we are all critical theoreticians and have some theoretical concept of what we are doing, enough to support our primary task of teaching and writing about literature itself—not teaching and writing about writing about literature. But most of the people questioning the validity of the Symposium had only a very general idea of the issues and writers being discussed, even though the greatest hostility came from some of the most distinguished and well-published members of the English Department's faculty. Perhaps one might surmise that it was the grand scale of the enterprise which alarmed these people; but I do not think that a symposium in critical theory from Plato to I. A. Richards would have provoked such a stir. Nor can I honestly say that these people were any more informed about the subject in May than they were in September, since their resistance to the new critical theory continued throughout the year and was evident in their absence from the lectures.

One cannot imagine teachers and researchers in the sciences, or even the social sciences, absenting themselves from equivalent theoretical lectures in their own disciplines or refusing to familiarize themselves with the latest theoretical approaches to their subject. Yet this attitude among most of the English faculty was certainly no different from that held by many of their peers at other academic institutions. Critical theory has its practitioners and followers, but it has a far larger number of critics and scoffers. One can conceive of all sorts of reasons for this rejection. The impetus for contemporary critical theory and most of its seminal texts travel from the continent, especially France, and there may be a xenophobic reluctance to apply foreign ideas to the literature of one's own language, especially in a nation that, as recently as a century ago, was still involved in assuring itself that it possessed a literature and intellectual life of its own; but these foreign ideas and approaches have by now been fully assimilated into the theoretical discourse of this country. Then there is the complaint of faddism. Structuralism and poststructuralism are trends in critical thought that will eventually give way to new approaches; but the very proponents of these schools of thought admit this fact. Theoretical trends come and go—continuously—and the academic community absorbs what is provocative and significant. Most crucial are the issues that are raised, the questions that are asked about texts and readers, for these are issues and questions that should have a bearing on the way we teach and write about literature. Perhaps one even might confess that these new theoretical approaches emerged in this country in a manner that smacked of elitism, supported by a small coterie that seemed to pride itself in its new learning and that seemed to speak a new critical jargon; but this hardly should be a reason for damning the validity of the ideas that were disseminated and developed. The most likely explanation is that the same reason for the resistance to the "old" New Criticism among scholars and teachers some decades ago is in operation today in the reaction to the new critical theory: it is difficult to have one's own training, skills, and thinking questioned and attacked. We must respond to this anxiety with sympathy, since to be able to write and talk about literature in a meaningful and profound way is the result of decades of thought and growth. No one can find it easy to agree that one's most basic intellectual assumptions are wrong–in many cases this charge is as untrue as it is tactless. The rhetoric of radical intellectual movements if often more violent than it need be. Proponents of recent critical theory at times seem to emphasize what must be discarded. Their true emphasis instead lies with expansion, with complementing and extending the more conservative dialogue that has endured in this country for decades.

The most heartening part of the Symposium was the large number of both graduate and undergraduate students who came to hear the lectures. For years, the English Department has been sponsoring lectures by reputable visiting scholars, but student attendance had always been sparse. The critical-theory lectures attracted crowds, often 200 students along with a number of faculty from various disciplines.

Where did these students come from? A number came from the new courses in critical theory, but these could account for only a small part of the audience. Others who attended undoubtedly were from classes in related disciplines. But most students came from the very courses taught by the antagonists of critical theory in the English Department. These students came because they were at the University to learn, and because they were curious, and because they had not yet entered into a single methodology or approach to literature. They came simply to hear, to understand, and to find out for themselves.

Considering the fact that more and more students are becoming interested in critical theory and considering the resistance of the majority of faculty in English Departments to this subject, one can readily understand the problems that have arisen. In spite of a basic conservatism, many departments are more ready to hire young faculty who have some knowledge of the new theory in addition to a more traditional specialization. Students, then, must to some degree go against the major current of the faculty with which they are studying to prepare themselves extensively enough to meet the challenge of the marketplace. They must also go against the main current of the faculty if they are to satisfy their own intellectual curiosity. But the enterprise is not, I think, disheartening, for their minds are certainly agile and bright enough to learn and understand both the new and the traditional. And must the two approaches be made to seem so separate? The problems debated today in critical theory are not exactly new to the study of literature, though the language and philosophical underpinnings may be. Perhaps once we have appropriated what is useful from the new and assimilated it into the never-ending discourse of literary study, and once theory becomes practice, we can discover that on some basic level we have, after all, every one of us, been engaged in the same intellectual pursuits and concerned with the same issues.

* * *

The papers in this volume are not presented in the order in which they were originally delivered, but have been arranged so that certain arguments can develop more clearly and so that approaches or methodologies can play off one another. The initial paper, Jonathan Culler's "Issues in Contemporary American Critical Debate," provides a clear overview of the present conflicts in literary study, focussing on the major issues argued by apostles of the new critical theory and the guardians of more traditional approaches.

For Culler, the first major issue concerns the task of criticism, an issue generated by the American propensity for "interpretation," which is itself a legacy of the New Criticism. The dominance of the New Criticism has been twofold, either to cause innovative critics to domesticate recent critical approaches to the act of interpretation, or to cause traditional critics to condemn new approaches when they cannot be appropriated in this manner. An interesting example of this appropriation is evident in the way critics have made deconstruction into a means of elucidating the text, even to the extent that deconstruction has become part of the work's meaning. Culler's second issue deals with critical discourse itself, whether it is to be considered a metalanguage which analyzes the object language of the literary text, or whether it is actually another level of literary textuality, sometimes even related to or entrapped by the very text it seeks to analyze. The argument against the second position can also be related to the American need for interpretation, for if critical and literary discourse mesh, the distance and objectivity necessary for interpretation are eliminated. The third issue that Culler confronts also can be related to the problem of interpretation: here he discusses the question of referentiality, "whether literary works tell us truths about the world, whether their function is to represent it, refer to it, make claims about it." Sometimes the need for a text to make statements or our need to interpret becomes so acute that we see the literary work as making pronouncements about other literature or even about itself as literature. The position that Culler defines here argues against literature as an end in itself and is both positivistic and moralistic in nature. The fourth issue that Culler discusses seems to develop from his three previous ones: here he discusses "the problem of the determinacy or indeterminacy of meaning," in many ways the central battlefield in much of the critical debate. Traditional critics argue against the subjectivity unleashed by the new critical methodology, the failure to recognize any consensus of meaning—especially attacked are the subjectivity of reader-response criticism and the free play of deconstructive readings. The argument for a consensus of meaning is, however, in its own way arbitrary and would limit discussion or interpretation to "well-defined boundaries," eliminating what lies beyond these boundaries both within and outside the text. On the other hand, Culler is quick to recognize that reader-response or deconstructive criticism in many instances is deterministic, imposing a certain structure upon the reader in the first case or a particular metaphysical focus on the text in the second.

Culler's final warning, that we be careful not to lose sight of the complexities of these issues, that we not let them be reduced to simplistic polemics in a war for truth and meaning, is a fine introduction to the papers that follow. These essays open up the critical debate through a variety of approaches and respond to such approaches in a manner that is cogent but not finally decisive; indeed, decisiveness is the very element the Symposium sought to avoid. They confront traditionalist positions that Culler outlines—the need for interpretation, objective critical language, referentiality, and determinacy—with great vehemence and sometimes anguish. The real issue, however, that finally emerges from this diversity of opinion may well be whether there is any such predeterminate truth to be found or whether our systems of thought, both inside and outside literary discourse, have led us to the wrong truths. If the latter is the case, then the investigation must focus, at least for a while, on our methodologies and systems of thought.

In his essay "The Ethics of Reading: Vast Gaps and Parting Hours," J. Hillis Miller both reiterates a few of Culler's generalizations about the state of modern criticism and then goes on to demonstrate the applicability as well as the ethical responsibility of the most controversial of the new approaches, "deconstruction," with a poem by George Crabbe. The aim of Miller's essay is to demonstrate that the "openness or 'pluralism' " characteristic of much modern criticism is compatible with "a firm ethical commitment in the teacher-critic"—an especially important argument in light of traditional critics' insistance that they are upholding "humanistic values" in their fight against recent methodologies. Miller is persuasive in stating that much of this fight is the result of a failure to read carefully "the texts of the new methodologies" and a failure to test the theory through interpretation of our literary canon. His choice of Crabbe's poem is somewhat arbitrary—the work is certainly not major—but the randomness of the selection might in itself be a good argument for the applicability of his method in general.

Miller takes Crabbe's opening claim that any life is coherent and continuous and therefore "narratable" in a logical sequential order, with all the links bound together, and he goes on to demonstrate, through his reading of the work, that "the more the storyteller or his protagonist try to fill in all the gaps by a careful retracing, the more they discover that inexplicable gaps remain." We ultimately are left with two differing spatial pictures of the protagonist at the beginning and end of the poem, with no valid explanation of why he "came to differ from himself," indeed with no real explanation of the very events he narrates which are meant finally to connect the two pictures. In claiming that the poem, "almost in spite of itself, deconstructs two of those cherished certainties of humanist literary study, the continuity of the self and the organic continuity of narrative from beginning to middle to end," Miller seeks to place the poem in the context of "western intellectual and literary history" with both its affirmation and "disarticulation" of these assumptions. To verify this point, he briefly discusses similar articulations and disarticulations in both Aristotle's *Poetics* and Sophocles' *Oedipus the King*. Miller's conclusions follow naturally from his demonstrations: each of the camps in the contemporary critical controversy argues for the exclusive influence of one of these "operations of writing and reading which have recurred throughout our history," yet both operations are inherent in the very language of literature. Those modern humanists who find truth, referentiality, propositions, logic, and coherence in the text seek to affirm what the text claims to perform; and those who argue for indeterminacy, self-reflexivity, contradiction, and decentering or deconstruction argue for what the text performs, often in spite of its claims. The true imperative, then, is ultimately linguistic, to which a traditional and limited sense of ethics must give way: "the ethics of reading is the moral necessity to submit . . . to the truth of this linguistic imperative."

Both Miller and Gayatri Spivak are important forces in this country in appropriating the writing of Jacques Derrida for American literary theory and criticism. Derrida's texts are, of course, basically philosophical discourses, and he seeks to expose and unwrite certain philosophical concepts in Western metaphysics; but what both Miller and Spivak have managed to do with their Derridean approaches is to open up the closure placed on texts by traditional interpretation. A certain dogmatism, a certain conventionality, often itself corrupting, a propensity towards partial readings which dismiss the inconvenient elements of a text, have now begun to give way to a critical discourse that is opening up the canon once again and that is forcing us to take heed of the dynamic quality of the language of literature, forcing us to recognize that what exists in our very reading is a struggle for meaning closer to our struggle for understanding the world outside the text than traditional mimetic interpretation allows. Certainly Spivak's essay, "Finding Feminist Readings: Dante--Yeats," is an exciting struggle to break through and recognize the limitations and contradictions in the thought and language of certain texts, especially as these problems relate to gender. For this reason, her essay is perhaps the least assertive, the most difficult to summarize, and the most dramatic in this collection.

Spivak's paper is a paper within a paper (really a paper as part of a paper within a paper), a commentary upon a commentary upon a commentary, which opens itself to the same type of deconstructive reading that she performs upon Dante and Yeats (note the qualifications of her original paper which she makes within the larger paper written three years later). Although Spivak is primarily concerned with feminist readers and the kind of reading they ought to perform upon canonical texts which exhibit "brutal sexism," both male and female readers must perform the same type of deconstructive reading if this new critical approach is to have any true humanistic value. Spivak attempts to bring together both feminist and deconstructive criticism, but the greatest value of her essay is in both broadening the possibilities and defining the applicability of deconstruction.

Her paper first warns against the type of deconstructive reading that frees an author from responsibility for his text by arguing that "the text deconstructs itself"—a methodology which "close[s] rather than complicate[s] discussion." Her own solution, influenced by her reading of Derrida's *Glas,* is for the critic to "write the theoretically impossible historical biography of that very self that is no more than an effect of a structural resistance to irreducable heterogeneity"—and for Spivak that biography must be of the feminist self (which she later suggests is almost an impossibility). In her own paper(s), the feminist self of Spivak responds to the masculine selves of Dante in *La Vita nuova* and to Yeats in *"Ego Dominus Tuus"* as each poet responds to a woman. Both of these writings, Spivak says, have a "*narrative* of self-deconstruction as their scenario; and, curiously enough, woman was often the *means* of this project of the narrative." It is the "reactionary operation" of objectifying, dispersing, or occluding woman that "holds the texts together." Spivak's analysis of these works is clever and intriguing; it is certainly worth the close scrutiny her formidable style requires to see how her deconstructive readings of these texts can bring together and separate autobiography (her own), biography (the poet's), culture, history, language, and literature. Perhaps one might think her open to the charge of marginality, of refusing to confront the central (traditional) themes and ideas of these works, but Spivak succeeds in making this centrality itself dubious. Her quotation from Foucault seems the best defense of her method: "the task is to mark . . . how 'discursive practices are characterized by the delimitation of a field of objects, the definition of a legitimate perspective for the agent of knowledge, and the fixing of norms for the elaboration of concepts and theories.' " But as Spivak claims, "we as readers," with all our "elusive historico-politico-economico-sexual determinations," must "bring the machinery of our reading and judgment" to the " 'minimal idealizations' " within "the shifting and abyssal frame" of the text. "The machinery is to look for identities and differences–to make connections."

To move from the earlier papers to the writing of René Girard may at first seem a movement from a larger theoretical debate to an institution in and of itself. Striking out in what often seem bold and imaginative ways, developing his own anthropology and theory of mimetic desire, Girard is nevertheless part of the contemporary theoretical scene. Though he is not easy to locate, many would like to call him a structuralist who works out the same basic structure of mimetic desire in a host of texts. But Girard denies such a label and even attacks some of the basic tenets of both structuralism and poststructuralism. Consequently, he must remain a significant figure in the ongoing discourse in critical theory, calling under scrutiny some of the claims of other critics but remaining independent of the most influential modes that have helped shape the contemporary critical scene. In his paper "Comedies of Errors: Plautus–Shakespeare–Molière," which appears in this volume, Girard attacks Lévi-Strauss, as the origin of a basic structuralist misconception, that of "binary differentiation." Even when discussing the many twins who appear in mythology, Lévi-Strauss sees them also in the context of differentiation. But for Girard, the point of twins–for example, the twins (or apparent twins) in the plays he discusses throughout his paper–is "the absence of difference." "Otherwise why resort to twins?" Girard attacks a more traditional kind of differentiation in criticism, that which resulted from "the romantic and individualistic revolution" and was used in criticizing such a play as *The Comedy of Errors* for the sameness or lack of individuality in its characters; and he also criticizes a new form of "the differential imperative" based on "the differential nature of language."

If at first Girard seems to be creating his own kind of structure which he claims keeps appearing in our great literature, then it is a structure which constantly seems to be collapsing into itself throughout each work, where the opposition and balance of forces are sucked inward into the sameness or oneness or undifferentiality of a single point of identity, meaning it is finally no structure at all. Girard draws his insight about differentiation and identity from anthropology, Freud, and great literature, and he applies it to plays by Plautus, Shakespeare, and Molière in a way that seems to expand these texts for critical discussion. Certainly Shakespeare's *The Comedy of Errors,* generally considered one of his weaker plays, is given new significance both by Girard's reading and by the way in which he relates the play to Shakespeare's other works in terms of its characters' struggle for differentiation in spite of the overwhelming force which brings them together into a state of identity. What we have is a crisis which results from "a collapse of cultural differences, destroyed by the mimetic reciprocity of competitive and conflictual behavior," the very crisis that is described in Ulysses' famous speech on "degree" ("which means exactly what is meant here by difference") in Shakespeare's *Troilus and Cressida.* Girard brings into his discussion the immediate source of Shakespeare's *Comedy,* Plautus' *The Menechmus Twins,* and also Plautus' *Amphytrion* which both influenced Shakespeare's play and was the direct source for Molière's *Amphytrion.* Girard relates Molière's play to Shakespeare's *Comedy* by observing that "Divine disguise, the supreme contrivance of comedy, amounts to the same thing as the accidental birth of twins. There is no more difference, really, between Amphytrion and Jupiter, than between the twins themselves." For Girard, "Both stories are unusually appropriate to the representation of mimetic desire," and both authors chose their traditional plots for this reason and improve upon their story's capacity for this representation, demonstrating an "amazing insight into the paradoxes of individual and collective behavior."

Unlike Girard, who is unfavorably disposed to the major concepts of recent critical theory, Murray Krieger attempts to mediate between the conventional and innovative, between the New Criticism and post-structuralism specifically, in his paper "An Apology for Poetics." This is no small task since much of the opposition to recent critical theory has been based upon the suppositions of the New Criticism. Krieger does not seek to compromise between these two approaches, nor does he try to reshape them to give the illusion of compatibility. What he argues for is a recognition that both approaches can work simultaneously, that though they are irreconcilable, one does not finally cancel out the other. Krieger's remarks, it seems to me, suggest a dynamic process in our reading of a poem, an interplay between referentiality and closure on the one hand and self-reflexivity and openness on the other—while one level deconstructs the other, it also asserts at least the temporary existence of the other level in the very act of deconstruction. Krieger's essay, like Spivak's, is written in an autobiographical context which gives an urgency to his words; but whereas Spivak's conflicts arise from being both a feminist and literary critic, Krieger's conflicts are the result of being influenced by a formalistic tradition that begins with Aristotle and reaches a kind of culmination with New Criticism and yet being attracted to and feeling the relevance of poststructural concepts and methodologies. What Krieger suggests is "a sophisticated view of language that knows of its metonymic condition and yet generates an internal play among its elements which appears to create a metaphorical identity that exists in the teeth of the principle of difference."

Krieger admits the validity of the principle of difference in all texts, literary and non-literary, but he also distinguishes poetry as having the capacity to create a presence, a reality of its own. Krieger asserts the aesthetic need of the "human imagination" for closure and referentiality, a need, I might add, that common sense and our own instinctive responses to literature tell us exists in spite of all our awareness of differentiality and gaps. This need, Krieger suggests, exists in authors as they write their texts and readers as they read these texts. But, at the same time, we must also be aware of the "paradoxical nature of language" (and here Krieger shows how his New Critical bent *can* mesh with poststructuralism) as it creates both a "self-sufficient presence" and yet remains a system of "transient and empty signifiers." Krieger blends New Criticism, poststructuralism, and also reader-response criticism when he puts the burden on the reader-critic and argues that these "special characteristics" are not so much in the literary work as in "our aesthetic habits of perception," which must recognize the "rather extraordinary activity we are performing in contributing to our own persuasion." In other words, we must allow ourselves to be persuaded by the text of its closure and referentiality at the same time we are aware of our being persuaded in spite of the text's openness and absences.

In his paper "How to Recognize a Poem When You See One," Stanley Fish discusses the activity of reading from a very different perspective than that of Krieger. Like Krieger, he emphasizes the significance of the reader's awareness, but for Fish the reader is basically an aggregate of social and cultural forces, the product of an interpretive community which tells him what to find in the text. In an interesting way, Fish undermines the inherent meaning in texts, their closure and referentiality, as do the poststructuralists; one even can say that the text becomes for Fish a series of signifiers without any immediate signifieds, and that it is readers, acting as products of their interpretive community, who attach the signifieds to the signifiers simply because they already know the kinds of signifieds which are available to them and those that they ought to employ. Certainly there is a strong validity to this argument, and one can apply it further to poststructuralist criticism: critics and students are being taught to see gaps or deconstructive elements in a text, and these are exactly what they find—in any text—just as Fish's students, as described in his paper, were all prepared at a given instant to apply certain established interpretive acts that they had inherited from their own intellectual community.

Fish shows how his students in a most amusing situation were ready to apply the kinds of significances to words and to find the larger structural patterns in the arrangement of those words that they had come to expect from the type of religious poetry they had been reading: "It is not that the presence of poetic qualities compels a certain kind of attention but that the paying of a certain kind of attention results in the emergence of poetic qualities." Fish's readers resemble those depicted in Barthes's *S/Z,* who come to the text with a plurality of codes already in them. For Barthes, however, readers' codes respond to codes already in the text; for Fish, the emphasis is basically on the codes readers bring to the text and with which they make a poem.

Fish's view of interpretation nevertheless does not open the door for the type of subjective reading feared by traditionalist critics. For Fish, subjectivity is not even an issue since "interpretive strategies" are basically "social and conventional." The act of seeing or reading a poem is "limited by the institutions in which we are *already* embedded," and thus our "interpretive strategies . . . are finally not our own." A community of understanding and opinion exists because understanding and opinion are a product of the community and not of the individual. The distinction between "subjective" and "objective" in literary criticism is misleading and prevents us from understanding how the interpretive faculty works. Fish's approach to reading may seem even more deterministic than that of phenomenological critics, and he may seem to avoid the issue of what readers do individually within the framework of an interpretive community; but he discusses the relationship of interpretation and community in a way that is more specific and focussed than Barthes's treatment of the same subject. In spite of our arguments about the plurality of codes and the absence or deferral of meaning, we share a culturally determined understanding of what texts generally mean and how most people respond to a given work. Indeed, even indeterminacy is becoming a shared experience because it is as much a product of the literary community as more traditional literary concepts.

Wesley Morris, in his paper "The Irrepressible Real: Jacques Lacan and Poststructuralism," returns us to the world of poststructuralist criticism with what seems to be a Lacanian reading of a passage from Addie Bundren's meditation in Faulkner's *As I Lay Dying*; but Morris uses this approach to turn poststructuralism upon itself and to develop certain aspects of Lacan, especially his concept of the "real," beyond what Lacan himself allows in his own discourse. Morris begins by developing from Saussure the idea of the arbitrary or " 'problematical' relationship between words and the 'Real,' " and then applies this idea to Addie's linguistic "freeplay" and use of absence, both of which denigrate Anse as a male part of the anatomy and castrate him on a verbal level. Morris then discusses Lacan's ideas of the Imaginary and the Symbolic in such a way that he is able to see "extreme poststructuralists" repressing "the Imaginary along with its focus on the realm of sensual experience." These "radical theorists . . . decompose the empirical into the absolute freeplay of the Symbolic, much as Addie playfully decomposes the image of the biological, bodily Anse into mere sound." This is the key point for Morris, since "Lacan's third realm, the Real . . . is defined by the problematical relationship between the Symbolic and the Imaginary. That is to say, the Real is that interface between Language as a differential system and the experiential world of the images of things." Morris confesses that for Lacan "Language as Symbolic Order has only an asymptotic relationship to material reality," but Morris argues that language "cannot free itself from that ground." In this context, we are better able to understand Addie's use of language as "her primary weapon"—"Addie's power play is logocentric"—not merely in the analyzed passage but throughout the book, after her death. For Morris, "The lesson of Addie Bundren is: one cannot close off the real world, the image-ing of experience. . . ." At this point in his essay, Morris uses this literary example to launch an attack against what he considers to be radical poststructuralists with their emphasis on "freeplay" and their "rejection of any suggestion of the Lacanian Real."

In the last part of his paper, Morris relates Addie, with her logocentrism, and Faulkner himself to the "masculine fantasy/nightmare of the Oedipal Age," which sees women as "castrated and castrating" and expresses the ideal of female wholeness, with its "postponed gratification." For Morris, this Freudian "myth is exposed in Lacan's definition of the Symbolic, since the Ideal whole is not a biological but a social, a linguistic fact." We have seen how Morris himself freeplays with Lacan, and at this point he seems to justify himself when he argues that even Lacan "is caught in this schema" since he marks the "entry into the Symbolic Order . . . by a crossing of the bar of repression, that socially-placed bar which protects the ego from its unconscious desires." Morris then states that "To some extent this argues that the very basis of Language is in metaphor, in the Ideal of wholeness . . . ," and cites "Derrida's accusation that Lacan's theory is logocentric"—indeed, that it is actually "phallogocentric." Towards his conclusion, Morris says that "To repress the problematical real castrates the Symbolic Order, leaving a substantial gap in the fabric of language." Of course the real is always problematic, in Lacan and in Morris, but Morris has opened up the perimeters of discussion and he has done so in a way that does not avoid the issues raised by poststructuralism and Lacanian psychoanalysis.

Whereas Morris uses poststructuralist concepts to attack poststructuralist excesses in his paper, Gerald Graff, who is one of the most articulate critics of many of the attitudes and dogmas expressed in the new theory, continues to make his arguments in a straightforward way that is captivating by the sheer common sense his method seems to convey. Graff's paper in this collection, "Literature as Assertions," should be seen as part of the dialogue that was carried on throughout the Symposium; indeed, one should match it up against the first paper in this collection, written by Jonathan Culler, whom Graff addresses in his talk.

Graff is actually attacking a position held by a line of theorists whom he claims begins with Kant, but the position in general is also assigned to many of the critics working in the new theory. Graff clearly articulates the position he attacks: "propositions stated or implied in literary works, even those which appear to make general claims about human experience, are not meant to be taken as serious assertions. Literary propositions do not make the kind of truth-claims, it is said, for which they might be liable if they occurred in non-literary forms of discourse." Graff argues that "anti-assertionists" often make this claim because they do not want to see "literature . . . degraded to the purely utilitarian level to which a practical and commercial society reduces all objects." Perhaps his most impressive point against this position comes midway in the paper when he claims "that literature differentiates itself from other modes not by refraining from assertion but by making a stronger, more universalizable kind of assertion, that it is *hyper*-assertive rather than non-assertive." Graff develops this point by arguing that conversations in literature are expected "to illustrate some point," while those in real life have no such "rhetorical purpose." In general, we see literature as having the potential for significance (even though all literature does not fulfill such potential), and this is an expectation we bring to virtually every text we read. Graff further argues that when "thematic assertions become complex, ambiguous, contradictory, plural, and even indeterminate, they do not cease to be assertions." Of course, the particular period and culture in which the work is written and the literary conventions of the time will determine how explicit such assertions will be. Graff makes his appeal to the experience of actual readers, and, drawing upon material from E. D. Hirsch and Teun A. Van Dijk, argues that "it is through propositional understanding that the dramatic materials of literary works are retained in memory and are made intelligible."

Graff cites an argument he has made elsewhere: that the anti-assertionist position has gained strength through a significant number of literary texts which themselves seek to frustrate efforts to reduce them to assertions but which do make assertions with their "anti-assertionist stance." His final and most challenging statement, one he has also developed elsewhere and one which relates to the ethics of reading discussed earlier in the volume by Miller, confronts an issue which must be further debated if much of the new critical theory is to have any lasting effect: "the link between literary works and the real world is through the assertions advanced or presupposed in the work. If literary works make no assertions, then they are trivial, and it is difficult to understand why so much time, effort, and attention has been expended on them." One of the questions this statement raises is what we finally do with assertions which the author may intend to be applied to the real world, but which we, as readers, cannot apply to our reality because of our own value systems or culture. Few modern readers of Dostoyevski, for example, can accept his religious assertions, yet there is a willing suspension of disbelief when we read his novels and accept his fictional universe wholesale (though we know it is not ours); nor do many readers accept the various cosmological assertions expressed in *Moby-Dick* as valid in their own world, though we do not hesitate to step into Melville's universe, white whale and all, while we are reading. The answer to this problem might be in some sort of experimental application of assertions to the world we inhabit. Though we finally disregard these assertions in respect to our own reality, we may accept them in a fictional context which would yet reflect the real world in both its ontological and psychological ranges. Or the answer may be in a simple act of faith, faith which allows us to reshape in our imaginations the real world into something between fantasy and fact, a literary world sharing the malleability of the first and reality of the second.

The final paper in this collection, Barbara Herrnstein Smith's "Narrative Versions, Narrative Theories," launches an attack on three popular concepts in contemporary theory of narrative: (1) that some sort of basic story, deep structure, or originary version exists for various kinds of narratives; (2) that a significant disparity exists between what Seymour Chatman calls "discourse-time" and "story-time," between the time it takes to read a story and the actual duration of the events of the narration; and (3) that a significant disparity also exists between the order in which events are narrated and the order in which they supposedly occurred. The last two concepts, both of them temporal, are used by theorists to argue for the "double-leveled model of narrative structure" of concept one. Smith's major arguments in response to these concepts is that any narration must be seen as "the verbal acts of particular narrators performed in response to . . . sets of multiple interacting conditions."

Smith does not mention Lévi-Strauss in her discussion of the first concept since her distinction between "deep structure" and "surface manifestation" (which she takes from Chatman) is concerned with the distinction between a basic story and its narrative version; but her comments are interesting to compare to the French anthropologist's assumptions and even methodology. Smith argues against the notion of an ideal Platonic form for any narrative or group of related narratives. Although this notion has been attributed to Lévi-Strauss, his analysis of myths shows him in agreement with Smith, since he works in terms of basic universal oppositions and tensions underlying a group of related myths and culture's attempt to construct within these mythic narratives some form of mediation between such forces. For Lévi-Strauss, *this* is the work's deep structure. But, interestingly, Smith's statement that any deep-plot structure is itself a retelling "by someone in particular, on some occasion, for some purpose, and in accord with some relevant set of principles," is a point one can make about Lévi-Strauss's structuring, which at times seems highly individual and the result of his own professional context and interests. Smith's remarks on this subject in relation to her own notion of "deep structure" are worth following a little further: "no narrative version can be independent of a particular teller and occasion of telling and, therefore . . . we may assume that every narrative version has been constructed in accord with some set of purposes or interests." For this reason, as well as others, "there is no single *basically* basic story subsisting beneath [any particular narrative] but, rather, an unlimited number of other narratives that can be *constructed in response* to it or *perceived as related* to it"—a statement which seems well supported in this essay by the example of folklorists' futile search for basic or originary versions of such well-known tales as *Cinderella*.

Smith believes that critical concern with temporal disparity between discourse-time and story-time is in part the result of early Formalist theory and in part the result of a mistaken expectation for temporal conformity or parallelism as the norm; this expectation is itself the product of seeing discourse "as consisting of sets of discrete signs which, in some way, *correspond to* . . . sets of discrete and specific ideas, objects, or events." The answer to these mistaken notions is a concept of language which sees utterances "as *acts* which, like any acts, are *performed in response to various sets of conditions.*" In this way, individual narratives could be seen "as the verbal acts of particular narrators performed in response to—and thus shaped and constrained by—sets of multiple interacting conditions" (conditions such as context, setting, the readers or listeners addressed, and the psychological variables of the narrator). Smith thus confronts a conflict developed in the pages of this volume, that between referentiality and pure textuality, and she further argues that the kind of study she suggests would diffuse the issue of the correspondence between language and the world since "the formal properties of an individual narrative would be regarded as *functions of all these multiple interacting conditions* rather than as *representations of specific, discrete objects, events, or ideas. . . .*"

In arguing against concepts that we now think of in terms of *sujet* and *fabula*, Smith, without stating that she is doing so, goes against a significant part of reader-response criticism, especially important elements in Ingarden's and Iser's phenomenological criticism. For her it is almost impossible to have straight chronological narration, and she doubts that even in a time-twisted narrative exists such a "prior and independent set and sequence of events." Like the phenomenologists, she states that much of our knowledge of earlier events "is usually *not* narrative in structure or given in storylike sequences: on the contrary, that knowledge is most likely to be in the form of general and imprecise recollections." But where she differs with the phenomenologists is in keeping this information in a scattered and not fully reconstructed form, as "variable inferences and constructs . . . that constitute our characteristic cognitive *responses* to narrative." Often readers have no reason "to arrest, stabilize, or verbally articulate this set of responses," and when they do, the amount of specificity of reconstituting depends on their role as reader or listener. Smith then states that reconstituting takes place to various degrees, depending frequently on the intentions of the narrator.

But for Smith concepts such as "dual time orders and underlying plot structures in describing and explaining the phenomena of narrative temporality" would be unnecessary if narrative were seen as a verbal act—as "*someone telling someone else that something happened.*" Such an approach "makes explicit the relation of narrative discourse to other forms of discourse and, thereby, to verbal, symbolic, and social behavior generally." Such an approach also opens up "the *particular* motives and interests of narrators and audiences and . . . the *particular* social and circumstantial conditions that elicit and constrain the behavior of each of them."

Smith's discussion suggests, then, two ways we could apply her general approach to issues discussed in a number of papers in this volume: (1) the " 'truth value' " of fictional propositions could be "reformulated in terms of . . . verbal transactions"; and (2) "narrative transactions" (and transformations) could also be understood in the context of verbal communication. I do not think that the first issue would either be solved or even deflected with this approach—we would still have the problem of referentiality in relation to speaker and listener and within the speaker's discourse—but certainly referentiality could now be seen in a more concrete and definite context. And certainly narrative transactions would still exist and have to be understood within the narrating itself; but again we might comprehend them more accurately by seeing them as part of the act of communication, of narrative discourse itself.

Smith's paper, like all the papers in this collection, posits no final answers or solutions—if final answers or solutions were possible, literary discourse would be superfluous—but it does open up the debate and give us further ways of trying to understand both the text and our responses to the text. What I believe is most exciting about the papers in this collection and the critical debate which today rages with such heat is the engagement and involvement they offer us all. I do not wish to go so far as to suggest that critical discourse should exist as an end in itself—its major purpose must continue to be the investigation of great works of literature. But our understanding of the nature of great literature must grow as cultures change, as various disciplines develop and offer us new insights into texts, and as the demands of our own age make new demands on our canon. Not only does critical discourse allow this adaptation of the text and thereby extend the reach of even our most powerful works, but in itself it offers us the experience of actively engaging in the formulation of ideas about literature, about the canon and the ways we respond to the canon. By allowing us to formulate ideas concerning the ways we respond to literature, critical theory helps us to formulate ideas not just about ourselves, but also about the mind itself, about mental responses to reality and to the transformations of this reality into text. The very questions of why and how we read and how we interpret or respond to the language of literature are part of the larger issues of epistemology and self-knowledge.

ISSUES IN CONTEMPORARY AMERICAN CRITICAL DEBATE*

Jonathan Culler

The invitation to participate in this series of lectures asked me to address the question of "The Critical Act." The four issues I propose to discuss do all bear upon this topic, but let me start with the topic itself: what is the critical act? If someone asked you what was meant by "the critical act," you would doubtless reply that it is what the critic does when he or she interprets a work of literature. This common reply involves an important assumption about literary criticism: that the task of criticism is to interpret.

1. This is the first issue: the task of criticism. Before the days of New Criticism no one would have taken it for granted that the critic's task was to produce new interpretations. Literary studies comprised a variety of activities–philology, literary history, textual criticism, literary biography, study of sources and influences, none of which was primarily directed toward interpretation; but New Criticism changed that, calling everyone to justify themselves and establishing a single standard of justification: these activities are of interest insofar as they contribute to interpretation. I, who grew up in the age of New Criticism, find myself assuming, for example, that the work of establishing a text is of interest only if it gives rise to new interpretations–an assumption that would shock any true textual scholar, whose goal is not new interpretations but authoritative establishment of an original text.

New Criticism so imbued us with the notion that all writing about literature is to be judged by its contribution to interpretation that we find it hard to conceive of other tasks or goals. Even those who themselves practice other kinds of writing pay homage to this standard. For example, Wayne Booth, who has spent his career investigating problems of narrative theory, has just published a large polemical work of literary theory entitled *Critical Understanding,* in which he apologizes for the sort of enterprise in which he is engaged. "Who would really want," he complains in his preface, "to write a long book of what current jargon might well call meta-meta-meta-criticism?"[1] This question reveals Booth's unquestioned assumption that the proper task of criticism is interpreting literary works. Non-interpretive studies are marginal though sometimes interesting; they ask what he calls "improper questions," but nevertheless may have a certain utility (this is the category into which *The Rhetoric of Fiction* and *The Rhetoric of Irony* would presumably fall). Writing about criticism is a distinctly poor third, parasitic and irrelevant. It is bizarre when someone as honest and lucid as Booth finds that his basic assumptions devalue the activity in which he is engaged—bizarre but not uncommon. American critics who have not been influenced by the continental tradition always apologize in the preface of a theoretical work for writing criticism of criticism. They assume that the critical act ought to be an act of interpreting a literary work, even though they find themselves led, for a variety of reasons, to undertake other projects which their presuppositions make it hard to justify.

This assumption has played a large role in determining the American reception of various critical developments. To the extent that they can be seen as methods of interpretation, they are treated as important--welcomed or combatted; to the extent that they can't, they are ignored. Thus, Hans Robert Jauss's admirable and ambitious *Rezeptionsästhetik,* with its attempt to work out the horizon of expectations against which works appeared, has attracted little attention, whereas its modest phenomenological adaptation, Wolfgang Iser's interpretations of English novels in terms of the reader's role in supplementing indeterminacies, has been welcomed and debated. Or consider deconstruction. I think that it is because it easily becomes a method of interpretation that deconstruction has succeeded in America in a way that, for example, Marxism and structuralism never have. Marxism is committed to the immense and difficult project of working out the processes of mediation between base and superstructure. When enlisted to interpret a particular work, it is bound to seem, as we say, vulgar. Structuralism is also committed to large scale projects, such as elaborating a grammar of

1. Wayne Booth, *Critical Understanding* (Chicago: University of Chicago Press, 1979), p. xii.

plot structure or the possible relations between story and discourse. Except in a few cases, these projects have not been taken up in America and structuralism has served the academy primarily as a set of categories which are "applied" in the analysis of literary works.

The power of the assumption that the task of criticism is to interpret literary works can be seen in the way various theoretical projects have been transformed into "approaches" or techniques of interpretation. Northrop Frye's poetics became myth criticism. More recently, deconstruction has been adapted to American purposes, taken up by old New Critics as a new mode of interpretation based on the insight that the language of poetry is the language of paradox. But it is not clear that Derrida's writings are in fact interpretations in any traditional sense. His treatment of Rousseau in *Of Grammatology*, for example, is part of an investigation of the place of writing in Western discussions of language and in particular of the way an idealized model of language has been preserved by attributing to writing certain problematical features of language and then setting writing aside as secondary and derivative. Derrida notes that certain key terms which Rousseau uses to describe writing, the noun *supplêment* and the verb *supplêer*, are used in discussing various other phenomena, and in following up these references in fictional, autobiographical, and expository texts, Derrida describes what he calls the logic of supplementarity, a general operation which we can now see at work in the most diverse texts. It is not by any means clear that Derrida has produced an interpretation of Rousseau; if it *were* an interpretation, it could be criticized on the grounds that it leaves out most of the contents of nearly every text he mentions. Derrida does not identify the thematic unity and distinctive meaning of any text but rather describes a general process through which texts undermine or reveal the rhetorical nature of the philosophical system to which they adhere.

This process of deconstruction often dispenses with deference to the text, for which it is criticized by those who assume that the goal of criticism must be to elucidate the meaning of a work and who thus argue that the critic ought to defer to the authority of what he is elucidating. But this absence of deference may be, precisely, a sign that Derrida is not engaged in elucidating what a text says. If he is rather investigating an uncanny logic that operates in texts whatever they say, then absence of deference might be precisely the right posture. Derrida's characteristic focus on the apparently marginal moments of a discourse and his weaving together of various textual strands to produce a signifying structure suggest that his writing works not to interpret a text but to identify a peculiar logic that energizes texts of very different sorts.

But when deconstruction comes to America a shift takes place, subtly inaugurated in Paul de Man's critique of Derrida in *Blindness and Insight,* which argues that Rousseau's text already carries out the deconstructive operations which Derrida claims to perform on it, so that Derrida *is* in fact elucidating Rousseau, though he claims to be doing something else because—as De Man puts it—it makes a better story. This displacement has since been transformed into a central methodological principle by J. Hillis Miller, who argues not just that the text already contains or performs the operation of self-deconstruction, in which a line of argument undermines the principles on which it is based, but that this undecidability "is always thematized in the text in the form of meta-linguistic statements."[2] In other words, the text does not just contain or perform a self-deconstruction but is about self-deconstruction, has it as a theme. Thus a deconstructive reading is an elucidation of what the text means. "Great works of Literature," Miller insists, "have anticipated explicitly any deconstruction the critic can achieve." Deconstruction, by these lights, does no more than bring out a meaning explicitly anticipated by the text; it is a special sort of faithful elucidation.

This assimilation of deconstruction, making it a form of interpretation, illustrates another aspect of this first issue, the task of criticism. The assumption that criticism must interpret is ultimately responsible, I believe, for a lot of the anger that contemporary criticism has generated. If we assume that the task of the critic is to tell us what the work means, then we will take anything the critic says about the work as a statement about its meaning. As my quotation from Miller shows, the critic is tempted to move from the discovery of a self-deconstructive movement in the work to an assertion that the work is about self-deconstruction. The critic is tempted to make this move by the prevailing assumption that any discovery about a work is of value only if it leads to a new interpretation, that a new interpretation is the payoff. But this is a very dubious assumption. No linguist would assume that

2. J. Hillis Miller, "Deconstructing the Deconstructors," *Diacritics* 5:2 (summer 1975), p. 31.

progress in describing the grammar of English should lead to new claims about the meaning of English sentences, nor would it occur to him to claim that sentences which manifest a particular semantic operation are *about* these semantic operations. Of course, in many cases there are good reasons for treating literary works as about their own structures and operations, but to take this connection for granted and to assume that every discovery about structure must be a discovery about meaning has unfortunate consequences. Whenever someone proclaims a discovery about the structure of a work and its relation to other discourses, there is the suggestion—because of our assumption about the task of criticism—that readers who have not seen this have been experiencing the wrong meanings all along. So Hillis Miller's investigations provoke the anger of many readers who have not read these texts as about self-deconstruction.

If we did not swiftly assume that critical statements about a work should be statements of its meaning, then we might avoid much of this pointless anger and see that there is no reason why new discussions of the structure of a work need imply that previous readers' experiences of it were wrong. For example, it seems to me that it would be quite plausible to claim that readers ought to think of characters in novels as people, while critics investigating the structure of novels must refrain from doing so. The most intense and satisfying reading experiences may depend upon what we call involvement with characters, but successful critical investigation of the structure and effects of a novel, as a literary construct, may require thinking of characters as sets of predicates grouped under proper names. Criticism advances by becoming increasingly formalistic, just as linguistics does. No one accuses linguistics of emptying language of all value by treating it as a formal system, but people accuse critics of emptying literature of its content by treating it as a system; they make this accusation because of the assumption that whatever critics write about a work is a statement of its meaning, the meaning it should have for readers. If we could suspend this assumption the situation of criticism and the pertinance of critical debate might be greatly enhanced.

One reason why there has not been perspicuous debate on this issue of interpretation and the task of criticism is that those who have championed non-interpretive projects have frequently themselves yielded to the temptations of interpretation, thus suggesting that it is indeed the payoff, the ultimate purpose of all writing about literature.

In *Critique et vérité* Roland Barthes distinguished clearly between *criticism*, which would assign meaning to works, and what he called a science of literature, interested in the conditions of meaning. "Ces deux discours," he wrote, "ne doivent être en aucun cas confondus, car ils n'ont ni le même object, ni les mêmes sanctions."[3] Yet in *S/Z*, which claims to describe the codes and hence the conditions of meaning of a *texte lisible*, Barthes ends by privileging one code, the symbolic, and producing a new and quite radical interpretation of *Sarrasine*. His own procedure confuses what he said should not be confused and feeds the assumption that the point of any form of literary study is to produce new interpretations.

American reader-response criticism is also afflicted with confusion on this point, as it simultaneously claims to describe how readers experience a work and to offer a new interpretation. Stanley Fish tried for some time to sustain both these claims—that he was describing how readers actually read and that he was offering a new reading—but the tension is most marked in Michael Riffaterre's new book, *Semiotics of Poetry*. Riffaterre claims to describe not how a few supremely erudite readers like himself read, but how all readers must read: the reader "is under strict control and guidance as he fills the gaps and solves the puzzle."[4] Yet Riffaterre loves nothing better than mocking the interpretations of previous critics and claiming to have solved a puzzle that has baffled previous readers.

Critical argument would be more productive, I believe, if critics observed the distinction between hermeneutics and semiotics. A lot of confusion might be avoided. But above all, what we need is to recognize the possibility and necessity of projects other than the attempt to produce new interpretations.

2. The second issue I would like to raise can be called for short the question of metalanguage: the question of the relation between the literary work and critical discourse.

In general, criticism relies on the assumption that its discourse is *about* literary language but not part of it: that critical discourse is a metalanguage which describes, interprets, and judges an object language,

3. Roland Barthes, *Critique et vérité* (Paris: Seuil, 1965), p. 56.

4. Michael Riffaterre, *Semiotics of Poetry* (Bloomington: Indiana University Press, 1978), p. 165.

and that between it and its object there is a difference in level which is also a difference in kind. For the New Criticism literature consists of pseudo-statements but critical discourse consists of real statements about pseudo-statements. For structuralism and semiotics and other systematic projects, the task is to construct a theoretically grounded, rigorous, explicit metalanguage that would describe the playful, evasive, paradoxical discourse of literature. But the rhetorical exuberance, the *literariness,* shall we say, of certain terminological proliferations, has led to the suspicion that the metalanguage might not be so different from literary discourse after all, that it too was a form of writing that shared many of the qualities of what it was supposed to analyze. In some circles this has now become the orthodoxy. In Lacan's lapidary, metalinguistic formula, "il n'y a pas de métalangage." A discourse proposed as metalanguage is in fact more language, governed by similar processes and mechanisms.

This questioning of the distinction between language and metalanguage takes various forms in recent American criticism. Let me quickly mention three: first, Harold Bloom's claim that poetry and criticism are both acts of misreading, misappropriation. Here criticism is not a metalinguistic statement produced from a position outside the process of poetic production but a continuation of the process of "misprision." Second, various critics—Geoffrey Hartman, Cary Nelson, and Ihab Hassan for example—have emphasized the literariness of the critical essay: criticism is essentially a literary genre and should not refrain from word play; it should exploit the literary resources of its language instead of pretending to be language of a different order. This is a "let it all hang out" school. "I must pun as I must sneeze," Hartman declares.[5] Third, other critics in the orbit of deconstruction or psychoanalysis, such as Paul de Man, Shoshana Felman, and Barbara Johnson, have emphasized not the creative freedom of the critics but rather the way in which they are trapped by the discourse they claim to be analyzing; instead of standing outside it, judging it, and interpreting it, they end up repeating in a displaced way the drama they claim to dominate. This third account, to me the most convincing, shares with the others the argument that the critical text repeats the operations of the discourse it claims to be describing. What is particular to this

5. Geoffrey Hartman, "Monsieur Texte: Epiphony in Echoland," *Georgia Review* 30:1 (spring 1976), p. 191.

account is the emphasis on the way in which critics are caught up in a tropological or figurative process at the very moment when they claim to be undoing figures, deciphering tropes in a non-figurative language. The argument here is similar to the psychoanalytic account of transference: the truth of the patient's condition is revealed not by the analytical discourse of the analyst (not by some metalinguistic statement of a master) but by the process of transference and countertransference through which the analyst gets caught up in a repetition (which he does not control) of the patient's drama. The structure of the drama is revealed by its repetition. Similarly, we discover decisive dimensions of the text by the way in which its logic uncannily reproduces itself in the critic's discourse.

There are thus good reasons to question the notion of criticism as metalanguage, but the situation is complicated by another factor. If criticism is metalinguistic in that it is about literature, what follows from the fact that literature too is often about literature. Literature too is often metalinguistic, citing and commenting on other texts, and on itself. It is a rare novel that fails to include remarks about the novel or discussions of its own procedures and, in particular, metalinguistic judgments and interpretations of its own plot and characters. The situation is thus rather complicated. On the one hand, the more literature talks about literature, the more the distinction between literature and criticism becomes problematic. But on the other hand, and this is important, it is precisely the authority of metalinguistic discourse within literary texts that justifies the authority of critical discourse. Critics never feel more secure in their judgments and interpretations, never feel more secure in their metalinguistic position, than when they can quote, from the text they are studying, passages that comment metalinguistically on it and say the same things about the work or about literary language that the critic wants to say. In the sentences of Hillis Miller's that I quoted earlier, Miller feels confirmed in his metalinguistic comments on undecidability by the fact that, as he put it, undecidability "is thematized in the text in the form of metalinguistic statements." Critics feel most solidly established in their metalinguistic critical position when they are discussing a work that itself contains an apparently solid, authorized, metalinguistic commentary. When there is an authoritative narrator who comments on the language of the characters and events of the novel, the critic can adopt and prolong this metalinguistic discourse; but when dealing with a work like *Finnegans Wake,* where there is apparently no authoritative metalanguage, or an ironic work where any discourse is open to doubt, the critic will feel more uneasy, as if he were just adding another voice to the polyphony of voices. He lacks assurances that he is indeed in a metalinguistic position, above and outside the voices of the text.

But this is a very paradoxical situation. The critic feels securely outside the text when his discourse is further development of a discourse represented and authorized in the text. And it is when his discourse doesn't correspond to an authoritative discourse in the text that he wonders whether his discourse is truly outside or inside the text.

This has various consequences: the notion of a metalanguage seems most solidly justified when there is a metalanguage within the literary work, but then the distinction between metalanguage and object language is not a distinction between criticism and literature. Indeed, it undermines that distinction, making the critical discourse just more of a discourse than already exists in its most authoritative form within the work. But on the other hand, if the best examples of metalinguistic statements appear *within* the literary work, then the notion of metalanguage itself is open to question, in that this supposedly superior discourse is part of the work and can always be read as such. We can treat the narrator as a sort of character whose statements are as much open to question as those of other characters. They can never be statements about the work as a whole since they are in the work. Indeed, a great deal of modern criticism has consisted of readings that question the authority previously granted to metalinguistic statements within works. We have learned that we need not believe a text when it tells us just what it means or how it functions.

I conclude from this—a most lame and impotent conclusion—that the distinction between metalanguage and object language is an essential feature of discourse but that it is highly unstable and confers no authority. Critical discourse positions itself metalinguistically, speaking about a text or group of texts, claiming a perspective on them that they do not have on themselves, but the claim to this outside perspective is always open to doubt. Others can usually show that the critic's claim to be outside is a delusion and that the position is already sketched in one way or another, enacted, even ironized, in the work itself.

Indeed, the best argument that criticism is not metalanguage comes from critics' dealing with one another. We are skilled at showing that other critics are not really in control of their discourse, that their descriptive categories are in fact rhetorical constructs that unconsciously reintroduce, for example, distinctions they claim to reject, or enact in some displaced way a literary scenario. We are skilled at reading the criticism of others as a literary, rhetorical, if not pathological discourse. Just as we can always show that the discourse of someone analyzing his own society is in some way the product of that society and that the claim to stand outside and judge it is in fact a way of acting within it, so we can show that criticism is structured by and suffused with those textual forces it claims to master.

But as I say, though the distinction between object language and metalanguage is unstable and what was thought to be the one can be seen as the other, it is still very important, and those who attempt to scrap the distinction risk depriving their discourse of all purchase. To accentuate the "literariness" of one's critical writing solves no problem at all, nor does it make one master of the situation. One's attempted literary effects may succeed or may fall flat; unless they entice the reader they will fail of effect since they lack the discursive leverage provided by metalinguistic claims. Harold Bloom is much more powerful and convincing when he claims to be analyzing poetry (writing metalinguistically) than when he tells the same stories in a science fiction novel *(Flight to Lucifer)*. His theory may deny the distinction between critical and literary writing and claim that all criticism is prose poetry, but the metalinguistic situation of his discussions of poems leads the reader to engage with them in a way that makes them more productive than his comparable fictional statements. The metalinguistic situation of criticism is important, though the authority of that position is always problematic.

3. A third issue, recently brought to the fore by Gerald Graff in *Literature against itself,* I am inclined to call the problem of referentiality, but there is a terminological problem here. Graff tends to talk interchangeably about the non-mimetic, the non-propositional, the fictional, and the non-referential. In any thorough discussion these would have to be distinguished, but the major issue seems to be whether literary works tell us truths about the world, whether their function is to represent it, refer to it, make claims about it. Once, Graff complains, plot and character were fictional but ideas and themes were real; literature had something to say about the world. Now it is fashionable for critics to claim that ideas themselves are fictions and that literature is only

about itself, and this, for Graff and others, destroys the *raison d'être* of literature and literary studies.

Whether or not that is so, Graff is right in his claim that critics who may proclaim the non-referentiality or self-referentiality of literary works usually end up by drawing from them some proposition, in particular propositions about the nature of language, literature, or representation. But the reason this is so is that critics generally interpret, and interpretation necessarily involves a positing of reference; to interpret is to treat the work as reflecting on or pronouncing on something, even if that something be language, or other literary works, or itself. Interpretation necessarily makes the work a source of propositions of some sort.

Why, then, do theories deny the propositionality or referentiality of literary works? The answer, and this is what Graff seems not to have grasped, is that progress in understanding literary structure and accounting for literary effects depends precisely on the denial that a work has a particular referent or is the assertion of a particular proposition. In the opening pages of *Le Père Goriot* an authoritative voice asserts "All is true." If a critic were to accept this referential, propositional claim, he would have to say that each element and detail of the novel is to be explained as simply a representation of the true events that are being recounted. Every detail is there because that is the way it was. Study of the novel as a literary construct cannot even begin unless this referentiality is denied, unless one is free to consider every detail as a literary device to be related to others, both in the novel and in other texts. Whenever anyone reads or interprets *Le Père Goriot* they will necessarily make some elements referential; which elements are made referential and propositional will vary from one reading to another. Are the propositions *Le Père Goriot* asserts about 19th century Paris? about paternity or ambition in general? etc. A fiction will be made to refer in various ways. Reference is inferred or produced in the process of interpretation, but this very activity of interpretation, as it has long been practiced, depends upon the undecidability of literary reference: the work does not itself have a particular reference but can be made to refer at various levels and in various ways.

It seems to me noteworthy that Graff himself, though he champions the idea of reference, does not actually propose a theory of the referentiality of literary works. He does not do so, though he chastises others for denying referentiality, because any theory would be wrong, untenable. Even the mildest formulation–that a literary work is always about something–is dubious insofar as it suggests that a particular reference is at the center of a work. In fact, any particular reference can always be shown to be questionable, by virtue of the reversibility of figurative language and the equivocal status of fictions. I am suggesting that the investigation of literary structure and the nature of literary language depends and had depended precisely on the possibility of studying any supposed referent as a literary device, a rhetorical strategy. Criticism advances by treating texts as complex constructions rather than as imitations of reality–just as linguistics advances by suspending the notion that a sentence is a representation of a thought and investigating the complex grammatical operations that determine its form.

On this issue also part of the confusion arises from the assumption that all writing about literature should be interpretation, a working out of what the reader ought to experience. When critics study nineteenth-century novels as elaborate self-referential, self-deconstructive structures, there is often a claim implied that any reader who experiences them as referring to a particular social reality is hopelessly deluded, but it ought to be possible to maintain both that reading and interpretation necessarily involve the positing of a referent, and that investigation of literary structure requires the displacement of any particular proposition or reference. Literary study has gained in range and subtlety from theories of language and literature that urge us to postpone as long as possible the moment of reference, the rush from words to world, and to concentrate on patterns of relations within texts and between them. Indeed, there seems to me no coherent and convincing alternative to anti-referential or propositional theories of literature–accompanied, of course, by an account of the referential movement in interpretation.

4. The final problem I wish to discuss is somewhat ill-defined because it is the intersection of a great many complaints about contemporary literary criticism and literary theory concerning the relationship between the literary work and meaning. One could call it the problem of the determinacy or indeterminacy of meaning. Contemporary theory is accused of inaugurating a riot of subjectivity by suggesting that the meaning of the work is what it means to the reader, or else by presenting accounts of language focused on the power of the signifier, said to produce an infinite play of meanings that can be arrested only by an act of arbitrary authoritarianism. Various theoretical currents come

together to create the impression that this is the tendency of contemporary theory. For example, Barthes' writings after *S/Z* tended increasingly to focus on individual pleasure, neglecting the general codes and systems which had previously formed the backbone of his work. Reader-response criticism, in emphasizing the dynamic aspect of literary meaning, has defined meaning as the experience of readers as they move through the text. Psychoanalytic thought has either stressed, as in France, the importance of connections established at the level of the signifier, or else, as in offshoots of American ego-psychology, claimed that the meaning of a text is the result of the reader projecting his own defenses and identity theme onto the work. Finally, a certain interpretation of deconstruction has inscribed it within this same tendency, partly because Derrida's own writings do exploit idiosyncratic and poetic devices, and partly because of passages like the influential statement at the end of the essay "La Structure, le signe, et le jeu dans le discours des sciences humaines," which for a long time was the only work of his easily available in English. "Il y a donc deux interprétations de l'interprétation. . . . L'une cherche á déchiffrer, rêve de déchiffrer une vérité ou une origine échappant au jeu et à l'ordre du signe et vit comme un exil la nécessité d'interprétation. L'autre, qui n'est plus tournée vers l'origine, affirme le jeu," which he has just before spoken of as "le jeu d'un monde de signes sans faute, sans vérité, sans origine, offert à une interprétation active."[6] This was often understood as a rejection of determinate meaning, a call for an interpretive freedom in which anything goes.

The question of the determinacy of meaning has become an important rallying point in American critical debate. The enemy, says E. D. Hirsch, are "cognitive atheists" who deny that a text has a meaning which the critic should attempt to discover and who thus, so the argument runs, undermine the very basis of critical inquiry and lead us into a solipsism and relativism where any text can mean whatever anyone wants it to mean.[7] The notion of determinate meaning does not

6. Jacques Derrida, *L'Ecriture et la différence* (Paris, Seuil, 1967), p. 427. The English translation appeared in *The Languages of Criticism and the Sciences of Man*, ed. R. Macksey and E. Donoto (Baltimore: Johns Hopkins University Press, 1970).

7. E. D. Hirsch, *The Aims of Interpretation* (Chicago: University of Chicago Press, 1976), p. 13.

involve the claim that every work has a univocal meaning: a work can include local or even systematic ambiguities as part of its determinate meaning; in this case, a work's true meaning includes a particular ambiguity. Nor is there a claim that we can necessarily discover a work's true meaning. But, the argument goes, a work must in principle have a true meaning or else everything totters.

If a work has in principle a determinate meaning, it is because there is something that determines it, something that is responsible for the true meaning. Unfortunately, the partisans of determinate meaning have not made much progress in determining what determines meaning. Is it the author's intention, the norms of language and genre, the comprehension of competent readers of the day? Booth, Abrams, and Hirsch—or BAH, to use a convenient acronym—are swift to identify regions of consensus and to point out that those who argue against the determinacy of meaning rely on the possibility of being understood and complain if their arguments are misunderstood or misrepresented. But in the absence of a compelling account of what determines meaning, what they describe is a situation in which meaning is in principle indeterminate but where in practice there is considerable agreement about meanings.

BAH claims that if meaning is not in principle determinate, then there is no control or interpretation and we find ourselves in a realm of whim and subjectivity. Certainly there do exist interpretive writings which strike one as idiosyncratic and unconvincing, which explore insubstantial connections or associations in the name of the free play of meaning. But in general BAH are not worried by the critic who says simply, without giving reasons, this is what the poem means to me, or this is a possible connection I would like to explore. BAH are worried by critics who give reasons, who argue for a particular determination of meaning and who cite in defense of their readings theories which they regard as excessive, inappropriate, pathological. The problem is not so much the indeterminacy of meaning as particular ways of determining meaning, as becomes clear when one looks at the critical tendencies that are cited as champions of the indeterminacy of meaning. When you abandon determinacy at one level you reintroduce it at another. For all their claims about the indeterminacy of meaning and the play of the signifier, psychoanalytic readings nevertheless follow certain characterizable moves and reach conclusions that form a predictable class. One may wish to reject them as improbable, unconvincing, based on dubious assumptions, etc. However, the problem is not subjectivity but precisely their recognizable, theorizable patterns.

Much the same is true in the work of American critics who champion subjectivity in the name of ego psychology: Norman Holland or David Bleich. Here is Bleich: "Reading is a wholly subjective process and what is perceived is determined by the rules of the personality of the perceiver."[8] We thought we were moving into the realm of anything goes, but this turns out to be a realm of even more rigid rules. The same thing happens in Holland's work. He denies that a text has a unity of its own; each reader unifies it in his own way by projecting his defenses, fantasies, etc. onto the text. The work's meaning is the product of what Holland calls the reader's own "identity theme." What is an identity theme? It is what you discover if you treat a person (his life history and behaviour) as a text and extract its unifying theme in best New Critical fashion. The claim that interpretation is wholly subjective turns out to depend on the possibility of objectively identifying the "true" unity of a reader's whole being.

The case of deconstruction is rather different, but once again the problem is not subjectivism or the randomness of "anything goes." Derrida's remark quoted earlier about the two interpretations of interpretation was usually interpreted as a call for uninhibited, creative interpretation, but in fact Derrida immediately continues, "ces deux interprétations de l'interprétation—qui sont absolument inconciliables, même si nous les vivons simultanément et les concilions dans une obscure économie—se partagent le champ . . . des sciences humaines." But "je ne crois pas pour ma part . . . qu'il y ait aujourd'hui à *choisir.*"[9] It is not a question of choosing either, in particular because no interpretation is conceivable in which the question of its truth or falsity is not prominently involved. If one tries to opt for free play, one can scarcely be assured of success.

In its dealings with texts deconstruction is not an instance of linguistic free play or of rampant subjectivism. Indeed, critics are rather more inclined to accuse it of a rigid determinism: it focuses on certain inescapable metaphysical oppositions at work in texts and thus brings critical argument back repeatedly to the same fundamental problems. Though it may concentrate on various systematically ambiguous

8. David Bleich, *Reading and Feelings* (Urbana, Ill.: NCTE, 1975), p. 3.
9. Derrida, loc. cit.

structures and terms—*supplément* in Rousseau, *pharmakon, pharmakos, pharmakeus* in Plato, *hymen* in Mallarmé—the play of these "undecidables" is highly determined by the exigencies of a textual logic that is the principal subject of interest and that is discussed in detail.

What is scandalous or threatening in deconstruction is not subjectivism or a critique of the determinacy of meaning so much as, on the one hand, an interpretive practice that treats meaning as subject to forces that the writer or speaker does not completely control and, on the other hand, a refusal to respect traditional proportions. In making some apparently marginal element the focus of attention and arguing for its subversive force, in seeking to display the heterogeneity of a text, refusing to strive to interpret it as a harmonious whole, or in calling upon difficult and "non-literary" theories in its arguments about literary texts, deconstruction violates various norms of critical writing.[10] This may be the real problem.

Indeed, I am convinced that critics who complain about relativism and subjectivism do so because they are unhappy with the position they would have to adopt in order to reject deconstructive readings. One critic who does not hesitate to take this stance is Ralph Rader, who formulates principles that others might like to espouse if they had the courage of their convictions. The goal of criticism, Radar claims, is to assign a work a single coherent meaning. "The understanding we have of literature and the pleasure we take in it . . . derive from . . . a comprehensive inferential grasp of the author's overall creative intention in a work, which allows us to eliminate in the act of reading any potential incoherencies and ambiguities which cannot be resolved within our appreciation of the whole."[11] Readers are indeed inclined to eliminate potential incoherencies which they cannot resolve within their comprehension of the whole, but few critics are willing boldy to propose this as a principle that *ought* to be followed. But, I believe, it is only in name of some principle such as this that BAH can reject critical readings which they mistakenly call subjective.

Rader's principle urges not merely the elimination of possible ambiguities of words, as when we come upon the word *bank* and eliminate the idea of a river bank because the First National Bank better fits our

10. See Jonathan Culler, *The Pursuit of Signs: Semiotics, Literature, Deconstruction* (Ithaca: Cornell University Press, 1981).

11. Ralph Rader, "The Concept of Genre and 18th Century Studies," in *New Approaches to the Eighteenth Century,* ed. Philip Harth (New York: Columbia University Press, 1974), p. 86.

appreciation of the whole. He urges us to eliminate quite massive facts about literary works—facts which can be ignored as "unintended negative consequences of the author's positive intention." Milton intended in *Paradise Lost* to portray an orthodox Christian God and to justify the ways of God to man. To many readers, however, God has seemed unattractive, or at least less attractive than Satan. Milton did not intend this, Rader argues; it was an unavoidable consequence of his various positive intentions, and for that reason it should be ignored.[12] Critics who use this potential ambiguity or incoherency in their interpretations are in error. But if it is indeed true that to portray an orthodox Christian God in an epic is necessarily to make him unattractive, then that is an interesting fact about God, language, representation, or the epic; it is certainly a topic worth discussing in one's account of *Paradise Lost*. Rader is trying to rule out of court precisely those facts and elements that deconstruction finds most interesting and revealing: elements which are indissociable from a particular project yet work to undermine that project: necessary yet unintended consequences of an author's positive intention.

Rader's principle would not, of course, resolve critical disputes, since one would still have to argue about what was the positive intention of any poem and which elements could be pleasurably experienced as contributions to that project; but the idea of such principles is precisely to place critical disagreement within well-defined boundaries, eliminating the extravagant, the subversive, and especially the foreign. The issue is whether this is the kind of criticism we want or whether we might not learn, whether we have not learned, much more about literature, about language and thought generally, from investigating the uncanny, the exorbitant, the paradoxical—the literary?

The four issues I have raised—interpretation and the task of criticism, metalanguage and the status of critical discourse, the referentiality of literature, and the determinacy of meaning—are of course related, but it seems to me that only by distinguishing them and examining each critically can one avoid the danger, encouraged by BAH and others, of seeing contemporary American criticism as a struggle between an obscurantist, theorizing, European nihilism and a virtuous, practical, native Know-Nothing pursuit of true meaning. American criticism would

12. Rader, "Fact, Theory and Literary Explanation," *Critical Inquiry* 1:2 (1974), pp. 26f.

suffer greatly if it were to loose sight of the complexity of the various critical issues by accepting this simplistic and polemical delimination of contemporary critical controversy.

THE ETHICS OF READING: VAST GAPS AND PARTING HOURS *

J. Hillis Miller

> A wicked book they seized; the very Turk
> Could not have read a more pernicious work . . .
>
> George Crabbe, "The Parting Hour"[1]

A distinctive feature of literary study in America at the present time is its internationalization. The result has been a fissuring of what not too long ago seemed perhaps about to become a seamless whole, whether under the aegis of literary history and the history of ideas, or under the aegis of the New Criticism, or under the aegis of the archetypal criticism of Northrop Frye. The diffusion in America of new linguistic theories of various sorts, of Slavic formalism, of phenomenology, of structuralism, of continental Marxism and Freudianism, and of so-called "deconstruction" has put an end, for the moment at least, to any dreams of unification. Nor can the various invading theories be reconciled among themselves. This penetration, fracturing, or "crazing" has made the institution of literary studies in America a house divided against itself, its domestic economy invaded by alien hosts or guests from abroad. These foreign imports have been around long enough now for their disruptive implications to be at least partly understood, and we are in the midst of the predictable negative reaction against them.

My purpose here is to investigate the question of the ethics of reading in the context of this situation. The phrase "the ethics of reading" might seem to be an oxymoron. The obligation of the reader, the

1. Ll. 355-56, *The Poetical Works,* ed. A. J. Carlyle and R. M. Carlyle (London: Oxford University Press, 1932), p. 229. Further citations from Crabbe's poem will be by line numbers from this edition.

teacher, and the critic would seem to be exclusively epistemological. The reader must see clearly what the work in question says and repeat that meaning in his commentary or teaching. He functions thereby, modestly, as an intermediary, as a midwife or catalyst. He transmits meanings which are objectively there but which might not otherwise have reached readers or students. He brings the meaning to birth again as illumination and insight in their minds, making the interaction take place without himself entering into it or altering it. It would seem that the field covered by reading involves exclusively the epistemological categories of truth and falsehood, insight and blindness. The teacher is a revealer, not a creator.

Nevertheless, ethical issues arise in all sorts of ways, both practical and theoretical, in the act of reading. Men and women have given up their lives over questions of interpretation, the reading of a phrase of scripture, for example. One expects reading in one way or another to have moral effects, for good or for ill. To the couplets, truth and falsehood, insight and blindness, themselves not quite congruent, must be added the pair good and bad, both in the sense of aesthetic judgment and in the sense of ethical judgment, and the pair speech and silence. These pairs cross the others widdershins, and no one of them may be easily twisted to superimpose exactly on the others in a single act of critical judgment. It is impossible to divide, discriminate, sift, or winnow the wheat from the chaff, true from false, good from bad, in a single moment of parting.

As a result, difficult questions arise in the attempt to adjudicate between epistemological and ethical responsibilities. Does a teacher or critic have an obligation to choose only certain works to teach or write about? Who has the right to set the canon and to establish the Index? Should "the state see to it," as Matthew Arnold thought? Is a good work always moral? Should a teacher or a critic keep silent if he is led, perhaps unexpectedly, to ethically negative conclusions about a given work? Should certain aspects of a given work be suppressed at a preliminary level of teaching, or should there perhaps be a hierarchy of works of increasing ethical complexity in a given curriculum? How is the need for a firm ethical commitment in the teacher-critic compatible with that openness or "pluralism" often said to be necessary to the sympathetic understanding of works from different periods and cultures? The commitment of both the scientific and religious strands of our American heritage to seeing and saying the truth fearlessly *(veritas vos liberabit; lux et veritas)* can easily, in a given teaching or writing situation, come to collide with concrete ethical responsibilities towards students and colleagues, no less a part of our heritage. Nor is this conflict external, between one critic and another, one teacher and another, one mode of criticism and another. The most intense conflict is likely to take place within the mind and feelings of a single person, in his or her attempt to fulfill incompatible responsibilities.

This problem is a universal one in humanistic studies. It arises in one way or another in any time, place, or culture, even in pre-literate cultures. Oral song or narrative, ritual performances, need interpretation too. Their interpretation may be problematic from the point of view of practical ethics in its relation to cognitive truth. The written text of *Beowulf* may be seen as a Christian interpretation which is also a distortion of the pagan oral poem on which it is based. Was that reinterpretation ethically justified?

The problem I am attempting to focus has, however, a particular context in the present state of humanistic studies in America. The concrete situation of teachers of the humanities is changing at the moment with unusual rapidity. More even than usual it seems as if we stand within the instant of a crisis, a dividing point, a "parting hour." Aspects of the change include the increasing emphasis on the teaching of writing (which may be all to the good if it does not involve the imposition of narrow notions of clarity and logic), the decline of enrollments in traditional courses in literature and other humanities, the catastrophic reduction of the number of positions open to younger humanists, and a conservative reaction in the universities. This tends to declare certain kinds of speculative questioning anathema. Perhaps this reaction is confined within the universities and colleges, a response in the 'seventies to the 'sixties. Perhaps it is part of much larger political shifts in our society as a whole.

One form of the closing of ranks is a return to basics in the name of a reaffirmation of traditional humanistic values, perhaps in the name of a reaffirmation of the faith in reason of the enlightenment. This tends to be accompanied by a rejection of "theory" as such and in particular by a strong hostility to certain fairly recent methodological developments in Europe and America. The latter have converged to put in question the most cherished stabilities of traditional humanistic studies in the United States: the stability of the self, the coherence of storytelling, the possibility of straightforward referential language, the possibility of a definitive, unified reading of a given work, the traditional schemas of history and of literary history which have formed the bases for the structuring of curricula in the humanities, for example the objective and definable existence of literary "periods."

Some of the methodological innovations which have challenged the traditional bases of literary study in America are scientific or claim to be part of the so-called "human sciences." These would include insights about the way language works from modern linguistics, from psychology, from psychoanalysis, from anthropology, from semiotics, and from common language philosophy, Wittgenstein and his progeny. Some of these methodological innovations are ideological or have developed from recent historical pressures. An example would be the newer forms of Marxist literary criticism which are beginning to be institutionalized in America and to exert force, particularly over younger teachers. A curious and I think important fact should be noted, however. Marxist literary criticism, both in its somewhat more naive traditional American forms and in the more sophisticated (sophisticated perhaps in the sense of "adulterated" as well as "wiser") newer forms influenced by semiotics, structuralism, Lacanian psychoanalysis, and so on, tends, strangely enough, to join forces with that conservative reaction to affirm more or less traditional notions of history, of selfhood, of the moral function of literature, and, most of all, of its mimetic or referential status. For Marxism, literature cannot help but reflect social and historical conditions and the superstructure of ideology these have created. Marxism here joins forces with the most traditional "humanism" against those methodological innovations I am describing.

Many of these have been imported from abroad, for example, phenomenology, structuralism, semiotics, and so-called "deconstruction." This is often held against them on the argument that methods brought in from old Europe cannot thrive in New World soil. Nevertheless, an internationalization in literary study is one of its most obvious features today, and this has concrete effects, for example in a tendency to weaken the departmental boundaries of the curricula devoted to national literatures. The transnational diffusion of literary theory and literary methodology occurs now more rapidly than ever before, in part because of technological developments: the rapidity of global transportation which can bring people together from all over the world for a conference anywhere in the world, electronic communication, the increased speed of translation, publication, and distribution, the improved teaching of foreign languages, at least in some schools and programs,[2] the development of international journals in the various branches of humanistic study. One example among many would be *Poetics Today*, published in Tel Aviv, but drawing together essays by scholars from all over America and Europe.

The internationalization of literary study has, as I have said, generated attacks from various directions in defense of those stabilities which seem endangered. These attacks are more or less reasoned or cogent, but their existence is itself an important symptom of our current version of the problem of the ethics of reading. Whether a given anathematizing of these new developments as immoral, nihilistic, or unAmerican is based on an understanding of them and is a genuine going beyond the challenges they offer, or is only a coverup, a repression, can only be told by a careful study of each case. It can be said, however, that the excommunications, extraditions, or convictions of heresy seem often to take place without a careful reading of the documents involved. At least so it seems on the evidence of the inadequacy of what is often said of them: "A wicked book they seized." The texts of the new methodologies must be mastered before they can be discussed, no easy task, since in part they have to do with the impossibility of mastery. Most of all, the readings of particular works which are derived from these theories or from which the theories derive need to be confronted in detail. The efficacy of a theory is to be measured by its results in interpretations. A theory as such cannot be confuted in isolation, for example by deploring its presumed destructive consequences, but only by showing in detail that the readings to which it leads are inadequate or wrong, untrue to the texts. It can also be supposed that young teachers and critics are more likely to have taken genuine stock of the new methodological developments before trying to go beyond them or to return in a new way to the old verities of literary study. For better or for worse literary study in America can

2. The recent statistics are appalling enough. In 1964 only one high school student in four studied a foreign language. Now the ratio has dropped to one in seven. In 1966, thirty-four per cent of American colleges required a foreign language for admission. Now only eight per cent do. (*The New York Times*, Saturday, November 10, 1979.) Nevertheless, the techniques of teaching foreign languages have greatly improved in America, and some students, in public as well as in private high schools, are given excellent foreign language training.

never be quite the same again. A difference, perhaps even a "vast gap" has been introduced. This separates us from the days of the New Criticism, Yvor Winters, R. P. Blackmur, and R. S. Crane. Any reconstruction is going to have to be reconstruction with a difference.

I propose to investigate the problem of the ethics of reading in this moment of our history a little more closely. I shall do so by way of an example, though with an awareness that my example, like any other, raises the question of exemplarity or of synecdoche. Is this part an adequate sample of such a vast whole? That issue is in fact exemplified and thematized within the poem I shall discuss as well as in my use of it.

Suppose there should fall into my hands "The Parting Hour," a poem by George Crabbe (1754-1832) published in *Tales* (1812). Should I teach it or write about it? What will happen when I do so?

It might be said that this poem is a marginal part of the canon of English literature, even more marginal a part of Western literature as a whole. No one and no institution or curriculum force me to teach or to write about this particular poem. There may be something willful or perverse in my choice of this example. This is to some degree true of any choice of an item for a syllabus, however, and this particular poem may in fact be a good choice. If even Crabbe offers support to those who challenge the assumptions of traditional humanistic study in America, then there may be some force in the challenges.

Crabbe's place in English literary history is an honorable but relatively small one. He is seen as a writer of narratives in verse of idiosyncratic distinction. His work moves across the transition in modes from eighteenth-century styles to verse stories by Wordsworth such as "The Ruined Cottage." There is a general sense that Crabbe's poems are of great interest and that he has perhaps not yet received his due. The debt of criticism to Crabbe will soon be at least partially paid off by Gavin Edwards of Saint Davids College, University of Wales. Edwards has a book on Crabbe in preparation, and my obligation to him is considerable. "The Parting Hour," in any case, is an admirable poem. It raises just those questions about the ethics of reading which are most my interest here and which, as I hope to indicate, are always present in literature and literary criticism in the West, for example in Aristotle's *Poetics* and Sophocles' *Oedipus the King*. Crabbe's poem is a good example of the way an apparently peripheral and unproblematic example in literary studies, taken more or less at random, always turns out to raise again all the most difficult questions about literature and about literary criticism.

"The Parting Hour" opens with no less than five epigraphs from Shakespeare, about each of which there would be much to say, as well as about the fact itself of the multiplication of epigraphs. It is as though Crabbe must try over and over to find a precursor fragment which will be a solid foundation allowing him to begin telling the story he has to tell. The text proper begins with a double claim: the claim that any human life, however strange, hangs together, and the claim that any human life is therefore narratable. It can be retraced later on as a continuous story which makes sense, has a beginning, middle, and end:

> Minutely trace man's life; year after year,
> Through all his days let all his deeds appear,
> And then, though some may in that life be strange,
> Yet there appears no vast nor sudden change:
> The links that bind those various deeds are seen,
> And no mysterious void is left between.
>
> (11. 1-6)

The opposition here is between strangeness and mystery; minutely traced causal continuity on the one hand, and sudden discontinuous change on the other, across the "void" or "vast gap." Though a given life may in one way or another be odd, if it is narrated with an absolute fidelity to detail it will hang together like the unbroken links of a chain. "Minutely traced": the figure is of one image superimposed on an earlier image and following it over again, like marked tracing paper over a previously made design, tracking it again with the utmost care as one follows the spoor of a beast. This is the image latently present in the Greek word for narrative or history: *diegesis*. On the other hand, if there is any failure at all in this tracing, the life will appear not strange but utterly mysterious, unfathomable. It will be broken by the abyss of a blank. Crabbe's image for this is what happens if one juxtaposes a vignette from the early life of a person with one from his old age without tracing minutely every event between. The opposition is between a continuous temporal line and the placing side by side of two spatial images separated by an unfilled temporal gap, like two portraits beside one another, in a diptych of "before" and "after." This graphic figure of the picture or of two pictures side by side Crabbe himself uses more than once during the course of the poem:

But let these binding links be all destroy'd,
All that through years he suffer'd or enjoy'd;
Let that vast gap be made, and then behold–
This was the youth, and he is thus when old;
Then we at once the work of Time survey,
And in an instant see a life's decay;
Pain mix'd with pity in our bosoms rise,
And sorrow takes new sadness from surprise.
(11.7-14)

This passage is curious in a number of ways. It opposes the line of the temporal continuity, within which binding links may be minutely traced, to the spatial juxtaposition, within a single instant, of two images from different times of a man's life. The two are separated by the blank of the temporal gap. The continuous narrative is by implication appeasing to the mind. It gives calm understanding, since the rationale of the movement of the person from here to there, from youth to old age, is all exposed. No gap for surprise and shock is left. On the other hand, the sudden exposure, across the gap, of the difference between youth and old age produces pain, pity, sorrow, a sadness generated by surprise. The terminology closely approximates that of Aristotle in the *Poetics* if we can understand "pain" to involve some fear for ourselves as well as pity for the degradation exposed in the juxtaposition of the two pictures: "This was the youth, and he is thus when old." The same elements as those in Aristotle are present but apparently in a criss-cross relationship, a chiasmus. In Aristotle's theory of tragedy it is the blinding revelation, the recognition *(anagnorisis)* of the links of connection binding apparently dispersed data together which produces the pity and fear appropriate to tragedy, for example in Oedipus's discovery that he has fulfilled the oracles, killed his father, and married his mother. For Crabbe, it is the vision of a non-connection, the confrontation of an unbridgeable gap, which produces these emotions, while the demonstration, by a careful retracing, of all the links of connection is appeasing. It abolishes mystery and satisfies the mind's need for rational understanding.

The chiasmus, however, is only apparent. After all, the Aristotelean recognition and reversal, showing how everything fatally hangs together and bringing the tragic hero down, not only produces pity and fear but also effects the catharsis of these emotions. This catharsis is a transformation or transport turning the painful emotions of pity and fear into the pleasure appropriate to a successful *mimesis*. This transport, as S. H. Butcher long ago recognized in his brilliant essay on the *Poetics*,[3] is in effect a metaphor turning this into that or carrying this over to that, renaming pain as pleasure. The image of the ship is of course one of Aristotle's basic metaphors in the *Poetics*. It serves not only as an example of metaphor but implicitly as a metaphor of metaphor. The same metaphor is woven into the text of his prime example of tragedy, *Oedipus the King*. It appears in the recurrent image of all the citizens of Thebes as frightened passengers on a ship steered, for better or for worse, by Oedipus. The chorus of Theban priests and citizens, all the citizens of Thebes, the actual audience in Athens watching Sophocles' play, all those who have read it or seen it or tried to translate it, down through Hölderlin and Freud to readers and interpreters of today, are carried by the ship, the vehicle Oedipus steers. We are taken where he takes us, in the tragic transport of our witness of the self-blinded hero at the end. We are, strangely, the tenor of that vehicle, the subject of the metaphor. We are what is carried over by it.

Where we are carried we know: "How can we ever find the track of ancient guilt now hard to read?" (*Oedipus the King*, 11. 108-09).[4] Oedipus is the type of the successful interpreter. He reads the various riddles and oracles right, puts two and two together to make a coherent story, the continuous track of a *diegesis*. He is so strongly motivated to obtain at any expense a rational understanding, an absolutely perspicuous vision of the whole line from here to there, that he is willing (or forced by his interpreter's zeal) to convict himself of the most terrible of crimes, parricide and incest, in order to preserve the values of clear and complete seeing through. These are just the values Aristotle says a good tragedy offers its spectators. The beast whose spoor he follows is himself, but only if he follows the track wherever it leads can full enlightenment take place, the audience be purged of pity and fear, the land of Thebes be freed from Apollo's plague.

3. S. H. Butcher, *Aristotle's Theory of Poetry and Fine Art; With a Critical Text and Translation of The Poetics* (New York: Dover Publications, Inc., 1951), pp. 113-407; see especially "The Function of Tragedy," pp. 240-73.

4. I am using the translation by Thomas Gould (Englewood Cliffs, N.J.: Prentice-Hall, Inc., 1970), p. 29. Further citations from *Oedipus the King* will be by line numbers from this translation.

In Aristotle's theory of tragedy, in *Oedipus the King* itself, and in the narrative theory proposed by Crabbe at the beginning of "The Parting Hour," the unbroken causal continuity of the plot is the necessary means of a transport which transforms pain into pleasure by giving full knowledge. The pleasure of *mimesis,* or what Crabbe calls minute tracing, is both for Aristotle and for Crabbe the pleasure of learning the truth about what is imitated. It is also the pleasure of rhythm or of the harmonious hanging together of the elements of the work. Crabbe in the opening lines of "The Parting Hour" implicitly reaffirms all Aristotle says in Section VII of the *Poetics* (1450 b 22-1451 a 15) about the primacy of plot. Plot is the soul of the work. For both, a good work should be like a living organism, with no discontinuities and nothing present which does not form part of an unbroken whole. It should have a beginning, a causally linked middle, an end, and an underlying ground or unifying soul binding all together and making it live. It should have a sufficient magnitude, "a length," as Aristotle says, "which can be easily embraced by the memory," so that it is "perspicuous."[5] The efficacy of a *mimesis* depends on our being able to see through it, to hold it all in our memory, or to "embrace [it] in one view" (p. 33): "the beginning and the end must be capable of being brought within a single view" (p. 91). This is just what Crabbe says in his emphasis on the need to see all the links that bind the various deeds of a man's life.

Crabbe's poem, Aristotle's *Poetics,* and Sophocles' *Oedipus the King* as interpreted by Aristotle are all versions of a certain system of concepts, figures, and narratives which have recurred in different ways throughout our history. That system includes just those assumptions about the continuity of selfhood, determinate univocal meaning in literary works, the sovereignty of reason, and the coherence of the march of history which, as I began by saying, seem most endangered by those methodologies imported from abroad. Crabbe's "The Parting Hour" states those assumptions with elegant economy in its opening lines. It presents itself as a promise to fulfill once more these millenial claims for the possibility of a narrative coherence. These are based on the necessary though sometimes hidden coherence of each man's or woman's life from one end of it to the other.

* * *

5. Butcher, *op. cit.,* p. 33. Further quotations from Aristotle's *Poetics* will be identified by page numbers in this translation.

Are the claims paid off, the promise fulfilled, the debt discharged, by the story Crabbe then tells? By no means. What happens, rather, is that the more the storyteller or his protagonist try to fill in all the gaps by a careful retracing, the more they discover that inexplicable gaps remain. The continuity of the story line and of the life is suspended, the line pulverized into static moments which do not hang together, like a rope of sand. Once the apparently innocent fissure of a parting hour has been inserted, the continuity can never be reestablished.

About the details of Crabbe's poem there would be much to say. Only an opening toward a full interpretation can be made here. Like others of Crabbe's narratives, "The Parting Hour" is a poem about thwarted or inhibited sexual desire. It is almost, one might say, the Oedipus story in reverse. It is the story of a man who does not marry the woman he loves because of a bar which is, metaphorically at least, that of consanguinity. Though Allen Booth and Judith Flemming are of different families in their village, they have loved one another almost like brother and sister as children and, as Gavin Edwards says, there is some vaguely Oedipal taboo opposed by the parents on either side against their marriage. In their old age they live together in a relation shown as entirely innocent sexually. She cherishes him in his feeble state as mother, sister, wife, though she is none of these. She is connected even more closely to him, in a nameless proximity or alliance, across the gap of their permanent difference and distance from one another: "No wife, nor sister she, nor is the name/Nor kindred of this friendly pair the same;/Yet so allied are they, that few can feel/Her constant, warm, unwearied, anxious zeal" (11. 18-21). "Few can feel her . . . zeal"—this seems to mean both that few people can experience anything like the strength of her feelings for him and that few people are so lucky as he in being the recipient of such zealous care.

"The Parting Hour" begins its narration proper with a reverse diptych. Not "This was the youth, and he is thus when old," but first Allen Booth in old age, cared for by Judith ("Beneath yon tree, observe an ancient pair—" [1. 15]), and then, in abrupt juxtaposition, Allen Booth as a child ("To David Booth, his fourth and last-born boy,/ Allen his name, was more than common joy" [11. 32-33]). The rest of the poem then attempts to fill in the void between the two pictures by showing the binding links joining the deeds between.

This attempt conspicuously fails. The way it fails turns on just that opposition, so important already in Aristotle, between what is conspicuous or perspicuous, what is theatrical, what can be seen or seen through, so that time becomes space, the diachronic synchronic, and, on the other hand, what can be told or narrated in a minute tracing which retains its diachronic sequentiality, like the links of a chain, one following another. Such a claim may be seen or seen through only metaphorically, as when one says, "I see it all now." The words "prospect," "prospects," "picture," "feature," and "scene" echo through the poem. These words keep before the reader the visual image for understanding. To understand is to read a picture. The poem demonstrates, however, that all the attempts by the poet-narrator and by the hero to bring into the light of clear-seeing the continuity of his life only makes more evident the gaps within it. These make his life not like a picture but like a sentence of faulty grammar, an anacoluthon beginning with one person or tense and shifting suddenly and unaccountably to another. The hour during which Allen Booth parts from his beloved on the beach and fares forth by ship to seek his fortune so that he may marry her inserts a void between them and within his life which can never be filled by any retrospective narration. His subsequent betrayal of Judith and of his community by marrying a Spanish Catholic maiden, fathering Catholic children, and converting to Catholicism only reaffirms the betrayal which occurred when he parted from Judith in the first place. Once he has left her he can never return to her and never return to himself, nor can he explain how he came to differ from himself, how he came to betray both Judith and himself;

> They parted, thus by hope and fortune led,
> And Judith's hours in pensive pleasure fled;
> But when return'd the youth?—the youth no more
> Return'd exulting to his native shore;
> But forty years were past, and then there came
> A worn-out man with wither'd limbs and lame. . . .
> (11. 181-86)

Two of Crabbe's four epigraphs from Shakespeare, chosen with admirable insight, provide models for this discontinuity. The first is from Imogen's speech in *Cymbeline,* I, 3. It opposes a "parting kiss" as the jointure between two words to the abrupt intervention of her father: "ere I could/Give him that parting kiss, which I had set/Betwixt two charming words—comes in my father." A "parting kiss" is an oxymoron combining joining and separation. The entrance of the father only anticipates the separation the kiss would have signalled, just as the loving separation of Allen and Judith is imposed by their parents' disapproval. They cannot marry until he has a fortune. Once something which does not fit the sequence has been inserted between two words, even a parting kiss, the grammar of the sentence of which they are part can never be satisfactorily completed. The sentence becomes a failure in following, which is the etymological meaning of the word anacoluthon.

In the second epigraph, from *Comedy of Errors,* V, 1, Aegeon tells how "careful hours with Time's deformed hand/Have written strange defeatures in my face," just as time changes Allen Booth from hopeful youth of fair prospects into an old man in no recognizable way like his former self. Far from being that principle of irresistible force making for form, for continuity, and guaranteeing them, as Crabbe's opening lines promise, time is for Crabbe, as for Shakespeare, a deforming power making things differ from themselves. The figure for this is the changes in a face, its "defeaturing," in Shakespeare's use of a word of which this is the first example in the O.E.D. The word shifts the understanding of a face from a visual image to an image of reading. This parallels the clash between picture and story, scene and narrative, theater and discourse, in Crabbe's poem. The face is not an image to see but a set of signs or features, a written text to decipher. The distinctive feature of the text written by time on a face is its unreadability, its disconnection from itself, its discontinuity with itself, its defeaturing. Allen Booth tries in vain, when he returns to his native shore after forty years' exile, "to trace/Some youthful features in some aged face" (11. 221-22).

Time for man is not a natural or organic continuity, nor is it ever a picture which can be seen at a single glance. Time for man is always experienced as some kind of sign, as a track to be followed, a line to be retraced, a face with features to be read. This means that time is always experienced as an incongruous repetition. It is experienced as a picture with gaps or as two pictures side by side which cannot be reconciled. This means also, as Crabbe's storyteller and his protagonist find out, discovering those gaps, discontinuities, incongruities, and incoherences which are intrinsic to any repetitive structure of signs. When one tries to retrace the line it never can be made to hang together. Far from doing what he promises at the beginning, showing the continuity of a life, all Crabbe's storyteller's efforts only make the "mysterious void[s] . . . between" more evident. His narration presents discontinuous vignettes rather than a continuous chain of events. There is no way to explain how or why Allen Booth came to differ from himself, why he married someone else, abjured his faith, failed to come back sooner, postponing from day to day and year to year the reunion that would heal the gap opened by the parting hour.

The temporal structure of "The Parting Hour" is strange enough. First the narrator presents the "ancient pair" beneath the tree. Next he leaps back to Allen Booth's childhood and the events leading up to his parting from Judith Flemming. Then he leaps forward forty years to Allen's return and to his attempt to pick up again the continuity of his life by returning to Judith. This he can do only if he can satisfactorily account for the intervening years and bring the past up to the present.

The narrative responsibility at this point shifts to Allen himself. He is shown compulsively telling his story over and over to Judith, "running it through" in the phrase from Othello's narration of his life to Desdemona Crabbe uses as his fourth epigraph (*Othello,* I, 3). Allen tells his story repeatedly in a hopeless attempt to get it right, to justify himself in his eyes and hers. The key term for this narration is the word "relate." It is a word for connection, for telling, and for family tie. The signal of the temporal incoherence of his "relation" is the shift back and forth between the past tense and the historical present. Only if his narrative can turn the past sequence of events into a present simultaneous possession can the relation succeed, but this can never happen, and so his relation vibrates between the two tenses, and must be repeated over and over without any hope of ever succeeding: "To her, to her alone, his various fate,/At various times, 'tis comfort to relate" (11. 309-10); "First he related . . ." (1. 313); "He next related . . ." (1. 372); "Here his relation closes . . ." (1. 434). Far from connecting the past to the present by a minute tracing of the intervening events, Allen only succeeds in bringing himself back to a present in which he is two persons, the faithful husband of his Spanish wife Isabel, father of her children, and at the same time the faithful fiancé of Judith. Whichever way he turns he must betray one or the other of them. Each is the dream which makes the other impossible as waking reality, and so his selfhood, his "life," is irrevocably divided, parted from itself. With that parting goes any hope of a coherent narrative with beginning, middle, and end:

> . . . how confused and troubled all appear'd;
> His thoughts in past and present scenes employ'd,
> All views in future blighted and destroy'd:
> His were a medley of bewild'ring themes,
> Sad as realities, and wild as dreams.
>
> (11.429-33)

Separated from his origin by his betrayal of his childhood love, Allen has no certain prospects or views toward the future. He can only hope for the "little earth" Cardinal Wolsey asks for in the passage from *Henry VIII* (IV, 2) Crabbe uses as his fifth epigraph to the poem. Allen Booth returns to "his native bay/Willing his breathless form should blend with kindred clay" (11. 189-90). The old folk of his native village say, "The man is Allen Booth, and it appears/He dwelt among us in his early years;/We see the name engraved upon the stones,/Where this poor wanderer means to lay his bones" (11.279-82). Only when Allen Booth is a dead body buried in a little plot of earth, a tombstone over his head with a single name engraved on it joining him to his family already buried there, can he be related enough to himself to be joined to anything or to anyone else without danger of parting from it or from her. He can be indissolubly wedded only to the "kindred clay."

"The Parting Hour" ends where it began, with the aged Allen Booth sleeping under a tree watched over by the unwearied care of his beloved Judith. Far from being an unequivocal ending tying Allen Booth's life together, this picture, the reader now knows, is the image of Allen Booth's disconnection from himself, as he dreams of his Spanish wife and children in the presence of the loving Judith whom he cannot help but betray as long as he is still alive. The poem ends with his waking from his dreams of Isabel to face Judith and cry, "My God! 'twas but a dream" (1.473).

"The Parting Hour" provides one striking image for this failure of narrative continuity. Allen is exiled for heresy from the Spanish colony where he has married and prospered. While he is poor no one pays any attention to him, but when he is wealthy they notice him and single him out for punishment:

> Alas! poor Allen, through his wealth was seen
> Crimes that by poverty conceal'd had been;

Faults that in dusty pictures rest unknown
Are in an instant through the varnish shown.
(11. 361-64)

It was lack of money which drove Allen away from England in the first place. If he had had enough of it he could have married Judith and maintained his continuity with himself and with his sworn fidelity to Judith. Money in the first life of Allen Booth stands for the missing principle of coherence. In his second life, however, when money is obtained it becomes the instrument of discontinuity, separating him forever from Isabel, from his children, and from his second self. The figure Crabbe uses seems an especially striking one when the use of the image of the "picture" elsewhere in the poem as a metaphor of a given state of a man's life is remembered. The attempt to varnish over a dirty picture only brings out its "faults." "Faults"–the word recalls "gaps" and "void" in the opening of the poem. Varnish may be taken as a figure for narrative, for the attempt to relate one thing to another in a sequential discourse. This attempt at varnishing over only brings out its impossibility. It reveals unbridgeable gaps, like geological faults in a terrain. Crabbe's "The Parting Hour," in its attempt to fulfill its promise of being able to show how a life hangs together, reveals the impossibility of fulfilling this promise. Any attempt to do so is a cover-up, a varnishing over. This infallibly betrays the hiatuses it tries to obscure.

"The Parting Hour," almost in spite of itself, deconstructs two of those cherished certainties of humanist literary study, the continuity of the self and the organic continuity of narrative from beginning to middle to end. It might be claimed that the poem is an aberration among those by its author or among those of its period, but this could be shown not to be the case. One need only think of the doubts raised about the unity of the self and about the cohesion of time by Locke, Diderot, or Hume, or in their different ways, by Rousseau and Wordsworth, to recognize that Crabbe's poem is a miniature version of one of the distinctive features of Pre-romanticism and Romanticism. This feature is the copresence of a powerful affirmation of the system of metaphysical assumptions of which Greek thought was one version, along with an equally powerful disarticulation of that system. This double affirmation and denial, tying and untying, in fact characterizes our own moment as I began by describing it. Without denying that there have been vast gaps and new beginnings both in linguistic history and in cultural history, this affirmation and denial may by hypothesis be said to form the unity in disunity of any "period" in Western intellectual and literary history, even that of the Greeks. The distinctiveness of any historical period, "the Renaissance," "Romanticism," "Modernism," or whatever, lies in its special combination of certain recurring elements rather than in its introduction of anything unheard of before. The gaps and discontinuities making linguistic and cultural history a vast anacoluthon are within each synchronic expression, making it heterogeneous, as well as in the diachronic movement from one expression to another.

* * *

I said this was true even of the Greeks. If one turns back to Aristotle and Sophocles and reads them more narrowly, in the light of what has been found in "The Parting Hour," in order to test the "sources" against their modern apparently subversive counterpart, one finds that Aristotle's *Poetics* and Sophocles' *Oedipus the King* are also coverups which reveal, in spite of themselves, what they mean to obscure. Far from subverting something unequivocal and whole earlier present in our culture, far from unravelling a seamless fabric, Crabbe does no more than repeat in his own way a gesture of unsuccessful varnishing over performed already by Sophocles and Aristotle in their own ways.

As a long modern tradition of the interpretation of *Oedipus the King* has recognized, the guilt of Oedipus may be a sin of interpretation. In order to bring everything out in the open, or to persuade himself that he has done so, he is willing, on not entirely convincing evidence, to convict himself of parricide and incest. The self-condemnation depends on a certain way of reading the various oracles, prophecies, and reports he is given. It is a way based on just that logocentric assumption of beginning, middle, and end which the Sphynx's riddle embodies and which Aristotle makes the logical or reasonable basis of a good plot. The fault in Oedipus's interpretation, revealed by the bringing to light, is there, for example, in the famous discrepancy between the two versions of the Phocal massacre. According to one version, Laius' murderers were many. According to the other version, there was but one murderer. As Oedipus himself says, "One man and many men just do not jibe" (1. 845). This discrepancy is never cleared up in the play.

Oedipus's self-condemnation is a glossing over of the contradictory evidence. It is an interpretation in excess of the facts he has. It is a varnishing over which reveals the fault in his story and his fault as a too arrogant interpreter. From Hölderlin through Freud to such diverse modern critics as William Empson, Thomas Gould, William Chase Greene, Karl Harshbarger, René Girard, Sandor Goodheart, Philippe Lacoue-Labarthe, and, most recently, Cynthia Chase in a brilliant article,[6] Romantic and Post-Romantic interpreters have in one way or another confronted the fact that Oedipus may not have had an Oedipus complex, that he may not have killed his father, and that his crime may be an error of misreading. For Hölderlin in "Remarks on *Oedipus*," "The *intelligibility* of the whole [play] rests primarily upon one's keeping before one's eyes the scene, in which Oedipus interprets in *too transcendent* [or *too infinite*] *a way* the word of the oracle and in which he is tempted to an act of *sacrilege* (Die *Verständlichkeit* des Ganzen beruhet vorzüglich darauf, dass man die Szene ins Auge fasst, wo Oedipus den Orakelspruch *zu unendlich deutet, zum nefas* versucht wird)."[7] As Philippe Lacoue-Labarthe comments, "The transgression, the sacrilege, would then be the excess of interpretation" (*ibid.*, p. 81). The intelligibility of the whole rests on keeping before one's eyes Oedipus's blind spot, the moment of his failure in intelligence, reason, and perspicuity, the moment when he commits the sacrilege of seeing himself as the sacred sinner who stands between men and the gods and who can, in expiating his crime, reconcile heaven and earth once more, appease the gods and cure Thebes of its plague.

For Cynthia Chase, following Freud, to leap all the way to the end of my line of commentators, the crime of Oedipus lies not in something he originally did, nor in its later repetition in his self-condemnation and self-blinding, but in between, in the interpretative connection of one with the other: "Like 'Emma''s typical 'psychoneurosis' [in Freud's

6. "Oedipal Textuality: Reading Freud's Reading of Oedipus," *Diacritics*, IX, No. 1 (Spring 1979), 54-68; see also Sandor Goodheart," Oedipus and Laius' Many Murderers," *Diacritics*, VIII, No. 1 (Spring 1978), pp. 55-71. Chase and Goodheart include references to the work of the other critics in their essays. Empson somewhere observes that Oedipus did not have an Oedipus complex, since he did not know it was his mother he married or his father he murdered.

7. Quoted and discussed by Philippe Lacoue-Labarthe, "The Caesura of the Speculative," *Glyph: 4* (Baltimore and London: The Johns Hopkins University Press, 1978), pp. 81-82.

Project of 1895], 'Oedipal' sexuality concerns a certain lag or limp of the subject in relation to structures of meaning. . . . An initial recollection of Sophocles' play gives us a 'first scene' in the murder of Laius, the Phocal crime, and a 'second scene' precisely in the drama itself, the moment of the legendary story chosen by Sophocles for representation on the stage; the quest for and recognition of the deed's agent and meaning. The accession to sexual awareness that converts an indifferent episode into a seduction in 'Emma''s case is paralleled in Oedipus' 'case' by an accession to genealogical awareness that converts an accidental manslaughter into patricide."[8]

* * *

If Oedipus was the first misreader of his own story, even when he apparently had come to see it most clearly, in his blindness, all the readers who come after, including those I have just been discussing, can do no more than repeat his gesture of a coverup which gives itself away through its own excess of repressive coherence, like a man who confesses to a crime by compulsively denying that he has committed it.

The first and most spectacular example of this was Aristotle when he chose *Oedipus the King* as the archetype of the perfect tragedy in the *Poetics*. The key word in the *Poetics* is *logos* in its various forms. The whole effort of the *Poetics* might be defined either as the banishing of the alogical or irrational from tragedy or as the argument that it is the function of tragedy to make the alogical logical, to bring into the light of reason what is dark, unreasonable, monstrous, incommensurate with the *logos*. The theatrical, what can be seen or seen through perspicuously, is implicitly identified by Aristotle with the reasonable or logical. In taking on *Oedipus the King*, with its play on blindness and insight and with its plot of the monstrous crimes of parricide and incest, with its one which is also more than one, with its dark illogic of family relationships in which a man's wife is also his mother, his children his siblings, Aristotle undertook to reduce a great deal of unreason to reason. In fact the remorselessly clear logic of Aristotle's exposition ("Aristotle is a skeleton," said Wallace Stevens[9]), is

8. Chase, *op. cit.*, pp. 57-58.
9. *Opus Posthumous* (New York: Alfred A. Knopf, 1957), p. 168.

everywhere threatened by a dark fringe of the alogical which is exposed, even by Aristotle, in the act of its coverup.

The alogical is dealt with in two ways by Aristotle, neither of which works as a successful varnishing over. One way is to banish it altogether, as when he says, categorically, that nothing irrational or that does not square with the reason should be presented directly on the stage: "The tragic plot must not be composed of irrational parts. Everything irrational *(alogon)* should, if possible, be excluded; or, at all events, it should lie outside the action of the play (as, in the Oedipus, the hero's ignorance as to the manner of Laius' death)."[10] Of course the whole theatrical force of *Oedipus the King* focuses on this irrational fact. The plot exists not to exclude it but to bring it into the light, not outside but inside the words and actions of the play.

The other way in which the irrational is dealt with in poetry, according to Aristotle, is by transforming it into something else through two puissant forms of metamorphosis or metaphor (which are really the same form). These are forms of change appropriate to poetry. They are performatives, ways of doing things with words which turn the alogical into the logical, the monstrous into the human, the pain of pity and fear into the aesthetic pleasure of a satisfactory denouement. These two forms of transforming are of course *mimesis* and *catharsis*. The remarkable thing about *mimesis* or imitation is that the pleasure of learning it provides is strong enough to counteract even the horrible or monstrous in the objects imitated: "Objects which in themselves we view with pain, we delight to contemplate when reproduced with minute fidelity: such as the forms of the most ignoble animals and of dead bodies. The cause of this again is," says Aristotle in his imperturbable way, "that to learn gives the liveliest pleasure."[11] In a tragedy, it is the *catharsis* which performs this transmogrification. "Even without the aid of the eye," says Aristotle, "he who hears the tale told will thrill with horror and melt to pity at what takes place. This is the impression we should receive from hearing the story of the Oedipus."[12] This pity and fear, however, are changed to pleasure as we learn, with Oedipus, the facts, tie them together rationally, and accept, in their *mimesis*, the reason even of such terrifying unreason as Apollo has imposed on Oedipus. We go forth in calm of mind, all passion spent.

10. Butcher, *op. cit.*, pp. 95-97.
11. *Ibid.*, p. 15.
12. *Ibid.*, p. 49.

Catharsis, however, as commentators on Aristotle have long recognized, is a homeopathic medicine. It cures by administering a small dose of the disease of unreasonable passion it would free us from. How can one be sure the dose is not excessive? The alogic of the theory of *catharsis* is like that of the killed virus as a vaccine. If the virus is truly dead it will have no effect. If it is alive it will cause the disease it is meant to cure. It must be both death and alive, absurdly or in contradiction to logic.

Everywhere in Aristotle's *Poetics* one finds the contradiction or alogic of an exclusion of the alogical which is at the same time an accommodation of it to reason. The pattern is there not only in the theories of *mimesis* and *catharsis,* but also in the historical sketch of the development of poetry and meter. This must show, and yet cannot show, how the natural became the cultural, just as *mimesis* itself is both natural to man, therefore part of nature, and at the same time reasonable and cultural, special to man alone, above brute nature. The same pattern is there in the aporias of beginning and ending which Aristotle's formulas encounter, as for example in the way the beginning must be both outside the play as its presupposed base and at the same time inside it, presented as part of the play. Aristotle is even led to recognize, absurdly, the possibility and even the existence, in the *Lynceus* of Theodectes, of a play which is all end or unravelling, since the beginning and the complication are presupposed as having happened before the play begins.[13]

The pattern of something alogical which is unsuccessfully covered over by logical reasoning is present, finally, in Aristotle's theory of metaphor. Here the neat logic of proportional or analogical metaphor (A is to B as C is to D) is undone by Aristotle's own recognition of the possibility of catachresis. This is the figure of speech in which one of the four terms is missing from the language and from our experience: "For some of the terms of the proportion there is at times no word in existence; still the metaphor may be used. For instance, to scatter seed is called sowing; but the action of the sun in scattering his rays is nameless. Still this process bears to the sun the same relation as sowing to the seed. Hence the expression of the poet 'sowing the god-created light.' "[14] Aristotle's theory of metaphor depends on a firm distinction

13. *Ibid.,* p. 65.
14. *Ibid.,* p. 79.

between literal and figurative. The theory is subverted when Aristotle recognizes the existence of words which are neither literal nor figurative. In the example Aristotle gives, "sowing" is not literal, since there is no literal word for the sun's shedding its rays, and not figurative, since the definition of a figure is that it is a metaphorical substitution for a literal word.

Aristotle's *Poetics* is not only surrounded by a fringe or margin of the irrational. It is invaded and its rationality everywhere undermined by various forms of unreason which it does not by any means wholly succeed in reducing to reason. Even Aristotle's logic cannot expunge or cover up the alogical in literature.

* * *

Beginning with an apparently marginal or innocuous example, Crabbe's "The Parting Hour," I have been led to recognize that not only in this poem but also in two grand precursor texts, the system of assumptions about selfhood, history, and literary form I began by describing is both affirmed and dismantled. If one should dare to extrapolate from these three examples, one might formulate this hypothetically as a general law for all texts in our tradition. If this law holds, then the conflict at this moment in American literary study between conservatives and deconstructers is only the latest example of a recurrent pattern in Western literature and literary criticism. If this should be the case, what then follows for "the ethics of reading"?

Two related provisional hypotheses about this may be briefly made in conclusion. The first is that neither the challenges to traditional humanistic certainties in contemporary American criticism nor the defensively aggressive reaffirmation of those certainties is willful, malicious, or blindly ignorant, nor is either something unique to our epoch, some unheard of nihilism, the "end of man," in one case, or a "new humanism" special to these far Western shores, in the other. Each position repeats operations of writing and reading which have recurred throughout our history. The perhaps necessary error or blindness of either is not to recognize the necessity of the other.

The second conclusion is embodied in that word "necessity." Both sorts of reading are necessitated by the words of the texts they treat. This means that reading is always an epistemological necessity before it is a matter of ethical choice or evaluation. More radically, it means that the ethics of reading is subject to a categorical imperative which is linguistic rather than transcendent or a matter of subjective will. Epistemology must take precedence over ethics in reading. One cannot make ethical judgments, perform ethical actions, such as teaching a poem, without first subjecting oneself to the words on the page, but once that has happened, the ethical operation will already necessarily have taken place. As Hölderlin says, in a phrase quoted by Paul de Man in a recent essay, "Es ereignet sich aber das Wahre." As de Man says, this can be freely translated, "What is true is what is bound to take place," which means that "reading . . . has to go against the grain of what one would want to happen in the name of what has to happen."[15] A reading is true as an acute angle is true to its model, or as one voice or word is true to another voice or word. The ethics of reading is not some act of the human will to interpretation which extracts moral themes from a work, or uses it to reaffirm what the reader already knows, or imposes a meaning freely in some process of reader response or perspectivist criticism, seeing the text in a certain way. The ethics of reading is the power of the words of the text over the mind and words of the reader. This is an irresistible coercion which shapes what the reader or teacher says about the text, even when what he says is most reductive or evasive. "Es ereignet sich aber das Wahre." The ethics of reading is the moral necessity to submit in one way or another, whatever one says, to the truth of this linguistic imperative.

15. In Carol Jacobs, *The Dissimulating Harmony* (Baltimore and London: The Johns Hopkins University Press, 1978), p. xi.

FINDING FEMINIST READINGS: DANTE-YEATS*

Gayatri Chakravorty Spivak

The fiction of mainstream literary criticism—so generally "masculist" that the adjective begins to lose all meaning (on this level of generality you could call it "capitalist," "idealist," or "humanist," as long as you show how)—is that rigorous readings come into being in a scientific field, or in the field of the legalistic demonstration of validity. The other view, coming from a mind-set that has been systematically marginalized, may just as well be called "feminist": that the production of public rigors bears the strategically repressed marks of the so-called "private" at all levels. It is not enough to permit the private to play in the reservations marked out by the subdivisive energy of critical labor: the olympian or wryly self-deprecatory touch of autobiography in political polemic or high journalism. It might, on the contrary, be necessary to show the situational vulnerability of a reading as it shares its own provenance with the reader. This is especially the case with feminist alternative readings of the canon that will not find their comfort in citing the demonstrable precedents of scientific specialism. Women must tell each other's stories, not because they are simple-minded creatures, but because they must call into question the model of criticism as neutral theorem or science. This essay is an exercise in allegorizing such a situation. It is hoped that the reader will learn the point of the awkward, elaborate yet marginal "autobiography" before he gets to the straight reading.

In the spring of 1977, I participated in a feminist literary criticism symposium. One of the principal papers was an excellent scholarly

*This essay in a slightly different form is forthcoming in *Social Text*.

presentation on Dante's *La Vita nuova*.[1] The paper took no stand on the brutal sexism of the tradition within which that text is situated. A woman in the audience asked at the end of the hour: "How can a woman learn to praise this text?" Before the speaker could answer, a distinguished woman present in the audience said, with authority: "Because the text deconstructs itself, the author is not responsible for what the text seems to say."

I was deeply troubled by that exchange. Here is male authority, I thought, being invoked by a woman to silence another woman's politics. Even at that, the most plausible way of understanding "the text deconstructs itself" is surely that the text signals the itinerary of its desire to be "about something," and that this itinerary must ruse over the open-endedness of the field of meaning; at a certain point, it is possible to locate the moment when the rusing reveals itself as the structure of unresolvable self-cancellings. Even if one honed a critical methodology sensitive and vulnerable to this understanding, there would remain the articulated specificity of the "somethings" that the text wishes, on one level, to mean, and with which it ruses. These are the "minimal idealizations" which constitute the possibility of reading.[2]

1. *Dante's Vita nuova:* A Translation and an Essay, tr. Mark Musa (Bloomington and London, 1973); further references are given as page numbers in my text. *La Vita nuova di Dante:* con le illustrazioni di Dante Gabriele Rossetti (Torino-Roma, 1903); cited in my text as D. I thank Ms. Gianna Kirtley for helping me with the Italian text.

2. Ignoring the ethico-political charge of such "minimal idealizations" sometimes affects the very finest readings with a formalist prejudice. In Shoshana Felman's brilliant treatment of *The Turn of the Screw,* for example ("Turning the Screw of Interpretation," *Yale French Studies* 55/56 [1977]), it is overlooked that the irony against the reading-enterprise is operated specifically through a female employee of a gentleman master. When Felman writes: "the 'governess' does govern" (p. 170), or that "the governess becomes, indeed, the *Master* of the ship, the Master of the meaning of the story (a master-reader)" (p. 173), we cannot help recalling the socio-sexual usage that fixes a great gulf between governess and Governor, mistress and Master. Indeed, in writing "In James's text as well as in Sophocles's, the self-proclaimed detective ends up discovering that he [!] himself is the author of the crime he is investigating: that the crime is his, that he is, himself, the criminal he seeks" (p. 175), Felman's otherwise impressively acute glance seems to miss that the governess in the James story is *not* allowed access to the Oedipal scene; unlike Oedipus, she does *not* know she is the criminal; and certainly is not allowed the privilege of punishing herself to save mankind, or even the story's world. Indeed Felman's essay does point out, although in a "sex-neutral"

Within a shifting and abyssal frame, these idealizations are the "material" to which we as readers, with our own elusive historico-politico-economico-sexual determinations, bring the machinery of our reading and, yes, judgment. As the choice of the strategic moment of the reply from the audience amply demonstrated, to know the limits of judgment is not to be able to help judging. "*La Vita nuova* should not be judged, for it, like all poetic texts, deconstructs itself" is, after all, a judgment, even in the colloquial sense; indeed, "the text deconstructs itself" is also a judgment, if only in the philosophical sense.

I confess that I was preoccupied that evening with computing the "practical" reasons for making the judgment in the *colloquial* sense rather than with the enclosure of metaphysics that made *philosophical* judgments inescapable at the limit. Both speaker and respondent were confronting tenure-decisions at the time. The institutional judgments involved in those decisions were carried out at least partially (and crucially) in terms of that very field of poetic language where judgment is supposed forever to be suspended or abandoned. As I walked out of the lecture room, I recalled the arrogance and anguish of the two women's judgments—expressed often in conversation—of the judges of their worth as judges of poetic texts.

"The poetic text should not be judged because it deconstructs itself," when used uncompromisingly to close rather than complicate discussion seemed, in that light, a wholesale exculpation of the text of one's trade, giving to the text a way of saying "I am not what I am not what I am not what I am not" and so on indefinitely or until the moment of suspended animation. When used in this way, the slogan seemed to fit only too well into the dreary scene of the mainstream pedagogy and

way, that the text's irony is against a governess who clutches the helm (phallus) too hard. Because she traces out in the text the intricate allegory of the flight of meaning, does she herself become a victim of the text's trap? We look in vain for a reading of the exclusion of Mrs. Grose (the illiterate housekeeper) and Flora (the girl-child) from *The Turn*'s allegory. Felman takes her place in the august company of the book's best readership: the Master-Author (Lacan, who is Master enough to forbid acknowledgment—"Lacan's works will be periodically referred to, not so much as an *authoritative* [italics mine] body of theoretical knowledge, but as a remarkably rich and complex analytical *text*" [p. 119]); the Author-Master (James, who is cited as authority against the critics' vulgar errors throughout the essay, and is finally shown as Master/dupe of his own fiction [p. 205]); and the governess, herself.

criticism of literature in the United States—hedged in as it is by "the autonomy of the text," "the intentional fallacy," and, indeed, "the willing suspension of disbelief." In such a case, the fear or contempt of what is taken to be the vocabulary and presuppositions of deconstruction that pervades mainstream American orthodoxy at the present time might be no more than a localized historical paradox. Is this how the situation of deconstruction should be understood?

All that summer and fall the problem haunted me, and that Christmas I thought I had found a formulation for it: deconstruction in the narrow sense domesticates deconstruction in the general sense. It is thus that it fits into the existing ideology of American literary criticism, which has already assimilated phenomenology's privileging of consciousness and is about to assimilate structuralism's apparent scientism. Deconstruction in the general sense, seeing in the self perhaps only a (dis)figuring effect of a radical heterogeneity, puts into question the grounds of the critic's power. Deconstruction in the narrow sense, no more than a chosen literary-critical methodology, locates this signifying or figuring effect in the "text's" performance, and allows the critic authority to disclose the economy of figure and performance.

I had read Derrida's *Glas* from summer 1976 to spring 1977. I thought I saw there a different way of coping with the sabotaging of deconstruction in the general sense by deconstruction in the narrow sense. Since the two are complicit and inseparably intermingled, the critic must write the theoretically impossible historical biography of that very self that is no more than an effect of a structural resistance to irreducible heterogeneity. I read *Glas* as an autobiography, "about" Hegel, Marx, Nietzsche, Freud, Genet et al.[3] Since a faith in the autobiographical self or in the authority of historical narrative is thoroughly questioned by the deconstructive morphology, Derrida's project was there taking the necessary risk of "demonstrating" how theory is necessarily undermined—as it is operated—by practice.[4] Rather than disclaim responsibility, Derrida was, I felt, now trying to write the limits of responsibility in different ways. He put it without rancor,

3. In "*Glas*-Piece: A Compte-rendu," *Diacritics* VII: iii (Fall 1977).

4. "What must be included in the description, i.e., in *what* is described, but also in the practical discourse, in the *writing that* describes, is not merely the factual reality of corruption and of alteration *[de l'écart]*, but corrupt*ability*" (Jacques Derrida, "Limited, Inc.," tr. Samuel Weber, *Glyph* II [1977], p. 218).

carefully preserving a legalistic metaphor of undisclosed hierarchies: "As always with a language, it is the *marriage* of a limitation with an opportunity."

Most of Derrida's work after *Glas* bears this mark of "historical" (auto)-biography. The essay from which I quote above begins: "I am introducing here—me (into) a translation," and ends: "not in order to decide with what intonation you will say, in the false infinity so variously declined of I—me: ME—psychoanalysis—you know."[5]

In my opening paragraph, I suggested that feminist alternative readings might well question the normative rigor of specialist mainstream scholarship through a dramatization of the autobiographical vulnerability of their provenance. It is no surprise, then, that as I pondered the exchange between my two colleagues, the "I/me" that I felt compelled to introduce in the space between deconstruction in the narrow and in the general senses (in itself not a hard distinction) was the subject of feminism. It is not one "subject" among many. It is the "object par excellence" as "subject." As such, the "gesture" of "reapply[ing] to a corpus the law with which it constitutes its object" can have for a woman a certain violence which is somewhat unlike the subtle language-displacement of the subject of psychoanalysis as critic.[6]

With the "subject" of feminism comes an "historical moment." No doubt any historical moment is a space of dispersion, an open frame of relationships that can be specified only indefinitely. Yet, as I argue above, the practice of deconstruction, like all practice and more so, undermines its theoretical rigor at every turn. Therefore, the trace of the self that struggles to define a historical moment, shoring up a space of dispersion even as that space gives the struggle the lie, must also go willy-nilly on record.[7] The answer from the audience had decided to

5. Jacques Derrida, "ME-PSYCHOANALYSIS: An introduction to the Translation of 'The Shell and the Kernel' by Nicolas Abraham," tr. Richard Klein, *Diacritics* 9:i (Spring 1979), pp. 6, 4, 12. Italics mine.

6. Ibid., p. 8.

7. A pre-deconstructive model of this is to be found in Heidegger's notion of the constitutive status of the necessary conflict between labor's worlding of a world and the self-secluding being of the earth; a non-deconstructive one in Deleuze and Guattari's formulation of the productive status of the ruptures between desire-production, disjunctive synthesis, recording, and conjunctive synthesis (Martin Heidegger, "Origin of the Work of Art," *Poetry, Language, Thought*, tr. Albert Hofstadter [New York, 1971]; Gilles Deleuze and Félix Guattari, *Anti-Oedipus: Capitalism and Schizophrenia*, tr. Robert Hurley et al. [New York, 1977]).

reduce that struggle out of the ordered field of deconstructive literary criticism. My task became to articulate a reading that was irreducibly marked and defined by the subject and "historical moment" of feminism.

(I have kept the paragraphs above and below untouched to convey a sense of the urgency I felt then. Today, three years later, I would write it a bit differently. There is no general "subject" of "feminism," no general "historical moment." I was in fact concerned with the practice of co-optation within the academic literary-critical scene in the United States, as it obtained inside rather elite circles. It is a concern that I have not relinquished, for, as I have argued elsewhere, to ignore one's own arena of practice and to turn to collectivities elsewhere might in the long run be a mistake.[8] Today I would be aware that it is a privileged arena, that the privilege of autobiography *to counter the rigor of the theoretical sanctions* is accessible to very few of the world's women. So much said, I would still endorse the energy of the readings themselves.)

Thus it was that I came to teach *La Vita nuova* at a Summer Institute that year. The specified title was "Recent Theories of Interpretation." I remarked on the first day that my task was to articulate a reading that was irreducibly marked and defined by the subject and historical moment of feminism. All but two of the men sought their pleasure and instruction elsewhere and dropped the class.

Assisted by that group of enthusiastic young women and two men, I read *La Vita nuova,* Yeats's *"Ego Dominus Tuus"* (which takes its title from *La Vita nuova*), and *A Vision* (which might recall the *Divine Comedy* in its title).[9] What we most especially remarked was that, apart from any tropological or performative deconstruction launched by the language of these writings, there was also a *narrative* of self-deconstruction as their scenario; and, curiously enough, woman was often the *means* of this project of the narrative.[10]

8. "Sex and History in *The Prelude* (1805): Books Nine to Thirteen," forthcoming in *Texas Studies in Language and Literature.*

9. The Rev. H. F. Cary's translation of the *Commedia* (New York, 1816), which Yeats is known to have used, was entitled *The Vision.* Yeats thought of himself as a subject, like Dante, of phase 17 of the Moon (Richard Ellmann, *Yeats: the Man and the Masks* [New York, Dutton paperback edition, 1948], pp. 236-37). The relationship between the definite and indefinite articles in the two titles is worth noting.

10. A reading such as Felman's (see n. 2) expertly describes the scenario but does not see the sexist charge.

As a group, the class agreed to produce papers that would fit together in a collection. I wrote a paper (Sections I to V of this essay) for the same deadline as the class, and it, like the rest of the papers, was subjected to class criticism. The resolve to produce a collective volume came to nothing, of course. The papers were too uneven, the participants without self-confidence, and I couldn't take "being a leader" seriously. In a society and institution which systematically rewards individual rather than collective excellence and originality, such a private act of utopian piety is, at any rate, useless.

I

Yeats needed ideal others. We know he knew of this need, diagnosed it often, made poetry, autobiography, and a vision out of it. "Say that my glory was I had such friends" ("The Municipal Gallery Revisited"). This Yeatsian sentiment expands until it takes in select inhabitants of history and myth, even wild swans and saints in a mosaic. How and why this need was needed is a question I must leave unanswered in this short piece. All I will say here is that Dante was perhaps the chief among these ideal others. Dante was a great nineteenth-century vogue. Emerson, Rossetti, and Longfellow translated him; Blake, Rossetti, and Gustave Doré illustrated him; Shelley, Matthew Arnold, and John Symonds wrote upon him; but Yeats seems to have liked him most because he loved the most exalted lady in Christendom. It was this love, thought Yeats, more than anything else, that allowed Dante as poet, though not as human being, to obtain "Unity of Being." In *A Vision,* Yeats writes: "Dante suffering injustice and the loss of Beatrice, found divine justice and the heavenly Beatrice."[11]

How is the figure of the woman used to achieve this psychotherapeutic plenitude in the practice of the poet's craft? This is the question I propose to consider in my essay. A greater question is implied within it. In Dante, as in Yeats, woman is objectified, dispersed, or occluded as a means; it is a reactionary operation that holds the texts together. If, as a woman, I deliberately refuse to be moved by such texts, what should I do with high art? As I have indicated, I am not unmindful of the deconstructive cautions against the feasibility of monolithic

11. *A Vision,* Macmillan paperback edition, New York, 1961), p. 44.

analyses: of "Dante," "Yeats," "myself," "art." In Derrida the reminder that all unified concepts such as these may be no more than textual ruses to postpone the possibility of a radical heterogeneity; in Lacan that they are the symbolic masquerade of the Imaginary. (Imaginary "relationships are constructed out of images, imaginings, imaginations and fantasy, but they are constructed in such a commonly unrecognized way that we are easily induced by our society to imagine them to be real, and hence go on treating them as if they actually were.")[12] Yet, as I have also indicated, the conservatism that has developed out of these potentially radical positions–the unexamined use of the argument that great texts deconstruct themselves, and thus that the canon might be preserved after all–will also not suffice.

If, as a woman, I refuse to be moved by such texts, what should I do with high art? That greater question I put aside as well, and come back to the lesser question: How is the figure of the woman used to achieve this psychotherapeutic plenitude in the practice of the poet's craft?

II

The title of Yeats's *"Ego Dominus Tuus"* (1917) is taken from Section three of Dante's auto-psychological tale *La Vita nuova*. The words are spoken by Love, whose Dantean description Yeats satisfactorily translates as "Lord of terrifying aspect."

Throughout *La Vita nuova,* one of Dante's strategies is the transference of responsibility. He repeatedly reminds us of the fragmented quality of his text and its inadequacy as a transcription of what really happened. In Section three, Dante's description of his first vision of Beatrice, for example, we read: "He [Love] spoke and said many things, of which I understood only a few; one was *Ego dominus tuus*" (p. 5; D 37).

12. It is difficult to find systematic definitions in Lacan. I therefore quote Anthony Wilden, "Culture and Identity: the Canadian Question, Why?," *Ciné-Tracts* 2:ii (Spring 1979), p. 6. I feel a certain solidarity with Mr. Wilden. As I translated the early Derrida, so he the early Lacan. He too seems to resist the elitist championship of his author, and to transpose the author's work into overtly political and situational categories that often lack "refinement of style."

"In dreams begins responsibility" (epigraph to *Responsibilities*) and this partially understood dream supposedly gives the first push to the previously composed collection of poems for which the prose text of *La Vita nuova* is a frame. Love and Beatrice may be dramatizations of the self-separation of auto-eroticism. For the vision in question resembles a wet dream. Dante sees Beatrice on the street, becomes drunkenly ecstatic, seeks the loneliness of his room, thinks of her, falls asleep, has a vision of fear and joy, and "a short time after this"—as the romantic novels say—, though still within the dream, cannot bear the anguish, and his drowsy sleep is broken.

In the dream, Love shows the poet his own bleeding heart, and makes Beatrice, held half-naked in Love's arms, eat it against her will. If I decide to describe the events of this dream-vision through psychoanalytic structures, I can treat it as telling the story of a fantasy where the woman allows the man to acquire a "passivity" that would prohibit "activity." By devouring Dante's phallus—the bleeding heart is a thin disguise—Beatrice "incorporates" him, "identifies" with him, acts for him.[13] It is, however, not a diadic but a triangulated transaction. Love is the lord who gives Beatrice this dubious power by showing Dante his heart as an already-severed "part object."[14] Through the intermediary of Love, the scene of a fantasmatic exchange is opened.

13. The classic argument for enabling incorporation-identifications is "Mourning and Melancholia," *The Standard Edition of the Complete Psychological Works of Sigmund Freud,* tr. James Strachey (London, 1957), vol. 14 (*Gesammelte Werke* [London, 1940], vol. 10). Incorporation as verbal cryptomania, traces of which one may find in Dante's text, is discussed in Nicolas Abraham and Maria Torok, *Cryptomanie: le verbier de l'homme-au-loup* (Paris, 1976). Derrida's introduction to this book has been translated as "Fors: the Anglish Words by Nicolas Abraham and Maria Torok," tr. Barbara Johnson, *Georgia Review* 31:i (1977). *La Vita nuova* may be considered Dante's act of mourning for Beatrice, incorporating her as a facet of his own ego-identification as poet. In that case, the mirror-image of Beatrice performing precisely that gesture of mourning for Dante's loss is a pertinent fantasy.

14. Melanie Klein developed the argument that the part-object, rather than necessarily an entire person, may be the object of affects. "My main conclusions on this theme: the primal internalized objects form the basis of complex processes of identification. . . . The inner world consists of objects, first of all the mother, internalized in various aspects and emotional situations. . . . In my view, the processes which Freud describes imply that this loved object is felt to contain the split-off, loved, and valued part of the self, which in this way continues its existence inside the object. It thereby becomes an extension of the self" ("On

Now that Beatrice has been unwillingly made to *introject*, Dante can *project*, create the text as product, begin to search for significance, analyze his dream, inaugurate a war against this integrated female (she's filled with the phallus now, after all). The war is also a self-glorification since it is his own phallus. The responsibility rests elsewhere, with the Master who perpetrated the curiously enabling castration of the poet. The woman's desire is nowhere in question, she remains mute, acts against her will, and possesses the phallus by a grotesque transplant.

Transferring responsibility, Dante allows himself a passive role. This particular theme of the passive role or pre-determined victimage of the author is repeated many times over in the text, although its credibility is much complicated.

In "The Seminar on *The Purloined Letter*," Lacan, without questioning or interpreting the Freudian suggestion that women hide their pubis by weaving a pendant phallus, calls the minister in Poe's story "feminine" when he begins to hide the letter in a certain way.[15] In that unquestioning spirit, one might say that Dante feminized himself as he chose for himself this passive role. If it is argued that tradition and convention allowed Dante to use this paradox of choosing passivity,

Identification," *New Directions in Psycho-analysis: the Significance of Infant Conflict in the Pattern of Adult Behaviour*, ed. Melanie Klein et al. [New York, 1955], pp. 310, 313). The part-object that is metonymic of the mother is of course the breast, as here the phallus is the metonym of the male. The curious thing is that Dante "object"-ifies himself so that Beatrice can be filled with his distanced "subject"-ivity.

15. Tr. Jeffrey Mehlman, *Yale French Studies* 48 (1972); "Le Séminaire sur *La Lettre volée*," *Ecrits* (Paris, 1966). The question Lacan does not ask would be: what is Freud that he needed to describe the woman's desire in this way? It is a question asked by Luce Irigaray in "La Tache aveugle d'un vieux rêve de symétrie," *Speculum: de l'autre femme* (Paris, 1974). Maria Torok's essay "La Signification de 'l'envie du penis' chez la femme" (in Nicolas Abraham, *L'ecorce et le noyau* [Paris, 1978]) seems, in the final analysis, unable to ask this question. She certainly takes the work of Melanie Klein and Ernest Jones forward by suggesting that the penis is no more than an idealized part-object, that although its fetishization requires the complicity of the woman its institutionalization is to man's advantage. But she never questions the sociality of what she seems to assume is the universally vicious imago of the mother—anal or phallic—and ends her piece, praising analysis because "it is meant to serve the cure" of penis-envy in women, with the highly ambiguous and possibly ironic condition that "the analyst be herself free from the phallo-centric prejudice, *as old as humanity*" (p. 171, italics mine).

another greater question looms: Why such traditions and conventions? A feminist-materialist analysis, menaced as it is constituted by deconstructive erasures, seems called for. Beatrice, then, can be said to *make* Dante act so. The story of Dante's extraordinary self-indulgence thus fabricates an excuse. Yet Beatrice herself does not act: she gives a greeting that is merely reported (sec. 3, p. 5; D 36). Her next gesture is the withholding of a greeting, and this withholding, too, is bypassed in Dante's narrative (sec. 10, p. 16; D 55). She is Dante's agent because she's a non-agent; by being an object who apparently regulates the subject's action, she allows the subject to deconstruct its sovereign motive and to disguise its masochism/narcissism.

In the dream following Beatrice's withholding of a greeting, Love appears again, suggests in Latin that the Beatrice episode might be a simulacrum, and tells Dante not to write her directly, but only through Love's mediation, for it is time to do away with simulacra (sec. 12, p. 17; D 58). Before the middle of the book, and while Dante is engaged in writing a poem, Beatrice's death is reported (sec. 28, p. 60-61; D 125).

Her beatification is a reduction of her proper name to a common noun, a possible word in the language, not necessarily indicating Miss Portinari, but signifying "she who gives blessing." (I interpret thus the ambivalent statement that introduces her in *La Vita nuova:* "She was called Beatrice even by those who did not know what her name was" (sec. 2, p. 3), and the accompanying disclosure of the poet's "animal spirit": *"Apparuit iam beatitudo vestra"*—now your beatitude has appeared (sec. 2, p. 4; D 34).

The common signification of her name as meaning "she who gives blessing" allows her to be placed within the anagogic Christian story, to be kicked upstairs or sublated, so that she can belong to God, the absolute male who might seem to stand outside the triangulated, analytical circuit of Love-Beatrice-Dante. The deprivation of her proper-ty, to put it formulaically, is her beatification. Her "proper name," that which is most proper to her, is emptied of its proper signification as her index, and restored back to the "common" language, where, miraculously, it becomes her definitive predication in terms of a non-indexical meaning accessible to dictionaries. The work is completed by death; through a numerological fantasy that has behind it the authority of the historical Imaginary of Christian doctrine; ending thus:

> This number was she herself–I say this by the law of similitudes *[per similitudine dico]*. What I mean to say is this: the number three is the root of nine for, without any other number, multiplied by itself, it gives nine: as we see manifestly *[come vedemo manifestamente]* that three times three is nine. Therefore, if three is by itself *[per se medesimo]* factor of nine, and by itself the factor of miracles is three, that is, Father, Son, and Holy Spirit, who are Three in One, then this lady was accompanied by the number nine so that it might be understood that she was a nine, or a miracle, whose root, namely that of the miracle, is the miraculous Trinity itself. Perhaps someone more subtle than I could find a still more subtle reason *[ragione]*, but this is the one which I see and which pleases me the most (sec. 29, p. 62; D 127).

Dante cannot describe this deprivation of Beatrice's property and identity in her glorification. But he also cannot allow his passivity to remain a full mask. The masculine figure of Love permits Dante to regain control. In Section nine, Love vanishes into him in a daydream. It is an unemphatic move, but it does reverse the reverse identification that Beatrice is made to perform in the initial dream.

It is, however, the play between Sections twenty-four and twenty-five that reflects the most resolute refusal-recuperation of control on Dante's part. In the former, Dante places the simulacra within the letter of the true and divine text and associates Beatrice with a Christ who is not named. "These ladies [Giovanna alias Primavera, and Beatrice] passed close by me, one of them following the other; and it seemed that Love spoke in my heart and said: 'The one in front is called Primavera . . . meaning she will come first on the day that Beatrice shows herself after the fantasy *[l'imaginazione]* of the faithful one. [Here too the proper name *Primavera*–Spring–is rendered into the common language as *prima verrà*–"will come first."] And if you will also consider her first *[primo]* name, you will see that this too means *Primavera,* since the name Joan *(Giovanna)* comes from the name of that John *(Giovanni)* who preceded the True Light' " (sec. 24, p. 52; D 110-11).

This is a moment of name-changing, a reminder of similitude and the authority of origins (as in Joan from John) rather than identity. "Love seemed to speak again and say these words: 'Anyone of subtle discernment, by naming Beatrice would name Love *[quella Beatrice chiamarebbe Amore]*, because she so greatly resembles me.' "

In Section twenty-five, which immediately follows this magnificent sublation, Dante asserts his own craftsmanly control. He places the figure of Love within the poetic tradition. He has been speaking, he says, of Love as if it were a thing in itself and a bodily substance. This is, of course, patently false. He cites examples from Virgil, Lucan, Horace, and Ovid, and explains that the figure named Love is allowed to exist, here as in any text, through poetic license. There is a further twist of the screw: "The first poet to begin writing in the vernacular was moved to do so by a desire to make his words understandable to ladies who found Latin verses difficult to comprehend" (sec. 25, p. 54-55; D 115). This is an argument against those who compose in the vernacular on a subject other than love, since composition in the vernacular was from the beginning intended for the treatment of love. At one stroke, Love (Master) and women are both brought under control. Some measure of superiority is still granted to the gentlemen's latin club, for Love speaks to Dante, though not invariably, in Latin. We remember with chagrin that Beatrice's august name had been given in the diminutive ("mona *Bice*" rather than Beatrice) in the previous exalting section.

And indeed, it is in the profession of writing that Dante comes into his own. The story of *The New Life* is openly declared to be a frame for a collection of poems previously composed, whose priority is, of course, deconstructed by placing it within the book's frame, and so on indefinitely.[16] The truth, or the adequation to truth of the frame narrative is disclosed through the following set: Memory is called a book whose privileged *reader*, though not the writer, is the autobiographer. Yet, we are in his power, for what we read in *La Vita nuova* is merely his own decision as to what is the gist of the pages of the book of Memory. This is the deconstructor's final gesture of retrieval. As author, he almost (though not quite) abdicates his sovereignty. "It is my intention to *copy* into this little book the words *I find written* under the heading [*Incipit vita nova*–the New Life begins] " (p. 3; italics mine; D 33).

16. For the deconstructive singularity of the frame or margin, see Jacques Derrida, "The Purveyor of Truth," tr. Willis Domingo et al., *Yale French Studies* 52 (1975); "Le Facteur de la vérité," *Poétique* 21 (1975); and "Le Parergon," *La Vérité en peinture* (Paris, 1978).

But the privilege of that *collective* readership is still in effect precariously maintained when textuality is said to extend beyond the bounds of the bound book. The very first poem within Dante's tale, and many of the others, are written for the brotherhood of fellow-writers and the fellow-servants of Love. (In my opening pages, I suggest that a certain use of the slogan "the text deconstructs itself" is an example of this abdication-recuperation topos, whereby the readership is recuperated even as individual sovereignty is disclaimed.)

As author, rather than merely as one of many readers, Dante exercises authority as well. It is of course abundantly clear that he is himself written into the anagogic text, just as Beatrice is put in her place there. Yet without Dante's book in hand, that text cannot be evoked in this instance. Thus, although the business of that higher text and Beatrice remains the first cause, nearly every section of *La Vita nuova* begins with: "moved by this thought I decided to write a few words." In addition, Dante analyzes each of his poems very strictly before or after he cites it, and when he does not, is careful enough to mention that that is only because the poem is obviously clear to all readers. It is not surprising that the book ends in a promise to write further: "I hope to write of her that which has never been written of any other woman." In Dante's text, Beatrice is fully sublated into an object—to be written *of*, not *to*.

And then the dumb broad is promoted yet further. She contemplates the One, but she does not understand him, for his predication is in Latin: *"qui est per omnia secula benedictus."* Thus, finally caught within the history of literary practice—that *entre-deux* between Latin and the vernacular—He is allowed to remain the agent. "And then may it please the One who is the Lord of graciousness that my soul ascend to behold the glory of its lady" (sec. 42, p. 86; D 164).

III

From such a text does Yeats borrow the title of his poem. What does the title conceal? Yeats's poem breaks into two voices, each the other's accomplice. Once again the self-separation of auto-eroticism, a longing for the self expressed in two ways. I resist here the hermeneutic seduction to show how that is so. Are the two together *Ego*? Does the title describe, rather, the relationship between those two voices, each claiming lordship over the other? Or, is the title descriptive of the theme of the poem—the urge to seek either the self, or its opposite. Clearly all this and more.

As a female reader, I am haunted rather by another question: Why are the names of the speakers, *Hic* and *Ille,* in Latin? It is not a very common thing in Yeats. Is this Yeats's version of Dante's dream? Where then, apart from those two lines in the poem:—"He found unpersuadable justice, he found / the most exalted lady loved by a man"—is the woman?

There are, as usual, at least two ways of constructing an answer to this question, a long way and, not surprisingly, a short. A long answer would be to say: it is indeed love that is Yeats's lord, but a love as much launched into the symbolic order of literary history—coming via Dante—as God, the true Lord, is at the end of *La Vita nuova.* One could then begin to formulate a feminist-psychoanalytic genealogy of the objectification of beloved (Maud Gonne), patroness (Augusta Gregory), and of the Mask and *Anima* as names for that mysterious female "thing" fallen or raised into multiplicity, of all of this as a refusal of action, the broaching of an ideology of victimage, disappointment, deception, the slow forging of a defeatist hero over against the folly of collective action, until the foolish and cowardly demos is shown to triumph in the name of comfort and brute loyalty in Yeats's very last poems.

The short way, on the other hand, would be to remember that *"Ego Dominus Tuus"* is the headpiece of a longer prose text, also with a Latin title—*Per Amica Silentia Lunae* ("By the friendly silence of the moon")—its two parts titled in Latin as well—*"Anima Hominis"* (man's soul), *"Anima Mundi"* (world's soul)—the whole text framed by two letters to a woman, her name disguised as a masculine name, "Maurice," within quotation marks. These letters are, indeed, "purloined or prolonged," as in Lacan's etymological fantasy in the essay to which I have already referred. I will not pursue that trajectory, for that will lead us back to the long way. I will propose rather that Yeats's technique of allusion—all that Latin is a sort of meta-narrative sign—here allows him to keep the woman out, to occlude, to neutralize, and thus to continue that entire history of the sublation and objectification of the woman.

To keep the woman out. Here the third woman in Yeats's life plays a role. She was caught on the rebound within the institution of marriage, and had a masculine nickname, "Georgie Yeats." She was the transparent medium through which the voices of Yeats's instructors, themselves at first dependent upon his own text, traveled: "On the afternoon of October 24th 1917 [Yeats writes in *A Vision*], four days after my marriage, my wife surprised me by attempting automatic writing. . . . The unknown writer took his theme at first from my just published *Per Amica Silentia Lunae*" (p. 8). We are back to *"Ego Dominus Tuus."* Is it the unknown writer who is Yeats's lord, is it Yeats who is his wife's lord? We are caught in another labyrinth of "I," "you," and mastery.

IV

The entire problematics of the objectification of woman is neutralized, encrypted, dispersed, and thus operated by the allusion in Yeats's title. In Dante, the point was not simply that the image came from outside, but that the image was of an unwilling Beatrice eating the poet's heart. Yeats's poem silently points to that image while ostensibly discoursing on the provenance of poetry.

It is not by chance that *Per Amica Silentia Lunae* is the agent, or non-agent, of *A Vision*. Even the non-Latinist female reader recognizes that the moon in the title is feminine, and remembers, of course, that the moon is Yeats's celebrated sign for subjectivity. This, then, is a subjective text, and the poet is of the moon/woman's party! I seem almost to lose my argument. I recover it, in part, by pointing out that it is when the moon is silent that the poet speaks. And then I remind myself that Milton's shadow is all over Yeats's work. Milton's blind Samson, absorbed with Delilah as Homer with Helen or Raftery with Mary Hines—all those eyeball-less poets singing of women—sings,

> The Sun to me is dark
> And silent as the Moon,
> When she deserts the night
> Hid in her vacant interlunar cave.
> (*Samson Agonistes*, 1. 86-89)

"Vacant" (meaning "vacationing") is almost Latin here, and the silence of the moon, within the well-known outlines of Yeatsian allegory, is anything but friendly, for it is the dark of the moon, close to pure objectivity, when what is not the self takes over.[17] Indeed, the objective sun is inaccessible, "the sun to me is dark." The Miltonic allusion carries a charge which complicates Yeats's "system." It is as if the poet wishes to force a personal "meaning" out of the impersonal truth of "allegory," to operate forcibly in spite of allegorical calculation. In those well-known lines from "The Tower," he repeats the gesture more openly

> But I have found an answer in those eyes
> That are impatient to be gone;
> Go therefore; but leave Hanrahan,
> For I need all his mighty memories.
> ("The Tower," lines 101-04)

Why should we believe this declaration of "finding," when all that the poet shows himself as manipulating is his own past creation Hanrahan? He must coax the fictive memory of his own creation to produce the desirable answer—not a dismissal but a resignation (that was the point about the benighted insurrectionists at "Easter 1916" as well—"they resigned their part in the casual comedy"), not a rejection but a conscientious renunciation, his own defeat not an objective fulfillment but a subjective loss:

> Does the imagination dwell the most
> Upon a woman won or woman lost?
> If on the lost, admit you turned aside
> From a great labyrinth out of pride,
> Cowardice, some silly over-subtle thought
> Or anything called conscience once.
> ("The Tower," lines 113-18)

In *Per Amica* as well, it is literary history, the record of subjective triumphs, rather than allegoric system that declares the silence of the moon to be friendly. The phrase is Virgilian, comes from Dante's guide. The Virgilian line is given in full within Yeats's text, in the opening sentence of "Anima Mundi," after an invocation of ruins, broken

17. It is to belabor the obvious that I am referring to the symbological fantasmagoria developed by Yeats in *A Vision* and most of his mature poetry.

architraves: "*A Tenedo tacitae per amica silentia lunae*" (*The Aeneid*, II, 255-56).

To read and undo that long problematic sentence in Yeats is another temptation I resist. I ask instead, who came from Tenedos by the friendly silence of the quiet moon? It is a moment of great cunning. The Argives arrive and free the Greeks from the wooden horse. Troy is destroyed. It is this scene of carnage in the name of the transgressing woman as sexual agent that is hidden behind that line. Yet, Helen is mentioned only twice, and incidentally, in the second book of the *Aeneid*. The hero recounts a dream of the mutilated Hector passing the relay to himself, Aeneas. The audience of one is Dido, a "lady in love," dressed in Helen's clothes brought from Aeneas's ship, caught in the in-fighting (moderated by a benign Zeus) between spiteful Juno and Venus; part of the story is a justification (provided by Aeneas's dead wife in yet another dream) for Aeneas's desertion of his wife in the face of the advancing Greek army. Whatever one makes of the *mise-en-scène*, the matter is a transaction between men, on the occasion here of a fallen woman, the harlot queen, as much a stereotype as the virgin mother. It is a transaction from Homer to Virgil to Dante to Milton to Yeats. Fill in the interstices and you have the Great Tradition of European poetry.[18] It is not for nothing that Yeats, allowing textuality though not ostensibly the sovereign author to triumph, looks for a reader at the end of "*Ego Dominus Tuus.*" What had been mere "magical shapes" has become, through the poem, "characters" to be deciphered. The figure of writing passes the relay to a mysterious future reader. And now,

> I call to the mysterious one who yet
> . . . standing by these characters, disclose[s]
> All that I seek; and whisper it as though
> He were afraid the birds, who cry aloud
> Their momentary cries before it is dawn,
> Would carry it away to blasphemous men.

18. As evinced, for example, in a title such as the following: Henry Walcott Boynton, *The World's Leading Poets: Homer, Virgil, Dante, Shakespeare, Milton, Goethe* (New York, 1912). Hugo and Verlaine on the matter of Troy might provide occasion for a comparable feminist excursus.

Like Dante or Poe's Minister, Yeats makes himself passive, "feminizes" himself. It is clearer at the end of *Per Amica* where Yeats writes, "I wonder will I take to them [my 'barbarous words'] once more, for I am baffled by those voices . . . or now that I shall in a little be growing old, to some kind of simple piety like that of an old woman" (p. 366).

V

What have I performed here? Tried to read two versions of the inbuilt exploitation of the figure of the woman in two autobiographical and self-deconstructive texts. What, then, must a woman do with the reactionary sexual ideology of high art? It is not enough to substitute "low" for "high," and perpetrate an ideology of complacent rejectionism, or an academic populist reverse sexism. On the other hand, it is also not enough to search mightily for a way of conserving and excusing the canon at all costs.

Is this dilemma itself symptomatic of the fear of the risks that all great changes might involve? Must one simply honor the breach between "the field of action" and "the field of art" and function by means of an ever-abreactive historical analysis, and try to undo deliberately structures of fear, desire and pleasure that, even if metaleptic, are beyond one's control? Whatever the program might be, it involves at least a decision to re-read "as a feminist." I am helpless before the fact that all my essays these days seem to end with projects for future work.[19] I seem to be surrendered to the Great Tradition in closing my piece with a promise.

19. It seems pertinent to mention the completion of one such project since this essay was written: a long article entitled "Displacement and the Discourse of Woman," forthcoming in a collection on displacement to be published by the Center for Twentieth Century Studies at the University of Wisconsin-Milwaukee. There is also 'Three Feminist Readings: McCullers, Drabble, Habermans," *Union Seminary Quarterly Review*; 35, i & ii (Fall & Winter, 1979-80), and essays on Marx, Freud, and Feminism to be published in *Voices of Feminist Scholarship* (University of Illinois Press) and on International Feminisms forthcoming in the papers of the first annual convention of the Marxist Union.

VI

Here ends the paper written in haste for a class deadline with a collective purpose out of a feminist anguish with academic deconstructive practice. Since then I have read it four times for money, once for an interview, once at a conference, once at a women's lunch. This is not to make a romantic disclaimer against what minimal effectiveness the essay might wield. This is simply to echo wearily that old pedantic sentiment: "to make changes would have been too drastic; I have let it stand as it was;"–except, nearly a year later, to add the paragraph on page 47.

I *would* like to touch, however, in a formal if not a substantive way, a few of the unanswered questions left in the earlier paper. For example: Why are the traditions and conventions of art so brutally sexist (page 52)? Here an immense work of genealogical investigation awaits us. Unfortunately, traditional positivistic historical (or herstorical) work of documentation and restoration remains caught in an ideology of cause and effect which catches us on the rebound into self-congratulation and cannot touch those metaleptic ruses of psycho-social structuring that represent themselves as the rigorous infallibility of that very historical method. (The dictionary meaning of "metalepsis" is "the substitution by metonymy of one figurative sense for another." Following Marx (the argument from fetishization, the money-form, and ideology), Nietzsche (the argument from genealogy and the true-false fiction), Freud (the argument from the unconscious and irreducible distortion *[Entstellung]*), and Heidegger (the argument from secondary dissembling and the double withdrawal), the poststructuralist tendency (Lacan, the later Barthes, Foucault, Deleuze and Guattari, Derrida) would present "cause" and "effect" as two such "figures." Thus the substitution of "effect" for "cause" which is one of the chief abuses of history would become a special case of metalepsis.) The present essay is a brief analysis of the discursive practice of two "literary" texts, an analysis permitted at least formally by the definition of the field of "literary criticism." The task is to analyze the discursive practice of "documentary" texts, and not merely from the point of view of the dominant "trope" or "rhetorical figure." (That would be to privilege the permissive discipline of "literary criticism" and thus neutralize genealogical analysis.) The task is to mark, rather, how "discursive practices are characterized by the delimitation of a field of objects, the definition of a legitimate perspective for the agent of knowledge, and the fixing of norms for the elaboration of concepts and theories."[20] And to avoid the quick citing of slogans (as in the comment from the audience at the feminist symposium) that will cut off such "non-literary" analyses, the following might be remembered: "The movements of deconstruction [or genealogical analysis] do not destroy structures from the outside. They are not possible and effective, nor can they take accurate aim except by inhabiting those structures. . . . Operating necessarily from the inside, borrowing them structurally, that is to say without being able to isolate their elements and atoms, the enterprise of deconstruction always in a certain way falls prey to its own work."[21] (In *Glas* Derrida undertakes such a *complicit* genealogical analysis of the history of philosophy.) If all analysis is a shoring up of a self in the midst of the irreducible and originary ruins of being, it seems necessary to acknowledge that analyzing, we borrow structures from that which we analyze, that the limits of judging can only be given in a judgment.

I had also not shown how *Hic* and *Ille*, the two voices of Yeats's poem, are each other's accomplice. Ezra Pound caught it in a jest when he called them *Hic* and *Willie.*[22] Here is a brief blueprint: *Hic* has arrived at *Ille*'s "summons"–he is what *Ille* wants (lines 7-10). Looking for the real face rather than a mask-image, *Hic* describes Dante as if Dante had made a mask: "he has made that hollow face of his / More plain to the mind's eye" (lines 21-22). *Ille* grants that original face as the place of the hunger that motivates the making of the stone image that *Ille* then presents as Dante's face:

> And did he find himself
> Or was the hunger that had made it hollow
> A hunger for the apple on the bough . . .
> (1.23-25)

20. Michel Foucault, "History of Systems of Thought" [summary of a course given at the Collège de France, 1970-71], *Language, Counter-Memory, Practice: Selected Essays and Interviews*, tr. Donald F. Bouchard and Sherry Simon (Ithaca, 1977), p. 199.

21. Jacques Derrida, *Of Grammatology* (Baltimore, 1976), p. 24.

22. Ellmann, *Yeats*, p. 197.

What then, one might ask, is the difference between the psychological status—this being a poem about the artist's psychology—of Dante's stone image and Keats's luxurious song? *Ille* does not deny *Hic* that Keats looked for happiness, but only that he found it. But *Hic* had already taken care of it in his adjective "deliberate" (line 54). All these slidings and blurrings of the two positions are kept at bay by the authority of the sententious binary opposition:

> The rhetorician would deceive his neighbours,
> The sentimentalist himself; while art
> Is but a vision of reality.
> (lines 47-49)

The final lines of the poem, like lines 7-10, can in principle be a description of *Hic,* in which case the aura of mystery is dramatic irony against the pompous *Ille,* as the aura of oppositions in the poem might be dramatic irony against the reader. Pound's mistake, if that is what it was, had been to take this duplicitous complexity for a mere failure of logic. Ours would be to take this labyrinth of self-deconstruction to be free of the charge that "communicates" the topos of the artist's negative capability at the expense of the repression or occlusion of the woman.

I shall end with the exquisitely orchestrated sentence in *Per Amica* that delivers *A Tenedo tacitae per amica silentia lunae:*

> I have always sought to bring my mind close to the mind of Indian and Japanese poets, old women in Connacht, mediums in Soho, lay brothers whom I imagine dreaming in some mediaeval monastery the dreams of their village, learned authors who refer all to antiquity; to immerse it in the general mind where that mind is scarce separable from what we have begun to call "the subconscious"; to liberate it from all that comes of councils and committees, from the world as it is seen from universities or from populous towns; and that I might so believe I have murmured evocations and frequented mediums, delighted in all that displayed great problems through sensuous images or exciting phrases, accepted from abstract schools but a few technical words that are so old they seem but broken architraves fallen amid brambles and grass, and have put myself to school

where all things are seen: *A Tenedo tacitae per amica silentia lunae.* (p. 343)

This attempt at reading will bring me back to some working hypotheses submitted at the opening of this essay: there remain the articulated specificity of the "somethings" that the text might mean, and with which it ruses. These are the "minimal idealizations" which constitute the possibility of reading. Within a shifting and abyssal frame, these idealizations and things are the "material" to which we as readers, with our own elusive historico-politico-economico-sexual determinations, bring the machinery of our reading and our judgment. The machinery is to look for identities and differences–to make connections. To choose not to read is to legitimate reading, and to read no more than allegories of unreadability is to ignore the heterogeneity and asymetry of the "material."

Yeats's sentence states a program, but obstacles are placed, in a mood of self-deconstruction, between the subject and his action. The program is, through making oneself passive, to pass from a limited *anima* to a general. The allusive metaphor chosen to describe the program is that stealthy entry into Troy.

One might say that, by this passively enhanced activity fabricated to get in touch with *Anima Mundi*–"the most exalted lady in creation," Yeats hopes to undo the harm that the language of abstraction and technique have done to the mind. He will, however, use that language, even if minimally and guarded with the "[nothing] but" construction–a little abstraction, "a few technical words . . . so old" (although "the subconscious" will hardly fill this bill)–"naturalize" it through an invocation of time's tyranny and a metaphor of ruins among brambles. Yet those old words only "seem" broken architraves, just as the wooden horse *seemed* innocent. We are free to imagine that Yeats dreams of making them the chief beam (arch + trave) of an edifice associated with the goal of all abstraction and technique: writing, "where all things are seen," *A Vision* between covers.

It must be emphasized that Yeats's sentence is a deliberate search for the areas of the mind thought to be almost beyond deliberation. "I have sought to bring my mind close to [certain kinds of mind], to immerse it [my mind] in the general mind where that mind [we know the antecedent, but in this masterfully clumsy prose the 'it' and the 'that' begin a sub-textual exchange, 'my mind' usurping 'general mind' and vice versa] *is scarce separable* from what we have begun to call 'the subconscious' " (italics mine). Indeed, the sentence moves toward *increased* deliberation. From an image of ideal others (within the larger movement, the predication of these others rises in rank from racial, sex-class-based, heterodox-professional qualities of mind; to trained and truant dreaming; to learned reference) to delight in chosen kinds of art to a judicious choice of language culminating, precisely, in a learned reference. What interests me specifically is that in Yeats's language, chosen from what is millenially available, the *anima*, end and means of the program, is elaborated into figures of woman; and that the historical signal, in Latin, and indirectly commanded by Dante, is that particular Virgilian-Homeric line.

COMEDIES OF ERRORS: PLATUS–SHAKESPEARE–MOLIÈRE

René Girard

The theater has always loved identical twins. They belong to the mythological sources of many traditional plots, tragic as well as comic. The twins must be as old as the theater itself. And they are as new as the most recent entertainment media, the cinema and television. There is no great career in comedy without a new version of the identical twins. The oldest extant version is *The Menechmus Twins* of Plautus. In *The Comedy of Errors* Shakespeare used it as a model and it is still a model today.

Why this popularity of the twins? Both Pascal and Bergson saw something intrinsically funny about two perfectly identical human beings. Quite a few people, indeed, are amused when they see identical twins side by side but this fact has nothing to do with the comedies of twins. If it did, the most successful works would show the twins together on the stage most frequently and for the longest possible time. Their creation would not be artistic in the full sense, it would resemble the exhibition of freaks in a carnival. Those critics who despise the comedies of twins believe that it does but they are wrong. Even in its most farcical form, this comedy has nothing to do with the mere spectacle of the twins' physical resemblance. Beginning with Plautus, it is an absolute rule that the twins must never appear together on the stage until the very last scene. If they did, they would be recognized as identical and the plot would collapse. The recognition scene is also a resolution. When it occurs the fun is over and it is not beginning as would be the case if the opinion of Pascal and Bergson, true as it may be, were relevant to the interpretation of this comic plot.

The true basis for this plot is the unsuspected substitution of the twins. Potentially disruptive consequences must result and they cannot result unless the substitutions are genuinely disconcerting to the people involved, including the twins themselves. The twins must interact with the same people repeatedly, but they must not interact with each other. They must not even suspect that they are in each other's vicinity and neither must anyone else. This requirement demands very special circumstances, which are not easily satisfied. As a result successive authors tend to reproduce the same plot with only minor variations. The twins have been separated from birth and they have lost sight of each other. They must have the same name, otherwise they would suspect the nature of the mistake when addressed by a stranger and they would clear up the confusion prematurely.

Things become more complicated if you have four twins instead of two, like Shakespeare in *The Comedy of Errors.* Why not quadruplets? Because we must have servants and masters. Two of the twins are slaves and their name is Dromio. Each Dromio is respectively attached to a gentleman in the other set, named Antipholus. All these twins got together at birth, then they were all in a shipwreck together and separate rescuers brought one of each set to Ephesus, and the two others in each set to Syracuse.

At the beginning of the play Antipholus of Syracuse has been looking for his lost twin all over the Mediterranean and his mood is one of discouragement when he lands in Ephesus, with his Dromio in attendance, naturally. Little does he know that his twin brother lives there, flanked by his own Dromio, a solid citizen and a married man, well known of everybody in town.

Many critics regard the device of the twins as artificial and cheap and they find it distressing that even a very young Shakespeare would make it cheaper still by having twice as many twins as the nearest competitor. Most do not even bother to justify their disdain but one who does is Harry Levin in his introduction to the Signet paperback of *The Comedy of Errors.* To achieve greatness, he claims, a comic writer must rely on contrivance rather than chance, on malice and mischief rather than sheer luck.

The distinction between contrivance and chance seems clear but it is not, at least in comedy. The comic contrivance par excellence is disguise. Shakespeare has a lot of disguise. So do the other great classical playwrights. In Beaumarchais' *Barbier de Sêville,* for instance, an old guardian and would-be husband keeps Rosalina a virtual prisoner in his house. In order to gain access to her, Almaviva, instructed by Figaro, impersonates first a drunken soldier, then a music master. Disguise is generally successful because it is the mainspring of comedy. Even the most improbable disguise, in the most improbable circumstances will insure the safe transfer of the disputed object from the old tyrant's hands to those of his handsome rival.

The most improbable and yet most successful disguise is that of a god; it is always perfect because a god can assume any physical appearance he chooses. In the story of *Amphytrion*, for instance, Jupiter assumes the features of the husband in order to propel himself into the bed of a still faithful wife, Alcmene. If you are a god you do not need to climb over high balconies, you do not have to feign suicidal despair or undergo any of the indignities to which the more ordinary lovers must submit.

Plautus turned this myth into a play. The Greeks had done it before but their work has not reached us. When Molière wrote his *Amphytrion*, many centuries later, he borrowed many things from Plautus. When Jean Giraudoux, in 1938, decided to write still another one, he made a list of all previous *Amphytrions* and the total, he claimed, came to thirty-seven. He had two good reasons, therefore, to entitle his play: *Amphytrion 38.*

In Molière, Jupiter presents himself to Alcmene as her husband, who happens to be back earlier than expected from a war to which the sly god had effectively arranged to dispatch the real Amphytrion. Unaware of dealing with a total stranger, the virtuous wife opens her arms to her divine guest.

This situation is less unique than it seems. In *The Comedy of Errors*, the twin from Syracuse is invited into his brother's house by none other than his brother's wife, Adriana, and the sister of the latter, Luciana. These virtuous women are deceived by the physical appearance of the visitor. The comic effect is very much the same as in *Amphytrion* even though in one case chance is responsible for the confusion and in the other the deception is intentional. In one case the visitor is in good faith, he too is deceived, whereas in the other he is an impostor. If Harry Levin were right, if the distinction between chance and intention were as significant as he claims, *The Comedy of Errors* and the *Amphytrion* of Molière would be at opposite ends of the comic spectrum; they would have little in common, and yet, in the two scenes I have in mind, at least, they are close to each other.

The truth is, of course, that Shakespeare borrowed that scene not from his most direct model, *The Menechmus Twins*, but from the Amphytrion of the same Latin playwright. Seeing its comic possibilities, just as Molière did, he decided to make use of that scene, and he found it easy because it is always easy to shift from the twins to the theme of divine disguise and vice versa. No professor of comparative literature was around to tell him not to do it.

A clever comedian will immediately realize that the comic possibilities of the twins and of Amphytrion are basically the same; that is why Shakespeare really borrowed indifferently from both stories when he wrote his *Comedy of Errors.* The idea of having four twins instead of two, for instance, is really another borrowing from *Amphytrion.* Jupiter takes an assistant divinity along on his pleasure trip, the god Mercury who assumes the physical appearance of Amphytrion's personal slave, Sosia.

The war to which the real Amphytrion has been dispatched really happens to be finished earlier than expected. When the real Sosia shows up at the gate, ahead of his master, the false one beats him black and blue; the outsiders are in and the insiders are out. His own wife and his own house, all the possessions of Amphytrion are in the hands of triumphant usurpers. The rightful owner is cast into outer darkness where he can do nothing, except of course take up the occupation that seems appropriate to that kind of place: screaming and the gnashing of teeth.

In *The Comedy of Errors* we have exactly the same reversal of outsiders and insiders. There too, the legitimate twins are forcefully kept out of their house while their illegitimate doubles inside make merry with the women. The cause is different but the result is the same. Divine disguise, the supreme contrivance of comedy, amounts to the same thing as the accidental birth of twins. There is no more difference, really, between Amphytrion and Jupiter, than between the twins themselves.

In *The Comedy of Errors,* and more generally in all comedies of twins, the characters deal with each other on the assumption that all of them are unique and immediately identifiable as such. If they did not cling to this assumption in the face of contrary evidence they would not become so confused. It takes more than the presence of undistinguishable twins, I repeat, to generate the comic effects; it takes this persistent refusal to acknowledge the possibility of beings, human or divine, less different from each other than we would like them to be.

The stubborn expectation of difference in the face of non difference is not reserved to the comedies of twins; it is a very Shakespearean predicament that appears not only in the comedies but in the tragedies and above all in the unclassifiable plays, the so-called problem plays that transcend all differences of genre because they focus on the dimension that is common to all and it is, I believe, the paradoxical relationship I am now trying to define. This non-difference occurs between antagonists who are not always physical twins but who literally turn into intellectual and moral twins in the process of fighting each other, of being each other's rivals. They desire the same object, they think the same thoughts, they resort to the same strategies, they regard each other with the same hatred and fascination; they are alike in everything including their belief in the reality and enormity of the difference between them. The paradox of the relationship becomes more extreme as the hostility intensifies; the delusion of individual difference heightens as more and more uniformity prevails.

The rivals themselves do not realize that their spirit of rivalry turns them into xerox copies of each other. The Ajax and Achilles of *Troilus and Cressida* are good examples. Ulysses does his best to bring the vanity of Ajax up to the level of Achilles', and he succeeds so well that Ajax resembles Achilles more and more, thinking of himself, all the time, a vastly different man. The envy each feels for the other gives to both an undeniable insight into the personality they have in common, which includes a common inability to turn this insight back upon themselves. We need uninvolved spectators to perceive all this and in this case they are the other Greek leaders who comment ironically on a circularity of judgment readily visible to anyone except to the judges themselves.

Ajax wonders in amazement at the immensity of Achilles' pride: "How should a man be proud? How doth pride grow? I know not what pride is." Nestor observes in an aside: "Yet he loves himself; is't not strange?" Then Ajax asks: "Shall pride carry it?," in other words, shall the pride of Achilles have the last word? And Nestor comments: "An't would, you'ld carry half."

This little jeu de scène reappears later. Shakespeare repeats the point again and again, with an almost didactic insistence that suggests its extreme importance. And it is essential indeed, not only to *Troilus and Cressida* but to the understanding of Shakespeare's entire work. Here is Ajax again, still speaking of Achilles:

A paltry insolent fellow!
Nestor (aside): How he describes himself!
Ajax: Can he not be sociable?
Ulysses: The raven chides blackness.
Ajax: I'll let his humours blood.
Agamemnon (aside): He will be the physician
that should be the patient.

In *Troilus and Cressida*, every comic or grotesque effect corresponds to an effort on Shakespeare's part to reveal the absence of a difference in which everybody believes. When the Greek leaders meet to approve the strategy of inflaming further the already smouldering rivalry between Ajax and Achilles, Nestor sums up the whole plan in terms that emphasize the reciprocity of the antagonists, as well as the emptiness of their struggle.

Two curs shall tame each other: pride alone
Must tarre the mastiffs on, as 'twere their bone.

For all the mad dogs of the Greek and Trojan army there is only one bone, the bare bone of pride. The key word in the play is "emulation." If you emulate someone, you pattern yourself on him, you follow the same rules of thinking and behavior. "Aemulari" and "imitari" are probably one and the same word. There is an imitation of rivalry that we do not perceive because it is conflictual. It is a major force in human relations and it operates like the twins of *The Comedy of Errors*. As it destroys existing differences, it increases the expectation of difference.

All sworn enemies in Shakespeare closely resemble each other and the perpetual misunderstanding between them is that resemblance, not some mythical difference that does not exist. This is true of Coriolanus and Aufidius, it is true of Goneril and Reagan, the rival sisters of *King Lear* who certainly deserve to be twins. In *Hamlet* the lack of difference between the two criminal brothers, old Hamlet and Claudius, is perceived only too clearly by the hero. And it is this unwanted perspicacity that accounts for the feebleness in him of the revenge spirit. Hamlet resembles his creator too much to be a good tragic hero.

Desire itself is conceived by Shakespeare as mimetic. The object of desire is determined by the model. If the model reaches for an object, his imitator will also reach for that object.

The Greeks want Helen back only because the Trojans want to keep her and the Trojans want to keep her only because the Greeks want her back. In this process of mimetic rivalry, the Greeks and the Trojans make each other alike; they are all united as well as separated by the same love/hate relationship. The same is true of the lovers who become the victims of their own mimesis, and who turn into prostitutes and pimps, just like the diplomats and politicians, as they vainly try to control the mimetic desire of others. As they fight more and more furiously, their common mimetic vainglory seems to make all the difference in the world when in reality there is none.

The tendency to reciprocity is one with the mimetic nature of desire. Just as the interference of the model exasperates the imitator's desire the interference of the imitator exasperates the model's desire. This model turns into an imitator of his imitator just as the imitator turns into a model of his own model. Hence the simultaneous evolution toward less difference and more illusion of difference. As the rivals keep thwarting each other, in their reciprocal imitation, they make each other more alike but, in each other's eyes, they look monstrously and even supernaturally different.

The mimetic desire of Shakespeare generates the ambivalent triangles of the comic and tragic theater more readily and efficiently than the Oedipus complex of Freud. No sooner does mimetic desire enter the stage than it becomes the stage of a theater. The play is always a play within the play. In *A Midsummer Night's Dream,* the preparation of the play within the play, the rehearsals of the craftsmen and the amorous entanglements of the four lovers are all examples of the same desire to impersonate the most prestigious models and to be translated into someone else. Bottom's desire for the theater forms a counterpoint with the theatricality of "true love" and all these desires finally blend into the madness of the midsummer night. The actor's boundless appetite for acting, his desire to monopolize all the parts, leads to the same results as Helena's fascination for her friend and rival Hermia.

Since the two boys are predictably in love with the same Hermia, the neglected Helena, too, must join the general desire and pay homage to Hermia. This docility of desire, this urge to follow the erotic trend as one would any other fashionable trend guarantees not the maximum harmony but the maximum disharmony. Desire cannot become a slave to fashion without becoming competitive and exposing itself to the perpetual interference of other desires. The lovers know this perfectly well and they are secretly disappointed if these sad consequences do not materialize. "True love" is a strange commodity that thrives exclusively on the endless "crosses" that it loudly bewails. Only obstacles and rivals can keep this metaphysical passion burning. Its ardor languishes in their absence and soon turns to a more promising or rather a more forbidding object, one that will provide the invigorating nourishment of rejections and rebuffs.

The net result is that mimetic relationships run contrary to all reasonable expectations. If you respond kindly to advances, if you are receptive and eager, you can expect fleeting interest at best followed by neglect and oblivion. You must show indifference and contempt and you will become the object of a frenzied passion. The soundest strategy, perfectly understood but not practiced by Cressida, consists in never showing one's true sentiment and behaving in a manner that contradicts one's actual desire. The Helena of *A Midsummer Night's Dream* not only does not practice this wisdom but she cannot get it straight, even when it is dinned into her ears by the more successful Hermia. She turns prayerfully to her rival as one would to an expert, to a theoretical guru, for a little seminar in the methodology of seduction:

> Teach me how you look and with what art you
> sway the motion of Demetrius' heart.

Hermia replies: "I frown upon him but he loves me still." This is the whole truth, of course, and nothing but the truth, but the dumb blonde immediately turns the whole thing around as she goes on raving:

> O that your frowns would teach my smiles such skill.

Hermia becomes even more specific:

> I give him curses, yet he gives me love.

But Helena will never learn:

> O that my prayers could such affection move.

Helena reminds me of those students who are so busy taking down every word of the teacher that they don't understand a thing. Demetrius reacts negatively to her because she acts enticingly, and he reacts positively to Hermia because she acts negatively. This systematic reversal of normal expectations is rooted not in differences between the four, or in the mischievous tricks of fairies but in the logic of mimetic desire.

It is exactly the same structure of misunderstanding as in *Errors* except that, in that play, the misunderstandings stem from the confusion of physical appearances only. It is the same reversal of all expectations. When the Dromios act like faithful servants, when they try to obey promptly and efficiently, they are rewarded with insults and beatings. When they become rebellious and saucy, they are treated with kindliness. The same thing with the other two twins. Being a man of wealth and a native of the town, the man of Ephesus expects friendliness and respect from his fellow citizens, but they treat him with diffidence and distrust. Being a stranger, the man from Syracuse expects to be treated as a stranger, but he makes the opposite experience:

> There's not a man I meet but doth salute me
> As if I were their well-acquainted friend;
> And everyone doth call me by my name.
> Some tender money to me, some invite me;
> Some others give me thanks for kindness;
> Some offer me commodities to buy.

This disconcerting experience is obviously rooted in not enough difference, rather than too much, and the misunderstandings are exacerbated by the expectation of difference. It is the same experience, therefore, as in the comedies of desire.

The device of the twins is not really a metaphor, or an allegory, or even a structural model of the mimetic process. A structural model is static and motionless whereas the device of the twins constitutes a source of misunderstanding structurally identical with the ones caused by mimetic desire and endowed with the same dramatic possibilities. That is why *The Comedy of Errors* develops along the same lines as the other comedies and the tragedies. The unperceived substitutions of twins trigger a local failure in the system of differences upon which all human communication and intercourse is based. The stubborn insistence on the integrity of difference, the will to persevere as if nothing had happened makes the problem worse and the confusion tends to spread to broader and broader areas through a kind of mimetic contagion. The resulting crisis is identical, really, with the midsummer night or with all the dramatic crises to which Hamlet's formula is applicable: "the time is out of joint." This crisis is a collapse of cultural differences, destroyed by the mimetic reciprocity of competitive and conflictual behavior. Ulysses, in *Troilus and Cressida*, gives a most elaborate description of this crisis that is also the most explicit from a theoretical standpoint. The cause of the crisis is the shaking, the vizarding and even the complete elimination of Degree which means exactly what is meant here by difference. Degree is the structural foundation of all human order. Degree is eroded and destroyed when it becomes a pawn and a prize in the frantic emulation of the mimetic rivals; all structural positions within the system lose their distinctiveness and everybody becomes the enemy twin of everybody else.

We do not see that all these plays are dramatically very close to each other because of extreme variations in scope, in style, décor and atmosphere. One deals with great affairs of state, another with the dreams and disputes of a few adolescents. But the dramatic process is the same and the comedy of the twins makes this process visible in its simplest outline. Too much presumption of difference, too much appetite for difference precipitates the loss of whatever difference there was in the first place, with consequences that can be comic or tragic according to the manner in which they are treated. The perpetual disappointment of expectations alienates the characters from each other and even from themselves.

The moment comes when the characters undergo a breakdown of personal identity. Then, anyone of them can exclaim, "Am I myself, are the others themselves?" In *The Comedy of Errors* this moment occurs at the same critical point as in the other plays. Dromio asks his master:

> Do you know me, sir? Am I Dromio, Am I your
> man, Am I myself?

His master tries to reassure him:

> Thou art Dromio, thou art my man, thou art thyself.

But he, too, undergoes a similar experience. He feels that his personality has been tampered with, metamorphosed, somewhat like Bottom in the

Dream. At that point, anything can happen to differences. They may vanish entirely and they may become so tangled up that monsters seem to proliferate. As the characters lose the stable perspective insured by their conviction of personal uniqueness and self identity, their ability to make the proper distinctions in the outside world is impaired. The formidable kitchen maid who pursues Dromio seems a kind of mythological monster to him, with a body as large, picturesque and diverse as a map of the entire world. Concurrently he feels transformed into a beastly creature, half animal and half human. The experience is a prefiguration of what happens to Bottom:

> I am an ass, I am a woman's man, and besides myself.

The prevailing mood, however, is not one of self examination but of mutual recrimination and scapegoating. Everybody is looking for a culprit. No one ever acknowledges the reciprocity of the mimetic process. The characters accuse each other first of double dealing, then of insanity, and finally of witchcraft. Their failure to perceive their mimetic similarity leaves them no choice but to accuse one another of inconsistency and treachery. Goblins and fairies may be invoked to account for the mischievous reversal of all the rules. In *A Midsummer Night's Dream*, the fairies are treated both as "real" characters and as a phantom generated by mimetic desire's natural aversion for its own truth. In *The Comedy of Errors*, just as in *A Midsummer Night's Dream*, the theme becomes more prominent as the crisis intensifies, but it does not crystallize into "real" characters. There is no need to provide for a supernatural "rationalization" of the mimetic process; the twins are sufficient to that purpose.

Doctor Pinch is finally called to the rescue. The man seems to perform simultaneously as a school teacher, a psychiatrist, a policeman, a religious exorcist and an independent businessman:

> Good Doctor Pinch, you are a conjurer,
> Reestablish him in his true sense again,
> And I will please you what you will demand.

The victims of the mimetic mania perceive each other as mystics in a trance, as regular madmen or as people possessed by evil spirits. Pinch alternates between taking the pulse of his patients and casting great curses against the demons entrenched in their bodies:

> Alas, how fiery and how sharp he looks!
> . . . . . .
> Mark how he trembles in his ecstasy!
> . . . . . .
> Give me your hand and let me feel your pulse
> . . . . . .
> I charge thee, Satan, housed within this man,
> To yield possession to my holy prayers,
> And to thy state of darkness hie thee straight;
> I conjure thee by all the saints in heaven.
> . . . . . .
> Ay me, poor man, how pale and wan he looks.

Ultimately, undifferentiation spreads to the entire city. Twins and non-twins alike are turned loose into the streets screaming and fighting insanely. Then comes the recognition scene, just in time to avoid a real disaster. This re-ordering *in extremis* parallels the rearranging of the four lovers at the end of *A Midsummer Night's Dream*.

The comedies of desire are richer, no doubt, and more subtle than *The Comedy of Errors* but the comic effects are structurally identical and it is wrong to dismiss the twins as an artificial device, unrelated to the great dramatic achievements of Shakespeare. When the twins are not there in person, so to speak, they remain present as a metaphor of the mimetic process, a metaphor that evokes a comedy of errors in a nutshell. Shakespeare's comedy of twins provides a simplified and therefore a highly readable version of something crucial and almost universally misunderstood in the Shakespearean conception of conflict and desire.

* * *

The story of the twins is remarkably suited to the representation of mimetic desire. But so is the story of Jupiter and Amphytrion. This myth is superior in one respect. Desire as such is part of the picture. Jupiter becomes undistinguishable from his rival because of his desire for Alcmene. In the story of the twins, desire has no place; it is an accident of birth that makes the twins undistinguishable.

But, still from the standpoint of mimetic desire, there is something deceptive in *Amphytrion*. The metamorphosis that produces the resemblance of the rivals is presented as a ruse of the god, a voluntary disguise. Jupiter is supposed to be in full control of the situation at all times. That is why he is a god, an omniscient as well as an omnipotent god. He manipulates others but he is not manipulated. He reaps all the benefits whereas all the unpleasant consequences of mimetic desire are the lot of Amphytrion. There is no symmetry between the rivals, no reciprocity.

This is contrary to the truth of the mimetic process. Would be manipulators abound, but they always end up manipulated, not by someone more clever or powerful than they are, but by the invincible circularity of the process. They are apprentice sorcerers, fanning the flames of a fire that finally engulfs everybody.

These consequences of mimetic desire are well represented by the confusion of the twins. No one who gets involved in the process can remain forever lucid about it. No one is on top of the situation.

In this respect, therefore, the farce of the twins is better suited than *Amphytrion* to the representation of the dramatic process. But *Amphytrion* is better suited in regard to desire itself which has no direct role in the story of the twins.

Both stories are unusually appropriate to the representation of mimetic desire. But they also have specific disadvantages as well as advantages and are not really interchangeable. In *Amphytrion* the unperceived substitution of one man for another is referred to its real cause, desire, but the consequences of desire are misrepresented. In the story of the twins, the real cause of the substitutions is suppressed; desire as such is absent but its consequences are faithfully represented.

In comedy, the implicit and often explicit goal of superior creation is the representation of mimetic desire. Authors such as Shakespeare and Molière turn to the traditional plots, such as Amphytrion or the story of the twins, as vehicles for this representation. If I am right, a great dramatist must deal with the comic plot he chooses, whichever it is, in such a manner as to improve its capacity for the representation of mimetic desire. I think this proposition can be verified in the case of both *The Comedy of Errors* and the *Amphytrion* of Molière.

Let us first consider Molière. In the *Amphytrion* of Plautus, Jupiter falls in love with Alcmene at some unspecified time. In Molière, he falls in love shortly after her wedding with Amphytrion. The god interferes with the couple's honeymoon. It is the sight of intense matrimonial bliss that excites his desire. There is less attraction for Alcmene herself in that desire than envy of a happiness from which the god feels excluded. Something similar happens to the Don Juan of Molière. He feels miserable at the sight of a loving couple and immediately attempts to seduce the woman.

Both Don Juan and Jupiter feel deprived. Jupiter feels deprived of his divinity, deprived by the happy lovers whose exclusive dependency on each other is a truly divine independence in regard to him. As a creature of desire, Jupiter cannot be a god. He tries to reconquer a divinity that continuously slips from his hands to reappear in the hands of those whose good fortune is an offense to him. Like all creatures of mimetic desire, Jupiter sees divinity outside himself, in someone else whose being he would like to possess because it appears divine. In order to absorb this being, desire is irresistibly compelled to mimic and imitate the possessor of that being. Jupiter's decision to impersonate Amphytrion has its exact counterpart in Helena's decision to impersonate Hermia. *I'd like to be to you translated* formulates the goal of desire in a language that already alludes to the possible consequences, the monstrous translation of the one who desires into someone else. The translation of Jupiter into Amphytrion is only one example among others, like the translation of Bottom into an ass.

Molière turned his Jupiter into a mimetic lover of the type Shakespeare also loves to portray. We can be certain of this when we analyse the French playwright's second departure from his primary source, the *Amphytrion* of Plautus. The complete success of his ruse does not suffice to satisfy the god. Alcmene belongs to him all right but the very means of her conquest empties it of significance. Alcmene cannot distinguish her divine lover from her human husband. Jupiter feels humiliated. Like all of us, he would like to be singled out; he wants "recognition" but he cannot get it because he cannot give up his disguise. If he disclosed the truth, the faithful wife would throw him out as the impostor he really is. In an amusing scene, Jupiter does his best to convince Alcmene he is not the one she thinks he is. The constraints of the situation make him sound terribly involved, abstract and *précieux.*

> Vous voyez un mari, vous voyez un amant;
> Mais l'amant seul me touche, à parler franchement,
> Et je sens, près de vous, que le mari le gêne.
> Cet amant de vos voeux jaloux au dernier point

> Souhaite qu'à lui seul votre coeur s'abandonne,
> Et sa passion ne veut point
> De ce que le mari lui donne.

There is no need to translate this French. It does not matter if you do not understand it; neither does Alcmene. It sounds a little like our recent critical discourse, and well it may since the purpose is the same. The purpose is to differentiate the lover from the husband. The purpose is to see a difference where, in reality, there is none.

Alcmene is too beautiful, innocent and serene to fall for this sophistry. Being marvelously immune to mimetic desire, she is also immune to the mystification of one-sided demystificators and deconstructors. In her magnificent response, she brushes off the unreal jargon of Jupiter and her naive trust in the reality she perceives firmly grounds her in a truth that remains alien to the ridiculous attempts of her husband and lover to differentiate one another.

> Je ne sépare pas ce qu'unissent les Dieux
> Et l'époux et l'amant me sont fort précieux.

> I do not separate what the gods have united;
> The husband and the lover are equally precious to me.

This is the simplicity of classical genius. Molière makes his god more human and his human couple more divine; he erases the difference between god and man. He makes his Jupiter comical by depriving him of his divinity, by making him as susceptible to jealousy as the husband he cuckolds. Amphytrion and Jupiter are more alike, in other words, than they are in Plautus; they are almost like twins.

If Molière brings his play closer to the twins, Shakespeare, in turn, brings his comedy of twins closer to *Amphytrion*. I have already observed that he borrows from the *Amphytrion* of Plautus almost as much as from his *Menechmus Twins.*

His major borrowing is the situation that is central to *Amphytrion*: the usurpation of the husband's role with the husband's wife in the husband's own house.

When Antipholus of Syracuse occupies this enviable position, he is absolutely charmed, or bewitched, in every sense of these words, not by his brother's wife, Adriana, but by her unmarried sister, Luciana.

Shakespeare did not minimize the erotic implications but he shifted them to the unmarried Luciana to develop them more freely. The impression made by Luciana is inseparable from the twin's amazement at the welcome he receives. Even though he does not know the young woman, she knows him well; she calls him by his own name, she invites him into her home. Ephesus is a strange town, with a reputation for witchcraft and Antipholus suspects some enchantment. He also feels enchanted by the enchanting Luciana. There is only one language for the seductiveness of Luciana and for the uncanny experience caused by the confusion of the twins.

> Teach me, dear creature, how to think and speak,
> Lay open to my earthly-gross conceit,
> Smothered in errors, feeble, shallow, weak,
> The folded meaning of your words' deceit.
> Against my soul's pure truth why labor you
> To make me wander in an unknown field?
> Are you a god? Would you create me new?
> Transform me, then and to your power I yield.

The Syracuse twin occupies here the position of Jupiter in *Amphytrion*. However different the two scenes are in other ways, they are alike in one major respect. The relationship of desire is experienced as a contact with the divine. In the case of *Amphytrion*, the myth itself supplies the theme of divinity. In the case of the twins, there is no such theme and Shakespeare must do the whole work himself. There is nothing gratuitous about the almost religious transfiguration of the desired object. It is the major process of the Western lyric. Shakespeare, like Molière, reveals more than its mythical roots. They reveal that the great mythical themes, like lyrical poetry, are rooted in the illusions of desire. They reveal more about the mimetic nature of these illusions than all our psychology and our sciences of man put together.

The great artist is free but his freedom moves along lines determined not by the mythical structure alone, not by the mimetic process of desire alone but by the ambiguous relationship of the one and the other.

At this point, an answer to the question "what is myth?" suggests itself. Myth is what the four lovers tell each other as well as Theseus and Hippolita when they wake up reconciled from the midsummer nightmare. They invoke fairies and goblins, they also complain about authoritarian fathers, like Freud, in order not to acknowledge the intolerable vanity and reciprocity of the mimetic process. The story of Jupiter and Amphytrion is one such story. And so is the story of the twins. Myth is a mask of the mimetic process, and, like all masks, it hides some features of the visage beneath and it reveals others. That is why myth is both appropriate and inappropriate as a vehicle for the representation of desire.

There are other indications in *The Comedy of Errors* that Shakespeare reads the farce of the twins as a fable of human desire. In *The Menechmus Twins* the first man who sees the twins together, at the end of the play, says to them:

> You two are more like each other than one drop of
> water or one drop of milk to another.

The drop of water reappears twice in *The Comedy of Errors* but its significance has changed. At the beginning of the play, Antipholus of Syracuse, the man in search of his brother, presents himself as follows:

> I to the world am like a drop of water
> That in the ocean seeks another drop,
> Who, falling there to find his fellow forth,
> Unseen, inquisitive, confounds himself.
> So I, to find a mother and a brother,
> In quest of them, unhappy, lose myself.

The search for the lost twin is interpreted as desire, or rather it is desire which is defined as a twin in search of a twin. Whatever it appears to be at first, the real goal of mimetic desire always turns out to be a twin. But the comparison of the twins with drops of water enables Shakespeare to express the undifferentiating effect of the mimetic process on everybody involved. If desire is a drop of water seeking more water it cannot achieve its goal without losing its distinctiveness. It is significant that the result of desire be presented not as the union of one drop with another single drop but as the dissolving of both into the ocean. The ocean corresponds to the contagious plague of mimetic desire that spreads to the community.

The ocean is not there in Plautus,but it is there again in *The Comedy, of Errors* when the entire metaphor reappears. This time, Adriana is speaking, to the wrong Antipholus and not, as she believes, to her husband whom she wants to rebuke for visiting women of ill repute and violating the sanctity of his marriage vows:

> Ah, do not tear away thyself from me!
> For know, my love, as easy mayst thou fall
> A drop of water in the breaking gulf
> And take unmingled thence that drop again,
> Without addition or diminishing,
> As take from me thyself, and not me too.

The goal that could not be reached in the first metaphor is already achieved. Two drops of water have become one without dissolving into the ocean. But there is no contradiction. It is matrimonial union that makes the difference. Husband and wife are viewed as a single body and a single person, as in the epistles of Paul. If one of the two partners surrenders to mimetic desire, the other too must suffer; the distinctiveness of both is destroyed. The husband who yields to the temptation drags his wife with himself into the ocean of mimetic undifferentiation. Both spouses are in the mess together, you might say, and, even though the mess is not of her own making, the wife cannot withdraw and become single again; she cannot recover the distinctiveness of the original drop that stood alone and unmixed outside of the ocean.

* * *

Not one but all critical trends are responsible for our failure to appreciate the significance of the comic twins, or doubles in our dramatic literature. Literary criticism as we know it is a product of the romantic and individualistic revolution. Like the mimetic lovers of Shakespeare we want ourselves and others to be uniquely different and original. Especially when we are most visibly enslaved by fads and fashions, we refuse to acknowledge our dependence on imitation and the predominance around us of the interchangeable and the identical, above all in our intellectual lives. We are not prepared for the study of the comic twins.

Our predilection for difference takes various forms at various times but it stays with us. For a long time, it took the form of "the great issues." All respectable drama was supposed to debate these great issues. The French were deadly serious about this. In each and every play they had to have a hero embodying "honor," for instance, and he would conquer "passion" which was embodied by someone else. Duty would settle accounts with pleasure. Love of country would have it out with love of the family. When people finally became tired of the great issues, the emphasis shifted to realism and psychology, but differences once more, especially individual differences, were all that mattered. In comedy, only figures such as Shylock or Tartuffe were praised; the less colorful characters were disdained.

The twins never do well with the critics. They did not look right as debaters of the "great issues," and with "individual differences" paramount, they became even more of an embarrassment. Anyone can see that. Some of you may remember the complete Shakespeare of Benjamin Harrison. In that almost venerable edition, *The Comedy of Errors* is declared "more appropriate to a New Years' Eve party than to a conference of critics." The advice may have been sound after all, considering the inevitable resemblance of the other critics to Benjamin Harrison himself.

In those days the plays of Shakespeare were checked at regular intervals for their level of "differentiation." Another fashionable word was "characterization." Benjamin Harrison had the four lovers of the midsummer night take a test of characterization, which they flunked. The dread literary disease of the time was a "character deficiency," we might say, or a "difference anemia."

Today, characterization is out and there is no market, fortunately, for a new and enriched version of *A Midsummer Night's Dream* but the differential imperative is still with us, although in a new form; it is even more entrenched than ever. In a negative form, at least, Professor Harrison was aware of difference as something that the literary text can eliminate. This is no longer true. Today, the differential nature of language, which is real enough, is taken as a pretext to deny the involvement of great literary works with the interchangeable and the identical. A simplistic methodology of pure difference and no identity dominates our literary criticism, the perfect philosophy, no doubt, for Helena and her friends. There are more Helenas than ever in Hermia's seminar and they still do not realize they are doing a comedy.

If you go straight to the source of some current critical schools, which is Lévi-Strauss, you will identify the reason for our inability to deal with comedy in general and with Shakespeare in particular. The structuralist method, as you know, is based on binary differentiation. When Lévi-Strauss analyses mythology he applies this differentiation to twins as he would to any other pair of associated entities. Like the god of Molière's *Amphytrion,* the Jupiter of anthropology tries to differentiate the twin who is the husband from the twin who is not with the help of his kinship rules. Here too, the result leaves something to be desired. The extreme frequency of twins in most mythologies does not go without saying. It calls for some explanation. When a myth resorts to twins, it must be trying to make a point and this point cannot be the difference between the twins, otherwise why resort to twins? The point is obviously the absence of difference. *The Comedy of Errors* is more fun than structuralism. It may be better anthropology as well, a better reading of the mythical text.

In a rather surprising gesture for an anthropologist, the later Lévi-Strauss condemns ritual for the same reason Professor Harrison disdained *The Comedy of Errors:* not enough differentiation.

If we shake off our methodological inhibitions, we will observe that the intensification of mimetic desire and the resulting confusion, in the comedies of Shakespeare, coincides not only with the dramatic process but also with the ritual practice of the old English folklore. Undifferentiation is a consequence of mimetic desire and a mythical theme, but it is ritual enactment as well which consists of parodic rivalry and conflict between the various groups of the community.

The four actors of the midsummer night have no thought for ritual when they plunge into the woods but their participation is insured by their very alienation from traditional custom. Their exclusive preoccupation with themselves and each other cannot fail to generate mimetic entanglements painful enough to qualify as the rigorous ordeal that the rites of passage into adulthood never fail to include. Ritual is an ancient mimetic crisis periodically re-enacted to prevent a new one from breaking out. The medicine is always the disease itself in a weaker and smaller dose. When ritual falls into disuse, a real crisis is bound to occur and great suffering lies in store, but it is not the end of the world because the real crisis will regenerate ritual; it, too, will serve as a model and be re-enacted. Ritual does not live forever; ritual is mortal but it is constantly reborn of its own ashes; its death opens the way to the catastrophic sequence that constitutes the origin and model of all ritual.

The circular pattern of the festive comedies, the constant presence of the ritual pattern and the perfect adaptation of its language of pollution and purification to plays which hardly mention it as a theme reveals the depth of Shakespeare's understanding. We are still unable to avail ourselves of that understanding because our anthropology, like our philosophy and our esthetics, is still dependent on a conception that separates mimesis and desire, the conception handed down from Plato and Aristotle. We even think we can "apply" to the superior and unified vision of Shakespeare such inferior and fragmented notions as Frazer's "vegetation cult" or the Oedipus complex of Freud.

As a result we do not perceive that the unity of mimesis and desire constitutes the intelligible aspect of Shakespeare's amazing insight into the paradoxes of individual and collective behavior.

AN APOLOGY FOR POETICS*

Murray Krieger

First I should like to place my theory between the New Criticism and certain elements of post-Structuralism by revealing those assumptions it seems to share with each of these positions, which I see as radically opposed to one another. Despite the fact that my early work was largely fashioned by New-Critical predispositions and despite a lingering sympathy with some of their central literary objectives, I have in at least two ways sought to differentiate my thinking from the New Critics'. Perhaps these modifications were performed in part to immunize this theoretical tradition from the assaults of those who would see in it undeniable tendencies toward mystification, but I like to think that my own transformations of the New Criticism borrowed from–if they did not anticipate–assumptions about language which post-Structuralism has now made commonplace among us.

The New-Critical aesthetic rested totally on a prior commitment to formal closure as the primary characteristic of the successful literary object. Its dedication to organicism, or to the peculiar sort of "contextualism" which I have described in many places elsewhere, gave to the poem the objective of self-sufficiency or of microcosmic perfection which, New Critics would claim, was the ultimate realization of the formalistic tradition from Aristotle to Kant to Coleridge and the organicists who followed. All borrowings from the world of actions, values, and language–as well as the borrowings from earlier poems–were to be radically transformed by the poet working in, as well as through, his medium into a world of its own finality sealed from his personal interests as from ours. Indeed, those venerable terms, "disinterestedness," "detachment," and "impersonality," all could be

*This essay is a recasting of remarks about my theoretical position delivered to a graduate student colloquium at the University of Michigan called to discuss a number of my recent essays.

invoked as assurances of the work's capacity to come to terms with itself. And yet, in its casuistic perfection, the world of the poem was to guide our vision by making itself normative of it. Consequently, although the existential was to be re-formed into aesthetic terms, through the work there was to be an existential projection after all.

It has now been a number of years and a number of writings of my own since I have come to reject an exclusive commitment to aesthetic closure of the New-Critical kind. The New-Critical position derived much of its strength from the claim that organicism is all or none and not a matter of degree; consequently, the poem could not be considered part open and part closed, so that an anti-New-Critical adjustment could not be achieved simply by moving from the emphasis on closure to the emphasis on openness. Instead, through the introduction of notions like self-reference, illusion, and metaphorical duplicity, I argued for a paradoxical simultaneity of utter closure and utter openness.

The argument proceeded in the following way: those moments during which the fictional world betrays a self-consciousness about itself as fiction remind us of the illusionary nature of that "reality" which seeks to enclose us. By a kind of negative reference, this reminder implicitly points to the world which the poem explicitly excludes in order to affirm its own closure. The world may be reduced to the stage in front of us, but so long as we are aware that it is only the stage in front of us, there is a world outside threatening to break in. Thus the work of art, as its own metaphorical substitution for the world of experience beyond, is a metaphor that at once affirms its own integrity and yet, by negative implication, denies itself, secretly acknowledging that it is but an artful evasion of the world. This claim to duplicity permitted me to allow the work to celebrate its own ways and the ways of its language unencumbered, without denying the ways of the world and *its* language. The work's very retreat from referentiality acted paradoxically to point it, through negative reference, to the world it so self-consciously excluded.

The second essential assumption of the New Criticism was its pre-established commitment to the poem as fixed object—a commitment which has effectively been attacked by much post-New Criticism as mere fetishism. The arguments against such reification as an act of uncritical spatializing of the language process have been often enough rehearsed and are well known. We are by now well aware of the extent to which the New Critics neglected the relation of art to the social process as well as to the psychological processes of human creation and response as these are defined by the flow of language as a governing force in human experiencing.

I would hope that my own theorizing has reflected these concerns. I have increasingly tried to dwell upon the poem as an "intentional object" only, an illusion of a single entity created through the complicity of the reader who, sharing the author's habit of seeking closure, allows the work—even as he does his share in creating it—to lead him toward the act of sealing it off within the aesthetic or fictional frame that his perceptual training leads him to impose. The metaphorical habits he has learned—from childhood, from religion, from previous traffic with the arts—lead him to seek an apocalypse, an end to history, in the work as he seeks in it to bring chronological time to a stop.

Such has been the human use of myth—the quest for the myths we need—in the western aesthetic since Aristotle formulated the distinction between history and poetry as they relate to time and to beginnings, middles, and ends. In thus emphasizing the poem as a will-o'-the-wisp, I have meant to reintroduce the temporal element, the element of process and of human experience, into our understanding of the literary work as it is created by the poet and created complicitously by us. Because I want to see the work as functioning within the metaphorical apocalypse we allow it to create for us even while it remains the unexceptional piece of language (running back into the past and forward into the future) which it would be were it *not* for us as aesthetically conscious readers, I am necessarily tempted to look for evidence of a self-conscious duplicity in the work as we come upon it and as we, in effect, ask it to do these things.

But I do not suggest that through these workings the aesthetic becomes a game of now you see it, now you don't. Rather I see the work as touching and unlocking in us the anthropological quest for that which marks and defines every moment of a culture's vision as well as of its inner skepticism that undoes its visionary reality with a "real" reality which is no less illusionary. The making and unmaking of our metaphors, our mythic equations, in experience as in art only reveal the primacy of the operation of the aesthetic in us all—and perhaps explain the extent to which our drive for art is accompanied by a cognitive itch which even the experience of art itself never quite eases, so that the need to experience more art happily remains.

These differences from the New Criticism allow me, I hope, to escape the difficulties arising out of its epistemological naiveté, leaving me less uncomfortable as I contemplate currently more fashionable theories about language with which I share large areas of agreement. Since the ascendancy of Structuralism more than a decade ago, critics in this country have had to come to terms with the Saussurean notion of verbal signs as arbitrary and as based upon the principle of differentiation. Thus what used to seem to be the simple matter of representation in language—the presence of a fixed signified in the signifier—is converted into a problematic. In the view of Structuralism, signifiers operate in a dynamic field of differentiation and have only arbitrary relations with their presumed signifieds. A culture's confidence in the identity and inevitability of its verbal meanings, rather than its confronting their differentiation and arbitrariness, only testifies to that culture's self-mystifications as it falls prey to the metaphysical habit of logocentrism. The wistful imposition of identity is accompanied by the ontological claim of presence, now to be undone by a shrewder philosophy of language that reminds us of the field of absence upon which the system of differences plays. Hence we have the rejection of metaphor for metonymy, and with the rejection of metaphor the removal of the ground on which the New Criticism rested. After all, how can one retain the central requirement of unity in metaphor—the overcoming of verbal differences by the fusion that overwhelms all boundaries that set words apart from one another—if the very basis on which words function subjects them indiscriminately to the Structuralist's "all-purpose differentiating machine" of which René Girard has contemptuously spoken?

Though I may be persuaded about language as the marshalling of arbitrary and differentiated signifiers, I would hold out for the possibility that a single verbal structure can convert its elements so that we read them under the aegis of metaphorical identity with its claim to presence. It is this hold-out claim to what the poem can persuade us its language is doing which ties me still to the New-Critical tradition despite my concessions to Structuralist theory. I seek to maintain this power for creating poetic identity in language despite language's normal incapacities, so that I do not see Structuralism or post-Structuralism as precluding a poetics such as the tradition since Kant and Coleridge has been seeking to construct. I grant that the conception of metaphor, with its illusion of presence, may well be a secular conversion of the religious myth of transubstantiation, so that we may wish to reduce it at once to nostalgic mystification. And we may then see such mystification operating in all our spatializing of verbal relations which would bring linguistic temporality to a stop in its attempt to redeem time. By confessing the illusionary nature of this metaphorical operation we help perform on ourselves, I am suggesting a sophisticated view of language that knows of its metonymic condition and yet generates an internal play among its elements which appears to create a metaphorical identity that exists in the teeth of the principle of difference. It is an identity that knows the world of difference, a metaphor that has known metonymy, a spatial vision which sustains itself only through the acknowledgment that all may be finally nothing but time. If it functions as what I have elsewhere called a "miracle," it can do so because it proclaims itself as miracle only while acknowledging that it cannot occur.

Clearly, what is at stake is whether there can be any claim for distinctions within the realm of signifiers, whether we can break off segments of language called poems as if they have something special in them. One of the ironies of Structuralism, it has often been pointed out, is the undifferentiating way in which it asserts its principle of difference (it was just this problem which prompted the Derridean critique of Lévi-Strauss). Eventually any poetics, but especially one like mine, must create its own ground by seeking discontinuities within textuality, at least for the momentary purpose of our aesthetic experience at the hands of a poem. This recurrent need, in our history, to establish a poetics perhaps accounts for the persistence with which theorists resort to a deviationist principle for distinguishing poems from other texts. And what for them sets poems apart must somehow be related to the power of converting differences into identities, the arbitrary into the inevitable—in short, verbal absence into verbal presence.

But these last years there have been assaults from several directions on the theoretical deviationism which for many decades had been a basic assumption for the dominant aesthetic. Some of these newer directions overlap one another significantly, and this is about what we should expect since most of them are related, one way or another, to that version of Structuralism which—in an anti-hierarchical spirit—rejects the literary work as an elite object and, consequently, rejects any collection of such works as a duly constituted canon.

First, the application of "information theory" is used by some as a monolithic model of interpretation which reduces all varieties of discourse to itself, searching out the cues for encoding (by the author) and decoding (by the reader) of the message which, as programmed discourse, the text presumably exists to communicate.

Second, the analysis of the process of signification leads others to apply their conclusions about the emptiness of signifiers—the absence of all signifieds from them—to words in poems as in non-poems. They judge the deviationist's claim to find a privileged fullness in poetic language to be a delusion and a fetish, a mystification. In poetry as in philosophy, they would deconstruct the metaphysical assumption that ontologizes verbal meanings.

Third, there are those who see all varieties of language as playing a similar role in culture's history, its way of meaning and of conceiving its reality. One can use what Foucault calls discursive formations to uncover the several archeological stages in our development. And there are no exceptions among those discourses contributing to, or reflecting, those formations.

Fourth, theorists may seek to deny the apparent meanings intended by all texts, reducing them to rationalizations of the author's "will to power." These critics are not satisfied with stopping the deconstructive process once assumed stable meanings have been changed into a textual play among signifiers; they rather pursue that process beyond all texts—until textual pretensions are traced to the political or psychological motive that puts them forward as its verbal disguise. For these critics, whether they derive from Marx or Nietzsche or Freud, there is no innocent text, no disinterestedness in its production or its reception: instead, though the text offers itself and its fiction as all there is, the author means to use it to manipulate the actual world, to imperialize the world his way. And poems, again, are no exception.

Fifth, there are those who analyze all texts as originating in tropes or in narrative structures. Such analysis bestows literary categories upon non-literary as upon literary texts, so that all texts are treated as similarly figured and similarly fictional. Consequently, there is no normal discourse from which poetic language could deviate, no neutral sequence of events on which we have not already imposed narrative and tropological shape. In effect, all language is deviation and there is no norm. Thus there is no neutral reference, so that we all speak in fictions, whatever truths we deludedly think we mouth. We have gone beyond Molière's Monsieur Jourdain who was surprised (and impressed) to learn that he had been speaking prose all his life; for in this view we have indeed, like all our fellows, been speaking—and writing—creative literature: poetry, fictions which we had been taking for sober referentiality. Where all are poems, there need be no special gift of poem-making.

Sixth, finally (and this also overlaps some of the others) theorists can consider all speaking and writing—or even, more broadly, all human activity—as indifferent parts of what I have earlier referred to as the seamless fabric of textuality, of course without distinctions within it: the world of words as text or even the world itself as text (the journal *Semiotexte* or the new, more radical journal, *Social Text*). We cannot, in this view, escape from experience, worldly and verbal or worldly *as* verbal, as a single capacious room composed of wall-to-wall discourse (to borrow Edward Said's phrase): the world as text, all of it just one hermeneutic challenge. Here is the farthest move away from any notion of the poem as a potentially discrete entity.

In all of these cases, the distinction-making power which would create a poetry and a poetics has been cut off. And, in light of the convergence of the several lines of recent theory upon these Structuralist or near-Structuralist notions, there would seem to be good reason to be persuaded by what they have taught us about the deceptive nature of sign-functioning and about the unified character of our apparently varied discourses at given moments in our culture. But I propose that we still worry about whether we wish to include literary discourse within this monolithic construct. Or, on the other hand, do we rather wish to see literary discourse as achieving a self-privileging exemption from that construct by manipulating all its generic linguistic elements until they are forced to subvert their own natures and do precisely what a Structuralist view of language would preclude them from doing: from functioning as signifiers that create and fill themselves with their own signifieds as they go, thereby setting this text apart from textuality-at-large as its own unique, self-made system? Without some such notion, are we capable of accounting for all that our greatest works perform for us? Do we not, further, have to recognize the peculiarly fictional, and even self-consciously fictional—which is to say self-referential—character of our most highly valued literature, even if we wish to grant to non-literature a fictionality and reflexivity which less sophisticated readings of would-be "referential" discourse did not used to grant? And are not literary fictions, with their peculiar self-reference, sufficient to separate the work which they characterize from the rest of discourse?

By urging the reflexivity of all discourse upon us, Structuralists and post-Structuralists have perhaps not leveled literature into common *écriture* so much as they have raised all *écriture* into literature. If these critics argue against the exclusiveness of poetry (that is, fictions, "imaginative literature") and rather seek to include a wide range of works by essayists, historians, philosophers, and even social scientists, they do so by treating these works as texts to which techniques of analysis appropriate to literary criticism may be applied. Even more, their techniques of deconstructing their non-literary texts, stripping them of their pretensions and reducing them to their naked fictionality, are to a great extent echoes of what poems have always been doing to themselves and teaching their critics to do to them. It is for this reason I suggest that, instead of the concept of literature being deconstructed into *écriture, écriture* has been constructed into literature. As a consequence, everything has become a "text," and texts—as well as the very notion of textuality—have become as ubiquitous as writing itself, with each text now to be accorded the privileged mode of interpretation which used to be reserved for discourse with the apparent internal self-justification of poetry.

I think, for example, of the work of Hayden White on history writing, in which he sets forth a number of models of narrative structure based on the several tropes (or master figures), modes of discourse which he treats as reflecting the modes of human consciousness. Obviously, his reduction of every historian's truth claim to be the illusions of the poet's fictions, his obliteration of the realm of neutral fact and of discursive reference, will not please many historians who take their truth-claiming function seriously. Indeed, it may well seem to condescend to non-poetic humanistic texts for us to cut them off from any truth claim by restricting them to the realm of fiction and to the metaphorical swerve of private consciousness. Whatever the deconstructive mood may suggest, the historian may well want us to believe his version of history over the versions of others, or the philosopher to make us accept his claims about the nature of language or of reality, so that either may well resent our turning him into a poet *malgré lui.* The literary humanist should understand that it may not be taken exclusively as flattery if he brings historians, philosophers, and other humanists under the literary tent, especially since they are so intent on their more direct objectives. Words like "fiction" and "illusion" should teach us that there is a negative side (from the cognitive point of view) as well as a positive side (from the aesthetic point of view) to being a maker of literary fictions, and others may not be as comfortable with the designation as we literary people are. The sober scholar in the non-literary disciplines, who does his careful work and makes his claims to its justness, may well feel that his discipline and its distinctive ambition are being trivialized by being treated as a fiction shaped by his tropological bent. And such attitudes, that would protect the distinction between—say—history and poetry, have had the history of literary criticism on their side since Aristotle initiated the distinction between history and poetry in Chapter Nine of the *Poetics*. Indeed, even earlier, Plato had inherited and severely contributed to the war between the philosophers and the poets in many places in his work, beginning most notably, perhaps, in Book Two of the *Republic*.

Such questions as those, for example, about the boundary between history or biography on the one side and the novel on the other, and about the applicability of narrotological analysis to each of them probably remain serious questions, despite efforts to collapse all discourse into undifferentiated textuality and all textuality into trope and fiction. Surely, even after we have granted that some fictional obfuscation, with its rhetorical swerving, takes place outside the realm of literary fictions, we may allow some remnant of the free play of fictional reflexivity to be left to the literary intent, and may allow it to be replaced by more precise and clearly aimed objectives in, say, historical studies. Our temptation to tell the historian what he is doing ought to subside, at least a little, before his own perhaps less subtle sense of what he is about. And the finally free-floating inventiveness of self-conscious make-believe in the literary text should also in the end be acknowledged as a thing apart, despite our best efforts to see in what ways these differing kinds of texts, produced in response to such varying purposes, may reflect on one another. Aesthetic foregrounding may well go on outside poems, but we do condescend to our writers in all the disciplines when we ignore, or deprecate, the several responses which the body of their works appears to be soliciting from their different readers.

So I suggest we respond critically to the enterprise, currently so common among us, that would undermine the poem's differentness from other discourse. What this enterprise has been seeking to accomplish is a deconstruction of the metaphysical assumptions behind the traditional aesthetic and its resulting claim about the poem's ontology:

the claim that the poem is a totalized structure, a self-realized teleological closure, a microcosm whose mutually dependent elements are cooperatively present in the fulfillment of their centripetal potentialities. Instead, the deconstructive move reduces the poem to a play of centrifugal forces such as characterizes general non-poetic discourse. Gaps appear everywhere—absences and emptiness—and we are to acknowledge these gaps for what they are, resisting our constructive tendency, imposed on us by centuries of self-deceiving habits of literary interpretation with their ontological assumptions, of trying at all costs to fill those gaps. For what we have taken to be the self-fulfilling and self-sealing poem is, like all discourse, mere vacancy, acknowledging an absence of substance, fleeing all presence as it leads us down the lines moving outward to the intertextual forces which become the code, but which permit no integrity, no free-standing sovereignty, to any would-be body operating within them. In this sense, the poem, as a construction of elements manipulated by art into a presence (according to the traditional older aesthetic), has been deconstructed into absences that can be made to point only to the code of writing itself.

But what of the need for closure, an aesthetic need felt by the human imagination, and the imagination's search for it in the objects of its experience? Should we not value, and set aside for separate treatment, those specially constructed objects that seem addressed to that aesthetic need? A criticism that preserves its own referential obligation to its literary object can treat poems as dislocations of language that enable language to create itself as a medium that can close off what Structuralists have shown to be normally open. The persistent impulse both on the poet's part to close the form he creates and on our part to close the form we perceive accounts for the internal purposiveness that, for Immanuel Kant, characterizes the aesthetic mode. Presumably it is this need to make or to find closure which leads us to the myth-making and, with it, the privileging of objects that recent deconstructionists would undermine.

The imagination's need to find closure may largely account for the role of the story—like that of the picture frame or the proscenium arch—in the history of culture. The inherent nature of narrative structure surely reveals a responsiveness to what Frank Kermode has called our "sense of an ending." The satisfying ending is one that fulfills internally aroused expectations, that realizes the purposes immanent in the story. From Aristotle's concept of denouement or falling action to the formal finality called for by Kant, and in the formalistic tradition that is indebted to both, we find the imposition of a mythic ending, a structural apocalypse, which cuts off the fiction from history. It acts, in effect, as an intrusion of the spatial imagination on the radical temporality of pure sequence, shaping time into the separateness of fiction. Linear sequence is suspended, transformed into circularity.

But there is something in literature that also keeps it open to the world, to language at large, and to the reader. As we contemplate the verbal object through our culturally imposed habits of perceiving what is presented to us as aesthetic, we must deal with the two-sided nature of its words, now that they have been, in spite of their normal tendencies, shaped into a poetic medium: they try to work their way into a self-sufficient presence, and yet they remain transient and empty signifiers. This is the paradoxical nature of language as aesthetic medium, and both sides must be exploited. Language is able to create itself into a self-justified fiction, but, because it is also no more than language—just words after all—it is able to display a self-consciousness about its illusionary character. Language seems in our best poetry to be both full of itself and empty, both totally here as itself and pointing elsewhere, away from itself. It permits its reader at once to cherish its creation as a closed object, one that comes to terms with itself, and to recognize its necessarily incomplete nature in its dependence on us as its readers, on literary history, on the general language system, and on the way of the world. We can see its words as uniquely apart from the world and the world of language, while we see them also as blending into those worlds.

Not that I am claiming these special characteristics to be *in* literary works so much as they are products of our aesthetic habits of perception—when dealing with such works—which seek to find them there. And part of our aesthetic habit of dealing with fictions is its self-consciousness about the occasion that sponsors it. In other words, the literary work persuades us of itself as a special object even as we retain an awareness of the rather extraordinary activity we are performing in contributing to our own persuasion. It is not fetishism when we recognize the tentative conditions that encourage the closure we celebrate, and when we accept the openness that surrounds the moment of our commitment to the closed object.

It is under these provisional conditions that we have learned to commit ourselves to the aesthetic response and to project upon the poem our grounds for it. Thus these conditions also qualify and complicate our sense of presence—of signifiers that have filled themselves with the signifieds they have created within themselves—within the play of words before us. And, despite arguments of both Structuralists and post-Structuralists, the illusion of presence emerges for us from the written as well as the spoken words before us. But it is always a presence sponsored *pour l'occasion* and co-existing with our awareness of the lurking absences that haunt both writing and speech (*écriture* and *parole*).

As has been suggested in post-Structuralist semiotics, the speaking voice may make us too ready to conceive the presence of the speaker, so that we concede too little to the anonymity of speech as it enters the network of all that is spoken or can be spoken; in consequence, so the argument runs, we would concede more if we were confronted by the silence of the apparently anonymous written page. But, on the other hand, a counter-argument might claim, speech may seem to be the more firmly tied to absence—the continuing fadings-away linked to temporal sequence—as the sounds dissipate in the air as they are spoken; further, the orphaned page, composed of visible (and invisible) traces left by an absent speaker, may nevertheless persuade us of a spatial simultaneity among its words as it takes its place within the physically co-present book. Let me turn the matter around again by adding that even speech, considered as a sequence of sounds, suggests a sensuous presence in its auditory phenomena that belie our sense of them as fleeting transparencies. As the poet dwells upon those characteristics, heard and seen, which turn words into sensory things, the signifiers can take on the weightiness of substance. In these ways, with the knowing cooperation of the reader-hearer, the word on the page *or* on the tongue can be made the occasion for our assigning a tentative spatial presence to it. But in remembering it also as being no more than word—the trace on the page, the buzz in the ear—we do not deny its temporality within the flow of our experience, worldly and linguistic: its elusive *un*presence despite our attempts to seize upon and fix it.

As I contemplate the possibility of conceiving speech as more likely to sponsor the feeling of absence than writing is, as well as the possibility of conceiving them the opposite way, I am aware that it has been my interest to dwell upon the poet's attempt to persuade us to break through to presence, whichever of the two is the case. I am aware, further, that in my career I have been concerned more with the presence of texts as discontinuous entities than with the speaking presence *in* texts of the authorial consciousness which is their point of origin. This fact only reveals my inheritance from the New Criticism and its obsession with isolated texts as well as my inheritance from the Anglo-American tradition dating from Bacon, which seeks to respond to empirical phenomena, rather than the French inheritance from Descartes, whose concern with the *cogito* and the resulting concern with consciousness can never long be shaken. It may be that the New Criticism has, after all, even shaped my differences from it just as, perhaps, critics of consciousness like Georges Poulet have helped shape the thinking of the post-Structuralists who have excluded consciousness as a controlling origin for the text.

There is yet another emendation I would make to the post-Structuralist's critique as it affects my claim—an unmystified claim—to poetic presence. I would argue that there is a major difference—not noted in post-Structuralist theory—between the generic difficulty with presence in our logocentrism and the special difficulty with presence in the language of poetry. It is not noted because one must distinguish poetic from other discourse (by means of a deviationist aesthetic) before being able to see the different sort of presence constructed by the poem. I have pointed out the usual assumptions about transparent representation—a signified fixed into presence within its signifier—assumptions which, according to post-Structuralists, we see our language as making, thanks to its implicit metaphysical assumptions. It is this presence which is to fall victim to the post-Structuralist's deconstructive enterprise. As a proponent of a deviationist theory of poetry, I could join in this enterprise while holding out for a special presence which a poem can build into itself by subverting and reworking the materials left it by those discourses which post-Structuralists have deconstructed in order to reveal the absences within them. The metonymic character of the usual sequence of signifiers, with their differentiations, can be transformed by the poet (so I would claim), who manipulates his verbal elements so that they may function as metaphorical identities, creating a presentation of signifieds through the generating powers of the signifiers with which those signifieds are perceived as being one. This poetic presentation feeds itself into a fullness out of the gaps of the failed *re*presentations in non-poetic discourse. If Derrida calls attention to our need to correct the naive feeling of presence in all texts constructed in the logocentric tradition of the West, de Man complains of the poet's arrogant effort to achieve the monistic presence of symbolism instead of accepting the allegory which is the appropriate way of language. Each of these denies simple presence by seeing all language as functioning in a similar way, but though neither would grant to poetry any privilege within the general realm of discourse, de Man's critique does attack verbal presence on rather different grounds, within the province of the self-privileging poet or the overreaching theorist who takes up the fight for privilege on behalf of the poet. And these are the grounds on which my own argument for poetic presence, without challenging Derrida's, can stand as an alternative to de Man's.

But the dream of unity, of formal repetitions that are seen as the temporal equivalent of juxtapositions, that convert the temporal into the spatial through the miracle of simultaneity—this dream persists, reinforced by every aesthetic illusion which we help create and to which we succumb. We cultivate the mode of identity, the realm of metaphor, within an aesthetic frame that acknowledges its character as momentary construct and thereby its frailty as illusion. But it allows us a glimpse of our own capacity for vision before the bifurcations of language have struck. The dream of unity may be entertained tentatively and is hardly to be granted cognitive power, except for the secret life-without-language or life-before-language which it suggests, the very life which the language of difference precludes. In poetry we grasp at the momentary possibility that this can be a life-in-language.

Let me suggest that, in our anxiety to resist the mystification of ourselves, we may concede too much to temporality when we grant it a "reality" which we deny to its rival category, space. Space, presumably, is an invention of the reifying act of mind in flight from confrontation with the world of fact which *is* the world of time. So the mystifications of the spatial imagination are, in the work of Paul de Man, deconstructed by our introduction of temporal facts. But we must wonder whether this deconstructive act is not a privileging of time that sets it outside the realm of mind and language while giving it ultimate control over both in spite of all our inventions. Is time any less a human category than space, to be given a secure ontological space which its own very meaning contradicts? Yet the spatial, as that which redeems time, must be taken as a delusion when considered from the temporal perspective, though—let us grant—this perspective may be no less fictional than the spatial. So the poem as language may well have a dual character, being seen at once as canonized text and as just more textuality, as words at once shaped into a palpable form of art and playing an undistinguished role in the network of discourse. This duality should not be broken up into separate choices: either a metaphorical delusion—the spatial simultaneity of the I AM—or the open flow of time which is to set the delusion straight. Instead, it is to be seen as two illusionary ways in which poetic texts seem at the same time to force us to see them as functioning. It is this self-conscious duplicity within both response and poem which leads me—despite whatever other changes my theory has undergone—to persist in seeing poetry still as a form of discourse whose functioning separated it from the rest.

In the original "Apology for Poetry," Sir Philip Sidney sought to maintain the place of poetry though it was being threatened by an austere philosophy that shut it off from the truth and would allow it no other proper function. This attack would exclude poetry from the rest of discourse, while our current theoretical movements would too readily absorb it into the rest of discourse. Any theory devoted to poetry must today argue for a separate definition of the poem, thereby justifying its own right, within the realm of language theory, to function as a maker of claims for its subject. Thus my apology is not for poetry, but for poetics, the theoretical discourse whose existence, resting on the assumption that there *is* a poetry, is threatened with every denial of poetry's separate place. In this way, having begun my career by commenting on the "New Apologists for Poetry," I now find myself an apologist—I hope not altogether an older apologist—for poetics. I can make my apology, I am now convinced, only by making the tentative, self-undercutting moves that separate me from those older new apologists and may seem at moments to align me with those who refuse to grant a separate definition to poetry *or* poetics. But my hold-out separatist tendencies invariably win out, so that, with whatever phenomenological concessions, I remain an apologist after all.

HOW TO RECOGNIZE A POEM WHEN YOU SEE ONE*

Stanley Fish

Recently I sketched out an argument by which meanings are the property neither of fixed and stable texts nor of free and independent readers but of interpretive communities that are responsible both for the shape of a reader's activities and for the texts those activities produce. In this lecture I propose to extend that argument so as to account not only for the meanings a poem might be said to have but for the fact of its being recognized as a poem in the first place. I would like to begin with an anecdote.

In the summer of 1971 I was teaching two courses under the joint auspices of the Linguistic Institute of America and the English Department of the State University of New York at Buffalo. I taught these courses in the morning and in the same room. At 9:30 I would meet a group of students who were interested in the relationship between linguistics and literary criticism. Our nominal subject was stylistics but our concerns were finally theoretical and extended to the presuppositions and assumptions which underlie both linguistic and literary practice. At 11:00 these students were replaced by another group whose concerns were exclusively literary and were in fact confined to English religious poetry of the seventeenth century. These students had been learning how to identify Christian symbols and how to recognize typological patterns and how to move from the observation of these symbols and patterns to the specification of a poetic intention that was usually didactic or homiletic. On the day I am thinking about, the only connection between the two classes was an assignment given to the first which was still on the blackboard at the beginning of the second. It read:

Jacobs–Rosenbaum
Levin
Thorne
Hayes
Ohman (?)

I am sure that many of you will already have recognized the names on this list, but for the sake of the record, allow me to identify them. Roderick Jacobs and Peter Rosenbaum are two linguists who have coauthored a number of textbooks and coedited a number of anthologies. Samuel Levin is a linguist who was one of the first to apply the operations of transformational grammar to literary texts. J. P. Thorne is a linguist at Edinburgh who, like Levin, was attempting to extend the rules of transformational grammar to the notorious irregularities of poetic language. Curtis Hayes is a linguist who was then using transformational grammar in order to establish an objective basis for his intuitive impression that the language of Gibbon's *Rise and Fall of the Roman Empire* is more complex than the language of Hemingway's novels. And Richard Ohmann is the literary critic who, more than any other, was responsible for introducing the vocabulary of transformational grammar to the literary community. Ohmann's name was spelled as you see it here because I could not remember whether it contained one or two n's. In other words, the question mark in parenthesis signified nothing more than a faulty memory and a desire on my part to appear scrupulous. The fact that the names appeared in a list that was arranged vertically, and that Levin, Thorne, and Hayes formed a column that was more or less centered in relation to the paired names of Jacobs and Rosenbaum, was similarly accidental and was evidence only of a certain compulsiveness if, indeed, it was evidence of anything at all.

In the time between the two classes I made only one change. I drew a frame around the assignment and wrote on the top of that frame "p. 43." When the members of the second class filed in I told them that what they saw on the blackboard was a religious poem of the kind they had been studying and I asked them to interpret it. Immediately they began to perform in a manner that, for reasons which will become clear, was more or less predictable. The first student to speak pointed out that the poem was probably a hieroglyph, although he was not sure whether it was in the shape of a cross or an altar. This question was set aside as the other students, following his lead, began to concentrate on individual words, interrupting each other with suggestions that came so quickly that they seemed spontaneous. The first line of the poem (the very order of events assumed the already constituted status of the object) received the most attention: Jacobs was explicated as a reference to Jacob's ladder, traditionally allegorized as a figure for the Christian ascent to heaven. In this poem, however, or so my students told me, the means of ascent is not a ladder but a tree, a rose tree or rosenbaum. This was seen to be an obvious reference to the Virgin Mary who was often characterized as a rose without thorns, itself an emblem of the immaculate conception. At this point the poem appeared to the students to be operating in the familiar manner of an iconographic riddle. It at once posed the question, "How is it that a man can climb to heaven by means of a rose tree?" and directed the reader to the inevitable answer: by the fruit of that tree, the fruit of Mary's womb, Jesus. Once this interpretation was established it received support from, and conferred significance on, the word "thorne," which could only be an allusion to the crown of thorns, a symbol of the trial suffered by Jesus and of the price he paid to save us all. It was only a short step (really no step at all) from this insight to the recognition of Levin as a double reference, first to the tribe of Levi, of whose priestly function Christ was the fulfillment, and second to the unleavened bread carried by the children of Israel on their exodus from Egypt, the place of sin, and in response to the call of Moses, perhaps the most familiar of the old testament types of Christ. The final word of the poem was given at least three complementary readings: it could be "omen," especially since so much of the poem is concerned with foreshadowing and prophecy; it could be Oh Man, since it is man's story as it intersects with the divine plan that is the poem's subject; and it could, of course, be simply "amen," the proper conclusion to a poem celebrating the love and mercy shown by a God who gave his only begotten son so that we may live.

In addition to specifying significances for the words of the poem and relating those significances to one another, the students began to discern larger structural patterns. It was noted that of the six names in the poem three—Jacobs, Rosenbaum, and Levin—are Hebrew, two—Thorne and Hayes—are Christian, and one—Ohman—is ambiguous, the ambiguity being marked in the poem itself (as the phrase goes) by the question mark in parenthesis. This division was seen as a reflection of the basic distinction between the old dispensation and the new, the law of sin and the law of love. That distinction, however, is blurred and finally dissolved by the typological perspective which invests the old testament events and heroes with new testament meanings. The structure of the poem, my students concluded, is therefore a double one, establishing and undermining its basic pattern (Hebrew vs. Christian) at the same time. In this context there is finally no pressure to resolve the ambiguity of Ohman since the two possible readings—the name is Hebrew, the name is Christian—are both authorized by the reconciling presence in the poem of Jesus Christ. Finally, I must report that one student took to counting letters and found, to no one's surprise, that the most prominent letters in the poem were S, O, N.

Some of you will have noticed that I have not yet said anything about Hayes. This is because of all the words in the poem it proved the most recalcitrant to interpretation, a fact not without consequence, but one which I will set aside for the moment since I am less interested in the details of the exercise than in the ability of my students to perform it. What is the source of that ability? How is it that they were able to do what they did? What is it that they did? These questions are important because they bear directly on a question often asked in literary theory, What are the distinguishing features of literary language? Or, to put the matter more colloquially, How do you recognize a poem when you see one? The commonsense answer, to which many literary critics and linguists are committed, is that the act of recognition is triggered by the observable presence of distinguishing features. That is, you know a poem when you see one because its language displays the characteristics that you know to be proper to poems. This, however, is a model that quite obviously does not fit the present example. My students did not proceed from the noting of distinguishing features to the recognition that they were confronted by a poem; rather, it was the act of recognition that came first—they knew in advance that they were dealing with a poem—and the distinguishing features then followed.

In other words, acts of recognition, rather than being triggered by formal characteristics, are their source. It is not that the presence of poetic qualities compels a certain kind of attention but that the paying of a certain kind of attention results in the emergence of poetic qualities. As soon as my students were aware that it was poetry they were seeing, they began to look with poetry-seeing eyes, that is, with eyes that saw everything in relation to the properties they knew poems to possess. They knew, for example (because they were told by their teachers), that poems are (or are supposed to be) more densely and intricately organized than ordinary communications; and that knowledge translated itself into a willingness—one might even say a determination—to see connections between one word and another and between every word and the poem's central insight. Moreover, the assumption that there *is* a central insight is itself poetry-specific, and presided over its own realization. Having assumed that the collection of words before them was unified by an informing purpose (because unifying purposes are what poems have), my students proceeded to find one and to formulate it. It was in the light of that purpose (now assumed) that significances for the individual words began to suggest themselves, significances which then fleshed out the assumption that had generated them in the first place. Thus the meanings of the words and the interpretation in which those words were seen to be embedded emerged together, as a consequence of the operations my students began to perform once they were told that this was a poem.

It was almost as if they were following a recipe—if it's a poem, do this, if it's a poem, see it that way—and indeed definitions of poetry *are* recipes, for by directing readers as to what to look for in a poem, they instruct them in ways of looking that will produce what they expect to see. If your definition of poetry tells you that the language of poetry is complex, you will scrutinize the language of something identified as a poem in such a way as to bring out the complexity you know to be "there." You will, for example, be on the look-out for latent ambiguities; you will attend to the presence of alliterative and consonantal patterns (there will always be some), and you will try to make something of them (you will always succeed); you will search for meanings that subvert, or exist in a tension with the meanings that first present themselves; and if these operations fail to produce the anticipated complexity, you will even propose a significance for the words that are *not* there, because, as everyone knows, everything about a poem, including its omissions, is significant. Nor, as you do these things, will you have any sense of performing in a willful manner, for you will only be doing what you learned to do in the course of becoming a skilled reader of poetry. Skilled reading is usually thought to be a matter of discerning what is there, but if the example of my students can be generalized, it is a matter of knowing how to *produce* what can thereafter be said to be there. Interpretation is not the art of construing but the art of constructing. Interpreters do not decode poems; they make them.

To many, this will be a distressing conclusion, and there are a number of arguments that could be mounted in order to forestall it. One might point out that the circumstances of my students' performance were special. After all, they had been concerned exclusively with religious poetry for some weeks, and therefore would be uniquely vulnerable to the deception I had practiced on them and uniquely equipped to impose religious themes and patterns on words innocent of either. I must report, however, that I have duplicated this experiment any number of times at nine or ten universities in three countries, and the results were always the same, even when the participants know from the beginning that what they are looking at was originally an assignment. Of course this very fact could itself be turned into an objection: doesn't the reproducibility of the exercise prove that there is something about these words that leads everyone to perform in the same way? Isn't it just a happy accident that names like Thorne and Jacobs have counterparts or near counterparts in biblical names and symbols? And wouldn't my students have been unable to do what they did if the assignment I gave to the first class had been made up of different names? The answer to all of these questions is no. Given a firm belief that they were confronted by a religious poem, my students would have been able to turn any list of names into the kind of poem we have before us now, because they would have read the names within the assumption that they were informed with Christian significances. (This is nothing more than a literary analogue to Augustine's rule of faith.) You can test this assertion by replacing Jacobs-Rosenbaum, Levin, Thorne, Hayes, and Ohman with names drawn from the faculty of the University of Michigan–Goodheart, Konigsberg, Super, Baker, Powers, and Weisbuch. Suffice it to say that it could easily be done (you can take the poem home and do it yourself) and that the shape of its doing would be constrained not by the names but by the interpretive assumptions that gave them a significance even before they were seen. This would be true even if there were no names on the list, if the paper or blackboard were blank; the blankness would present no problem to the interpreter, who would immediately see in it the void out of which God created the earth, or the abyss into which unregenerate sinners fall, or, in the best of all possible poems, both.

Even so, one might reply, all you've done is demonstrate how an interpretation, if it is prosecuted with sufficient vigor, can impose itself on material which has its own proper shape. Basically, at the ground level, in the first place, when all is said and done, "Jacobs-Rosenbaum Levin Thorne Hayes Ohman(?)" is an assignment; it is only a trick that allows you to transform it into a poem, and when the effects of the trick have worn off, it will return to its natural form and be seen as an assignment once again. This is a powerful argument because it seems at once to give interpretation its due (as an act of the will) and to maintain the independence of that on which interpretation works. It allows us, in short, to preserve our commonsense intuition that interpretation must be interpretation of *something*. Unfortunately, the argument will not hold because the assignment we all see is no less the product of interpretation than the poem into which it was turned. That is, it requires just as much work, and work of the same kind, to see this as an assignment as it does to see it as a poem. If this seems counterintuitive, it is only because the work required to see it as an assignment is work we have already done, in the course of acquiring the huge amount of background knowledge that enables you and me to function in the academic world. In order to know what an assignment is, that is, in order to know what to do with something identified as an assignment, you must first know what a class is (know that it isn't an economic grouping) and know that classes meet at specified times for so many weeks, and that one's performance in a class is largely a matter of performing between classes.

Think for a moment of how you would explain this last to someone who did not already know it. "Well," you might say, "a class is a group situation in which a number of people are instructed by an informed person in a particular subject." (Of course the notion of "subject" will itself require explication.) "An assignment is something you do when you're not in class." "Oh, I see," your interlocutor might respond, "an assignment is something you do to take your mind off what you've been doing in class." "No, an assignment is a part of a class." "But how can that be if you only do it when the class is not meeting?" Now it would be possible, finally, to answer that question, but only by enlarging the horizons of your explanation to include the very concept of a university, what it is one might be doing there, why one might be doing it instead of doing a thousand other things, and so on. For most of us these matters do not require explanation, and indeed, it is hard for us to imagine someone for whom they do; but that is because our tacit knowledge of what it means to move around in academic life was acquired so gradually and so long ago that it doesn't seem like knowledge at all (and therefore something someone else might *not* know) but a part of the world. You might think that when you're on campus (a phrase that itself requires volumes) that you are simply walking around on the two legs God gave you; but your walking is informed by an internalized awareness of institutional goals and practices, of norms of behavior, of lists of do's and don't's, of invisible lines and the dangers of crossing them; and, as a result, you see everything as *already* organized in relation to those same goals and practices. It would never occur to you, for example, to wonder if the people pouring out of that building are fleeing from a fire; you *know* that they are exiting from a class (what could be more obvious?) and you know that because your perception of their action occurs within a knowledge of what people in a university could possibly be doing and the reasons they could have for doing it (going to the next class, going back to the dorm, meeting someone in the student union). It is within that same knowledge that an assignment becomes intelligible so that it appears to you immediately as an obligation, as a set of directions, as something with parts, some of which may be more significant than others. That is, it is a proper question to ask of an assignment whether some of its parts might be omitted or slighted, whereas readers of poetry know that no part of a poem can be slighted (the rule is "everything counts") and they do not rest until every part has been given a significance.

In a way this amounts to no more than saying what everyone already knows: poems and assignments are different, but my point is that the differences are a result of the different interpretive operations we perform and not of something inherent in one or the other. An assignment no more compels its own recognition than does a poem; rather, as in the case of a poem, the shape of an assignment emerges when someone looks at something identified as one with assignment-seeing eyes, that is, with eyes which are capable of seeing the words as already embedded within the institutional structure that makes it possible for assignments to have a sense. The ability to see, and therefore to make, an assignment is no less a learned ability than the ability to see, and therefore to make, a poem. Both are constructed artifacts, the products and not the producers of interpretation, and while the differences between them are real, they are interpretive and do not have their source in some bedrock level of objectivity.

Of course one might want to argue that there is a bedrock level at which these names constitute neither an assignment or a poem but are merely a list. But that argument too falls because a list is no more a natural object—one that wears its meaning on its face and can be recognized by anyone—than an assignment or a poem. In order to see a list, one must already be equipped with the concepts of seriality, hierarchy, subordination, and so on, and while these are by no means esoteric concepts and seem available to almost everyone, they are nonetheless learned, and if there were someone who had not learned them, he or she would not be able to see a list. The next recourse is to descend still lower (in the direction of atoms) and to claim objectivity for letters, paper, graphite, black marks on white spaces, and so on; but these entities too have palpability and shape only because of the assumption of some or other system of intelligibility, and they are therefore just as available to a deconstructive dissolution as are poems, assignments, and lists.

The conclusion, therefore, is that all objects are made and not found, and that they are made by the interpretive strategies we set in motion. This does not, however, commit me to subjectivity because the means by which they are made are social and conventional. That is, the "you" who does the interpretative work that puts poems and assignments and lists into the world is a communal you and not an isolated individual. No one of us wakes up in the morning and (in French fashion) reinvents poetry or thinks up a new educational system or decides to reject seriality in favor of some other, wholly original, form of organization. We do not do these things because we could not do them, because the mental operations we can perform are limited by the institutions in which we are *already* embedded. These institutions precede us, and it is only by inhabiting them, or being inhabited by them, that we have access to the public and conventional senses they make. Thus while it is true to say that we create poetry (and assignments and lists), we create it through interpretive strategies that are finally not our own but have their source in a publicly available system of intelligibility. Insofar as the system (in this case a literary system) constrains us, it also fashions us, furnishing us with categories of understanding, with which we in turn fashion the entities to which we can then point. In short, to the list of made or constructed objects we must add ourselves, for we no less than the poems and assignments we see are the products of social and cultural patterns of thought.

To put the matter in this way is to see that the opposition between objectivity and subjectivity is a false one because neither exists in the pure form that would give the opposition its point. This is precisely illustrated by my anecdote in which we do *not* have free-standing readers in a relationship of perceptual adequacy or inadequacy to an equally free-standing text. Rather, we have readers whose consciousnesses are constituted by a set of conventional notions which when put into operation constitute in turn a conventional, and conventionally seen, object. My students could do what they did, and do it in unison, because as members of a literary community they knew what a poem was (their knowledge was public), and that knowledge led them to look in such a way as to populate the landscape with what they knew to be poems.

Of course poems are not the only objects that are constituted in unison by shared ways of seeing. Every object or event that becomes available within an institutional setting can be so characterized. I am thinking, for example, of something that happened in my classroom just the other day. While I was in the course of vigorously making a point, one of my students, William Newlin by name, was just as vigorously waving his hand. When I asked the other members of the class what it was that Mr. Newlin was doing, they all answered that he was seeking permission to speak. I then asked them how they knew that. The immediate reply was that it was obvious; what else could he be thought to be doing? The meaning of his gesture, in other words, was right there on its surface, available for reading by anyone who had the eyes to see. That meaning, however, would not have been available to someone without any knowledge of what was involved in being a student. Such a person might have thought that Mr. Newlin was pointing to the fluorescent lights hanging from the ceiling, or calling our attention to some object that was about to fall ("the sky is falling," "the sky is falling"). And if the someone in question were a child of elementary or middle-school age, Mr. Newlin might well have been seen as seeking permission not to speak but to go to the bathroom, an interpretation or reading that would never occur to a student at Johns Hopkins or any other institution of "higher learning" (and how would we explain to the uninitiated the meaning of *that* phrase).

The point is the one I have made so many times before: it is neither the case that the significance of Mr. Newlin's gesture is imprinted on its surface where it need only be read off, or that the construction put on the gesture by everyone in the room was individual and idiosyncratic. Rather, the source of our interpretive unanimity was a structure of interests and understood goals, a structure whose categories so filled our individual consciousnesses that they were rendered as one, immediately investing phenomena with the significance they *must* have, given the already-in-place assumptions about what someone could possibly be intending (by word or gesture) in a classroom. By seeing Mr. Newlin's raised hand with a single shaping eye, we were demonstrating what Harvey Sacks has characterized as "the fine power of a culture. It does not, so to speak, merely fill brains in roughly the same way, it fills them so that they are alike in fine detail." The occasion of Sacks's observation was the ability of his hearers to understand a sequence of two sentences—"The baby cried. The mommy picked it up."—exactly as he did (assuming, for example that "the 'mommy' who picks up the 'baby' is the mommy of that baby"), despite the fact that alternative ways of understanding were demonstrably possible. That is, the mommy of the second sentence could well have been the mommy of some other baby, and it need not even have been a baby that this "floating" mommy was picking up. One is tempted to say that in the absence of a specific context we are authorized to take the words literally, which is what Sacks's hearers do; but as Sacks observes, it is within the assumption of a context—one so deeply assumed that we are unaware of it—that the words acquire what seems to be their literal meaning. There is nothing in *the words* that tells Sacks and his hearers how to relate the mommy and the baby of this story, just as there is nothing *in the form* of Mr. Newlin's gesture that tells his fellow students how to determine its significance. In both cases the determination (of relation and significance) is the work of categories of organization—the family, being a student—that are from the very first giving shape and value to what is heard and seen.

Indeed, these categories are the very shape of seeing itself, in that we are not to imagine a perceptual ground more basic than the one they afford. That is, we are not to imagine a moment when my students "simply see" a physical configuration of atoms and *then* assign that configuration a significance, according to the situation they happen to be in. To be in the situation (this or any other) is to "see" with the eyes of its interests, its goals, its understood practices, values, and norms, and so to be conferring significance *by* seeing, not after it. The categories of my students' vision are the categories by which they understand themselves to be functioning as students (what Sacks might term "doing studenting"), and objects will appear to them in forms related to that way of functioning rather than in some objective or preinterpretive form. (This is true even when an object is seen as not related, since nonrelation is not a pure but a differential category—the specification of something by enumerating what it is not; in short, nonrelation is merely one form of relation, and its perception is always situation-specific.)

Of course, if someone who was not functioning as a student was to walk into my classroom, he might very well see Mr. Newlin's raised hand (and "raised hand" is already an interpretation-laden description) in some other way, as evidence of a disease, as the salute of a political follower, as a muscle-improving exercise, as an attempt to kill flies; but he would always see it in *some* way, and never as purely physical data waiting for his interpretation. And, moreover, the way of seeing, whatever it was, would never be individual or idiosyncratic, since its source would always be the institutional structure of which the "see-er" was an extending agent. This is what Sacks means when he says that a culture fills brains "so that they are alike in fine detail"; it fills them so that no one's interpretive acts are exclusively his own but fall to him by virtue of his position in some socially organized environment and are therefore always shared and public. It follows, then, that the fear of solipsism, of the imposition by the unconstrained self of its own prejudices, is unfounded because the self does not exist apart from the communal or conventional categories of thought that enable its operations (of thinking, seeing, reading). Once one realizes that the conceptions that fill consciousness, including any conception of its own status, are culturally derived, the very notion of an unconstrained self, of a consciousness wholly and dangerously free, becomes incomprehensible.

But without the notion of the unconstrained self, the arguments of Hirsch, Abrams, and the other proponents of objective interpretation are deprived of their urgency. They are afraid that in the absence of the controls afforded by a normative system of meanings, the self will simply substitute its own meanings for the meanings (usually identified with the intentions of the author) that texts bring with them, the meanings that texts *"have"*; however, if the self is conceived of not as an independent entity but as a social construct whose operations are delimited by the systems of intelligibility that inform it, then the meanings it confers on texts are not its own but have their source in the interpretive community (or communities) of which it is a function. Moreover, these meanings will be neither subjective nor objective, at least in the terms assumed by those who argue within the traditional framework; they will not be objective because they will always have the product of a point of view rather than having been simply "read off"; and they will not be subjective because that point of view will always be social or institutional. Or by the same reasoning one could say that they are *both* subjective and objective: they are subjective because they inhere in a particular point of view and are therefore not universal; and they are objective because the point of view that delivers them is public and conventional rather than individual or unique.

To put the matter in either way is to see how unhelpful the terms "subjective" and "objective" finally are. Rather than facilitating inquiry, they close it down, by deciding in advance what shape inquiry can possibly take. Specifically, they assume, without being aware that it is an assumption and therefore open to challenge, the very distinction I have been putting into question, the distinction between interpreters and the objects they interpret. That distinction in turn assumes that interpreters and their objects are two different kinds of *a*contextual entities, and within these twin assumptions the issue can only be one of control: will texts be allowed to constrain their own interpretation or will irresponsible interpreters be allowed to obscure and overwhelm texts. In the spectacle that ensues, the spectacle of Anglo-American critical controversy, texts and selves fight it out in the persons of their respective champions, Abrams, Hirsch, Reichert, Graff on the one hand, Holland, Bleich, Slatoff, and (in some characterizations of him) Barthes on the other. But if selves are constituted by the ways of thinking and seeing that inhere in social organizations, and if these constituted selves in turn constitute texts according to these same ways, then there can be no adversary relationship between text and self because they are the necessarily related products of the same cognitive possibilities. A text cannot be overwhelmed by an irresponsible reader and one need not worry about protecting the purity of a text from a reader's idiosyncracies. It is only the distinction between subject and object that gives rise to these urgencies, and once the distinction is blurred they simply fall away. One can respond with a cheerful yes to the question "Do readers make meanings?" and commit oneself to very little because it would be equally true to say that meanings, in the form of culturally derived interpretive categories, make readers.

Indeed, many things look rather different once the subject-object dichotomy is eliminated as the assumed framework within which critical discussion occurs. Problems disappear, not because they have been solved but because they are shown never to have been problems in the first place. Abrams, for example, wonders how, in the absence of a normative system of stable meanings, two people could ever agree on the interpretation of a work or even of a sentence; but the difficulty is only a difficulty if the two (or more) people are thought of as isolated individuals whose agreement must be compelled by something external to them. (There is something of the police state in Abrams's vision, complete with posted rules and boundaries, watchdogs to enforce them, procedures for identifying their violators as criminals.) But if the understandings of the people in question are informed by the same notions of what counts as a fact, of what is central, peripheral, and worthy of being noticed—in short, by the same interpretive principles—then agreement between them will be assured, and its source will not be a text that enforces its own perception but a way of perceiving that results in the emergence to those who share it (or those whom it shares) of the same text. That text might be a poem, as it was in the case of those who first "saw" "Jacobs-Rosenbaum Levin Hayes Thorne Ohman(?)," or a hand, as it is every day in a thousand classrooms; but whatever it is, the shape and meaning it appears immediately to have will be the "ongoing accomplishment" of those who agree to produce it.

THE IRREPRESSIBLE REAL: JACQUES LACAN AND POSTSTRUCTURALISM

Wesley Morris

> He did not know that he was dead, then. Sometimes I would lie by him in the dark, hearing the land that was now of my blood and flesh, and I would think: Anse. Why Anse. Why are you Anse. I would think about his name until after a while I could see the word as a shape, a vessel, and I would watch him liquefy and flow into it like cold molasses flowing out of the darkness into the vessel, until the jar stood full and motionless: a significant shape profoundly without life like an empty door frame; and then I would find that I had forgotten the name of the jar. I would think: The shape of my body where I used to be a virgin is in the shape of a   and I couldn't think *Anse*, couldn't remember *Anse*.
>
> (William Faulkner, *As I Lay Dying*)

Language: Revenge, Oedipus, Culture

The moral of Addie Bundren's meditation on language and life in *As I Lay Dying* is: "Never let a man choose your signifiers for you." This is a question of character or characterization raising the issue of just who pulls the strings on those bundles of words we readers call by proper names, and Faulkner here muddles the issue by giving us a character who seems to be fully aware of the power of language, who manifests a firm understanding of Saussure's concept of the "arbitrary" relationship between signifiers and signifieds. There is, of course, an ambiguity in Saussure's theory that extends the "arbitrary" notion to the relationship between words and the real, experiential world. On the one hand, the arbitrary nature of the signifier/signified relationship has nothing whatever to do with the real world; rather, it narrowly describes a "conventional" (cultural) connection between an accoustical image and a mental concept, between sound and sense. But a mental concept can be thought of as a sense-image, as intentional, as sense experience of the real world, and it is not clear in the characterization of Addie Bundren which notion of the arbitrary confronts us. Most obviously it is the narrower Saussurean doctrine that would allow us to characterize Addie's language as "freeplay." But Addie's manipulations are more complex than this; she is engaged in the power play of revenge (one of Faulkner's obsessions, according to John Irwin), and this must be read in the extended sense of the arbitrary, as describing a "problematical" relationship between words and the "Real."

The distinction between these two concepts of the arbitrary is crucial, and I find the passage from Addie's dying thoughts very instructive for contemporary literary critics. Our attention is drawn to the open space in the text, to an "absence," to a critical moment of choice in the paradigmatic, or selection, phase of verbal expression. The blank can, indeed, we feel that it must, be filled, and the available fillers are many. Addie says she once had the proper term, her husband's name, "Anse," but she forgot it. In order to forget it she first decomposed its referent, an image of the real, sensible Anse. Therefore, Anse is doubly absent in this syntagm, banished through forgetfulness. But as a result of Addie's action the reader knows that the image of Anse and his name are absent, for what remains is neither word nor image, signifier nor signified, but the "significant shape" of absence, an ineradicable mark, a palpable, contextual nothingness. It is on this hinge that the aggressive play of Addie's Freudian joke swings. She cuts loose the signifier, "Anse," from its signified so that it returns to the realm of freeplay, of *"differance."* This Derridean move is designed to unleash the free flow of metonymic substitution, the endless displacement of one signifier by another. But freeplay may never be as unlimited as the Yale Derrideans lead us to believe; in the case at hand, we cannot completely forget the "original" signifier, "Anse," nor its ghostlike signified, which most adequately fills the significant shape or syntagmatic slot, even though we are, through Addie's powerful forgetting, barred from articulating that taboo name.

The reader, admittedly, has no experience of Anse Bundren, although a mental image of Anse is formed even by the most unimaginative undergraduate. How may we speak of a "real" Anse, or, more broadly, of the "Real"? We are led by the syntagmatic force of the passage to substitute for the name, Anse, a signifier referring to a particular part of the male anatomy. Technically, the word we must select is not a metonym but a more intimate synechdoche that signifies a Kleinian part-object: the penis. This, however, is too clinical a term to do justice to the emotional pitch of Addie's meditation on her marriage. My choice (though each to his or her own favorite in this freeplay) is "prick." Once this option is exercised we read the phrase in two ways, two directions. First, clinically, horizontally, it is: "The shape of my body where I used to be a virgin is in the shape of a penis. . . ." Secondly, wittily, vertically, we rewrite the phrase to take advantage of the rules of free substitution, to equate the substitute part-term and the whole-term that it replaces, so that the phrase reads: "Anse is a prick."

Verbal wit of this sort teases us into freeplay. Roland Barthes calls it the "pleasure of the text"–a corruption of Derridean freeplay into sexual foreplay. But, by definition, foreplay is prelude to something, and an overindulgence in the joy of verbal wit distracts us from the darker side of Addie's thoughts. The phrase "shape of a penis" is a definition, a definition of the phallic image, and it is what I would like to call the "image-ing" function of this passage that too much erotic wordplay represses. Here we are confronted by a problematical relationship between words and the real world, not just between signifiers and signifieds. We have narrowed the relationship of words and world to that between words and phallic images of the real world. What is missing from this particular passage is the link that narrows the gap even further; I will call it the "phallic word," the significant shape of a textual absence.

The phallic word is literally repressed by Addie; as Jacques Lacan describes such repression, the phallic word is a signifier which has "slipped under the bar" (the Saussurean bar that Lacan reads as emblematic of repression) in order to function as a signified–as if it were no longer mere sound but substance. This is a cultural, not a poetic, "as if" commitment, for the phallic word has been censored leaving a substantial gap in the text where "penis" ("prick") ought to be. Thus we "read" a graphic image-ing of the lack of (a) penis and not merely the verbal definition of a phallic image. The opening in the text negatively images the substantial part-object.

Addie's puzzling reference to words becoming "shapes," or "vessels" should be much clearer to us now. Words do have an image-ing capacity; under the pressure of repression words take on a phallic or iconic function; they draw us toward or intend substance. Here, the opening in the text is not just any openness but represents for us a complex, culturally-motivated image of vaginal emptiness or castration. Addie describes herself in marriage as "unvirgin"—a double negation (which does not yield a simple positive), an absence of an absence. Moreover, Faulkner attributes to the character of Addie this act of negative image-ing, the graphic removal of the substantialized (phallic) word. It is Addie who censors, unsexes her text, and as a result, Addie emerges, darkly, as something more than a playful wit. She is almost a caricature of the castrating female.

If we read her chapter carefully, we begin to see Addie as something of a projection of Faulkner's male fantasy/nightmare. She is the domineering wife/mother who represses—oppresses—her entire family. But Addie is more than a product of Faulkner's chauvinism; she is a prisoner of her own culture-bound language, of the male-oriented society from which she draws her images. She is forced to condemn herself in her own voice, with words that are not wholly her own. Because of this she is the most fascinating character in the novel, but even to speak of her as fascinating in this manner is to fall victim to cultural repression—stereotyping. To some extent Faulkner's strategy is to disguise the darker implications beneath the verbal wit, to disguise his and his culture's obsessive belief that vaginal or virginal openness represents desire and pleasure but also sin and the threat of emasculation. Such is, sadly, the primordial law of our Oedipal Age.

Lacan's World

There is insufficient space here to draw fully the outlines of the Oedipal Age, although I hope to work in that direction. If one reads all of Addie's chapter, some sense of the complexity of this culture-concept emerges, a sense of the problematical relationship between language and reality interwoven with psychoanalytical issues of ego development, socio-economic exchange (giving and paying), and political power struggles. All of this rests heavily on the graphic image of feminine lacking, and, consequently, on the Oedipal law that treats children as compensation for that lacking while it also doubles the bonds of enslavement through the debt the woman incurs to her husband for his masculine expenditure in the production of those children. There is sympathy in Faulkner's insight here, a sympathy that may rescue him from total blindness.

But I will stay on a more focused issue: the illumination of the fundamental problematics of language and reality in the revisionist Freudianism of Jacques Lacan. I want to devote a few pages to the definitions of what Lacan calls the Imaginary, the Symbolic, and the Real, and then to speculate on Lacan's problems in accepting the direction of his own theory.

The Imaginary for Lacan must not be equated with that mystical "imagination" bequeathed to us by the Romantic poets. Lacan intends no god-like creativity, nor that form of image-making which intuitively penetrates beyond the veil of the familiar to the essential, vital forces of nature. The Imaginary defines a stage in the process of human maturation (roughly from six to eighteen months) which also we must not confuse with Romantic self-consciousness. The Imaginary is a pre-existential stage of thrownness, a stage of consciousness without an ego which resembles the consciousness described by Sartre as an empty wind blowing toward objects. For Lacan, this stage is a precondition for social belonging and for the development of the ego based on three factors: (1) consciousness as the imprint of images on the brain, as sense perception, which includes the experience of one's own image in a mirror; (2) a state of narcissistic/aggressive flux wherein images are freely exchanged and there is a confusion of the mirror image of the self as a whole, integrated being with the images of other wholes; (3) the interplay of biological need (for food, warmth, etc.) with non-mirrored perception of one's own body as separate, non-integrated parts, hence, as lacking, or even as decomposing. Clearly, this third category problematizes the others, instituting a gap in consciousness between the images of wholes and the perception of parts. This gap Lacan calls the "scene" of desire (though not yet desire in its full development). The Imaginary is the stage of close, sensual interaction between the conscious organism and its environment, yet it posits no self-reflexive ego.

The Symbolic can be defined as the stage which follows the Imaginary, yet the Symbolic does not supplant the Imaginary. Lacan's concept of the Symbolic owes much to a broad tradition in European philosophy; for example, it is the stage of existential thrownness described by Heidegger and Sartre; it is also reminiscent of Hegel's phase of the unhappy consciousness and, therefore, it defines a self-reflexive ego and its desire for an impossible Ideal. Lacan's Symbolic embodies both a Sartrean sense of ego-lacking and a dimension of social belonging like that of Lévi-Strauss's mythic deep structures. Finally, it describes the fundamental drama of Freudian repression, and, for Deleuze and Guattari, it is the scene of political oppression.

To the degree that the Symbolic defines the conditions of social belonging, it is best described as the stage of the accession to Language, of entry into the Symbolic Order (a cataclysmic event like that described by Lévi-Strauss as mankind's accession to Language in one giant step). Hence, Language as Symbolic Order appears to be "given" to humankind—a Heideggerian characterization that is not incorrect if we avoid seeing this "given" as metaphysical. We would do well to remember Derrida's claim that Language did not fall from the sky; it was produced. The important factor here, however, as it is for all poststructuralists, is that the Symbolic Order is not our personal property; Lacan calls it the "discourse of the Other," of the social order, perhaps, which situates power and authority outside the ego. The old Romantic interplay between the inner and outer worlds, between the soul and nature, is transformed by Lacan into the drama of a violent penetration of consciousness by an alien force, an opening of the private mind to the world. That precise sense of violation torments Addie, not just sexual violation by Anse, nor simply the hollowness of the word, "love," but the treachery of what she calls "older words," something utterly devastating. Addie's response is egocentric and vengeful, a bitter affirmation of herself. Her second son, Darl, however, is driven mad by the loss of self implied in the violation of the private inner by the public outer. Derrida's brilliant analysis of Husserl in *Speech and Phenomena* demonstrates this problem in the freeplay of the first person singular pronoun, "I." This linguistic shifter, so authentic, so personal and intimate as each of us speaks it, turns out to be just another signifier prostituting itself for any speaker's ego-desire.

On the accession to Language, to the Symbolic Order, the ego is forever divided against itself, named by names that are never its own, forever incomplete, lacking, castrated. Building on the gap of part/whole located in the Imaginary stage, complicating that gap by encoding it in a cultural message, the Symbolic establishes the rules of social communication and exchange, an economy of desiring and thus of producing and consuming, of substituting part-objects for other part-objects in an insatiable longing for the impossible ego-ideal of the whole. Again reflecting Sartre, as well as Lévi-Strauss, Lacan dissolves all possibility of a Kantian or Husserlian transcendental ego; ego-identity is a social (linguistic) given so that the ego is never in full possession of itself. This intensifies the narcissistic/aggressive competition of the Imaginary stage, naming with a common name not only the subject, the "I," but also the part-objects that the subject lacks in its struggle for the ego-ideal. The images of integrated wholes from the Imaginary become impossible dreams, like crumbling role-models, but competition is preserved, on the basis of narcissistic/aggressive drives, because the desired objects, even the common names, must be possessed by the desiring ego, and these objects seem "always already" to belong–wrongfully, oppressively–to others, to those in authority.

Lacan's system is classically Freudian, Oedipal, but it is also simply classical. The naming of the ego with a name not the ego's own comes through the posing of a double-edged question, the same question in two forms. As the discourse of an authoritative other, the question is a withering challenge: "Who are you?"; but since there is no transcendental ego to which such a challenge may be directed, the more accurate form of the question is Delphic, self-reflexive, and hermeneutical: "Who am I?"–a universal question. For the divided ego the answer is' "I am one who desires *as* and *what* others desire." Such an ego is frustrated by proprietary rights, by the ownership of forbidden objects. Desire cannot be assuaged, signifier must narcissistically/aggressively replace signifier, and, in the Freudian model, son must replace father. Symbolically, in "name" only, of course. In this Oedipal cycle of struggle and displacement the social order finds its motivating force to produce and to consume.

The Symbolic Order, therefore, is fundamentally repressive of the ego-ideal of wholeness; it is also repressive of the entire realm of the Imaginary, and this is crucial. There is a remnant of Romanticism in Lacan's system, an anti-social bias (after all, the social, Symbolic Order is anxiety-ridden). There is an honest Utopian longing for a simpler age, for the Imaginary. I do not want to push this idea too far, and the Utopian Romanticism of the theory is most clear in post-Lacanians like Deleuze and Guattari, but this Romantic drift reminds one of the infamous Rousseauistic nostalgia charged against Lévi-Strauss. More importantly, the threat of such a Romantic impurity in Lacan's theory explains the tendency of more extreme poststructuralists to repress the Imaginary along with its focus on the realm of sensual experience. This reveals the pressure of Derrida's radical disciples; it results in an overestimation of Lacan's attempt to debiologize Freud. The goal of these radical theorists is to decompose the empirical into the absolute freeplay of the Symbolic, much as Addie playfully decomposes the image of the biological, bodily Anse into mere sound.

We must avoid this repression if we are to grasp Lacan's third realm, the Real, for the Real is defined by the problematical relationship between the Symbolic and the Imaginary. That is to say, the Real is that interface between Language as a differential system and the experiential world of the images of things. The Real, of course, does not describe an atomistic connection between particular signifiers and signifieds, nor between names and particular things. This is not a naïve picture-theory realism. The Real is best thought of as what Wittgenstein called states of affairs, as arrangements of the images of things which define the horizons of our familiar environment. These states are largely unconscious, "given," like the cultural myths Lévi-Strauss reconstructs from patterns of behavior, those myths that think their ways into our minds without our knowing it. Or they are like the operational discursive systems that we call knowledge, sometimes even Truth, what Michel Foucault labels *epistemes*. The Real mediates our experience, establishes order and meaningfulness among humans in their human world. Perhaps we must understand the problematical Real in the sense of a Sartrean situation, or in the Heideggerian sense of historical being-there, or, finally, as a structure of cultural definition and bias like that defined by Edward Said in *Orientalism*. Lacan argues that Language as Symbolic Order has only an asymptotic relationship to material reality; true enough, but it cannot free itself from that ground.

Repression: Faulkner, Lacan, the Yale Derrideans

Unless we grasp the dimensions of this problematical Real, we cannot accurately read Addie's chapter in *As I Lay Dying*. Faulkner gives us here a complex character who emerges directly out of language theory. On the one hand, Addie is a Romantic sensualist who rejects words because they are nothing more than sounds designed to fill the gaps in people's experience. On the other hand, she is a language sophisticate who uses words iconically, or phallically, for revenge and self-promotion. Addie is a powerful and threatening figure who whips her young students until they bleed, who intentionally marks (inscribes, writes on) their flesh the message of her sensible presence. Language is her primary weapon even when she seems to be acting in the world of pure sense experience. Therefore, the "promise" she extracts from Anse and her children, to bury her with her own family in Jefferson, Mississippi, to remove her bodily remains "outside the circle" of the Bundren family unit, must be read as a verbal contract with profound experiential effects. She bargains for power by setting her gifts of children and work as a wife (that is, her life, which she sees as "getting ready to stay dead") against Anse's agreement to perform certain specified ritualistic acts after she is dead. But there is more, for the revenge she seeks rests on her manipulation of the others through a language she believes none of the others fully comprehends, and it is here that she makes her fatal mistake. Her revenge rests on the necessity of repressing the Lacanian Imaginary (that is, the problematical Real), and this repression makes her vulnerable not simply to Anse but, more dangerously, to the misogynistic tendencies of the author.

Thus Addie's life evolves into a pattern of balancing accounts, what she calls "cleaning her house," and this is crucially–even cruelly–interwoven with the promise. For example, the promise can be fulfilled only after her death, and this allows Addie to linger (in Heidegger's sense of presencing) beyond the grave in a privileged position of authority. This privilege also explains the ambiguity of the book's title, the problem we have with narrative point of view: "dying" is grammatically a lingering, a process synonymous with living. Even though Addie has been pronounced dead by the country doctor, Peabody, relatively early in the novel, her dying/lingering/living pervades the entire book, just as her single meditative chapter (placed after her death) dominates all of the others. Addie's lingering is a symbolic presencing, a violation of real time and fictional chronology, that both defies the decay of bodies (represses the Real or the image-ing of reality) and establishes an enduring, closed family structure centered around herself even though she is, paradoxically, buried "outside the circle." Addie's power play is logocentric, to use Derrida's term, and it will succeed only if she can involve the others in its mystical implications. Or, and this is the same thing, her plan will work if the author fails to extricate himself from the fascination (fear and desire) his character holds for him.

The difficulty of the journey to Jefferson, therefore, is less important to Addie's revenge than the fact of a symbolic and ritualistic commitment by her family to her desires. Her philosophy of "getting ready to stay dead" along with her logocentric revenge makes Addie the author/authority of a family story ("text") which must have an absolute ending, a family story fixed and contained within itself as an icon to her logocentric privilege. It is an effort at composition designed to repress decomposition, to stop the freeplay of metonymic signifiers. It is also an aesthetics of closed narrative form that all readers of Faulkner know he rejected. Yet insofar as Addie dominates the novel Faulkner allows her plan to succeed–until the last moment.

Motivated by a variety of selfish interests, the family commits itself to the journey. Her children, who are in many ways merely extensions of her personality, comprise a catelogue of near-allegorical types in this symbolic enterprise. The oldest son, Cash, shapes her coffin with unique care as his performance of iconic worship. His effort is directed toward defiance of the decay of her body. The name, "Cash" moreover, suggests a neutral medium of exchange, ambiguous as to value, and the character's simple, empirical, and pragmatic personality implies a kind of innocence which has no proper name, no real character other than that of its function. Conversely, Darl is a child of experience, the object of Addie's hatred and the primary cause of her vengeance. Darl, then, is a disruptive element in the family; hating his brothers and sister, he would take Addie away from them by burning her body in Gillespie's barn. It is this act, of course, that results in his being purged from the family (committed to an asylum). Yet Darl's madness is expressed through his mystical withdrawal and his loss of self, his sense of being, in the freeplay of language. Must we not see Darl, therefore, the only character whose name Faulkner deliberately corrupts, as a warning to the others about freeplay and repression of the Real? Darl stands as a poetic corrective to Cash's empiricism and pragmatism, but a corrective gone too far.

The third child, Jewel, the issue of Addie's adulterous affair with Whitfield, is the child of passion and Romance. Jewel would stand for intrinsic (not exchange) value if it were not for the hypocrisy of his father which undercuts Addie's Romanticized version of their sexual encounters. It is Jewel who initiates the debit system of the family economy, Addie's debt to Anse. And Jewel, the passionate, Oedipally obsessed child must ritualistically rescue Addie from water and fire in another worshipful, Addie-centered, act of devotion. The fourth child, Dewey Dell, is a mere negation of the debt incurred with Jewel, but this has a positive function in the family unit even as it cancels out Dewey

Dell's personality. The only daughter of the Bundrens is an exchangeable integer of potential, mindless fecundity who serves as cook and maid thereby foreclosing any future need for a replacement for Addie. The last child, Vardaman, remains for the reader an innocent without strong identity. Even his proper name recalls the tradition of naming after a popular political figure, yet it is Vardaman who most graphically, experientially, acts out the family's repression of the Lacanian Real when he, urged by Darl, drills holes in his mother's coffin so that she can breath.

Addie's logocentric designs on her children succeed in closing the circle around her absence/presence, succeed in stopping the free flow of signifiers through iconic repression, succeed in turning all passion incestuously inward. Nevertheless, she underestimates the empirical naivete of Anse, who is able not only to bury (forget/repress) Addie's body but also to work a clever exchange with her name: substituting the impersonal, relational, "Mrs. Bundren" for the iconic, personal "Addie" and then attaching the now absolutely free signifier of relation to the nearest convenient signified, body. No sooner has Addie been removed "outside the circle" than Anse introduces his children to the "new" Mrs. Bundren. Addie is displaced from authority, from logocentric privilege, in a move so sudden and inexplicable, a move totally unprepared for by the novel's plot, that we are tempted to see it as Faulkner's revenge. Addie's linguistic power, her very character, dissipates as quickly as her body; her Romantic logocentric plot is crushed by an intruding author who turns the final joke. Yet the alternative to logocentricity for Faulkner is clearly not freeplay, for that way Darl's madness lies. The lesson of Addie Bundren is: one cannot close off the real world, the image-ing of experience, simply by repressing its problematical nature.

Here again we should find the literary example instructive for literary theorists. Even with the Derridean caution against logocentrism, the Symbolic Order cannot be used to help us forget a troublesome mortality; such repression only further imprisons us, as Fredric Jameson claims, in the anxiety of the Nietzschean absurd. It is even more important to realize that rhetorical gamesmanship is never innocent, and it is morally irresponsible to act as if it were. This charge of irresponsibility has been directed toward the freeplay philosophy of Derrida, but I believe Frank Lentricchia argues persuasively, in his *After the New Criticism,* that Derrida never attempts to justify so extreme a position.

Lentricchia's analysis puts the blame elsewhere, specifically on the Yale school critics who have become fascinated with the idea of freeplay and devote much of their considerable polemical energies to a rejection of any suggestion of the Lacanian Real. These critics defend a philosophy that sounds much like traditional Existentialism; they commit themselves—heroically—to a continually renewed confrontation with what they call the "abyss." But this Existentialism has undergone a shift in focus from its source in the 1940's; no longer concerned with the absurdity of the phenominal world, this new Existentialism founds itself on the overzealous repression of reality. The abyss, a concept borrowed from Derrida, is a textual matter, a linguistic or rhetorical nothingness. The abyss is freeplay unbound, a form of Nietzschean madness, certainly, and troublesome whenever one wishes to make value judgments.

The crucial principle of the Yale critics, which they all share to some extent, is a fascination with rhetoric, a result of Paul de Man's theoretical efforts in his influential book, *Blindness and Insight.* De Man is the ultimate deconstructor, able to find abyssmal freeplay in any text whatsoever. This means that all writers have a bit of Derridean insight in the midst of their blindness, even Derrida. But by deconstructing Derrida (on Rousseau) de Man radicalizes freeplay into a philosophy of language that merely extends an old New Critical idea: that of the privileged (aesthetic) functioning of poetic discourse. This is de Man's point of greatest vulnerability for a perceptive historical theorist like Lentricchia. As de Man disestablishes ontological referentiality, and with it the authenticity of the author, in order to elevate rhetorical play to a position of authority-for-the-moment, he props his theory, Lentricchia argues, on a concept of freedom that is the basis for all "formalist, idealist, and aestheticist positions after Kant." De Man's theory of rhetoric is New Critical ambiguity writ large. No longer is the discrete poem the locus of "undecideables," of words cut free from referentiality, sealed off from ordinary experience and authorial intention, now *all* language, all writing is so idealized.

The Yale critics, of course, are no unified school, as any of those I will mention below would quickly say, yet the mistake of Addie's forgetfulness of the Real and the fascination with mere idealized word-games, the flirtation with a poetical madness very like Darl Bundren's, lurks within their writings. In the approach of J. Hillis Miller, who often serves the group as spokesman, the aim of literary criticism is to be "uncanny" (an idea borrowed from Heidegger and Freud); Miller likens interpretation, the search for meaning, to an endless unravelling of the insubstantial thread of Ariadne. In his *Georgia Review* readings of Wallace Stevens, Miller extends Stevens's aesthetics in order to become a critical denier of rocks, the obverse of Dr. Johnson, a playful, lonesome, sophisticated wanderer in a forest of signifiers. In search of the abyss, lured by it, yet frightened of it, the uncanny critic seeks a profundity of meaning which defies expression, which is a form of overdetermined meaningfulness that, in fact, does not exist except in the blank spaces between words, an argument that should remind us of Mallarmé's Symbolist Ideal of pure poetry. This is, in the tradition of de Man, rhetoric for its own sake.

Rhetoric is also the obsession of Harold Bloom, although in his hands, as in Faulkner's, wordplay has a darker, more sinister side. Bloom is a complex figure whose career has undergone rather profound changes of focus that I will not attempt to outline here. Lentricchia's reading of Bloom in *After the New Criticism* has already intelligently set the record straight; my attention, therefore, will be limited to Bloom's more recent work which, under de Man's influence, seems to both reject and accept the radicalized version of Derridean freeplay. Bloom finds freeplay uncomfortable; absolute freeplay is absolute anxiety submerged in narcissistic/aggressive competitiveness between the ego and its predecessors (father figures). Beneath the rhetorical freeplay for Bloom is a traditional I-thou struggle, an existential dilemma, that tends to draw us back toward the Lacanian Real. Yet there is a certain insubstantial air to Bloom's real-politics, to his importation of the Freudian family romance, the Oedipal triangle, into de Man's rhetorical playfulness. Bloom offers us little more than a thematics of freeplay; it even has a name: the anxiety of influence. This brings history in by the back door, brings in a concern with the past, with the continuity of tradition, with real, historical individuals who can be "named" as authors of particular texts, but Bloom's historicism is rarified, purified by a radical version of freeplay. His sense of history is wholly literary, appropriately a page torn from T. S. Eliot's "Tradition and the Individual Talent" and reflecting Eliot's conservative religious commitment to Tradition. Perhaps more accurately, Bloom's history of anxiety rediscovers his earlier allegiance to Northrop Frye's literary universe, to Frye's mythical order of writing, which Geoffrey Hartman once characterized as a forerunner of the structuralist fascination with the Symbolic Order. Bloom's revolutionary, rebellious existential personalism here gives way to rhetorical gamesmanship, to the idea of "misreading" as a form of creative power play. One overcomes one's literary predecessors by taking their words right out of their mouths, but, of course, such misreading is justified by the Derridean dictum that words can never belong to anyone. One wonders, then, why this theft occasions so much anxiety? Whatever the vacillations in Bloom's theory on this point, it is clear that the hint of the Lacanian Real receives only glancing treatment. Bloom insists that his Oedipal drama is played out upon a natural, a "real" stage, but the rhetorical reductiveness of this primal scene mystifies reality, leaving us with little more than verbal play, mere wit. The Bloomian critic all too often demonstrates his agility simply by tracing key words from poet to poet and designating this anxiety. Even Bloom, everywhere cautious of the Derridean extreme, falls victim, like Addie, to a forgetful repression of the Real.

My final example, Geoffrey Hartman, seems the most puzzling of the Yale critics. Perhaps the group's most perceptive reader of poetry, Hartman is a reluctant theorist who lapses into an embarrassed confessional pose when he writes about the philosophy of interpretation. In this he reflects the general anti-theoretical bias of the Yale critics—a bias that takes the form of promoting criticism to the honorific level of poetic creativity. Hartman openly confesses this in his assertion of an inferiority complex *vis-à-vis* literary texts and a superiority complex *vis-à-vis* critical texts. In his practical criticism, however, Hartman shows himself to be a learned scholar of deep sensitivity; he is able, for example, to present us with a remarkable reading of Keats's autumn ode wherein his inferiority complex mixes with Keatsian negative capability to yield a most suggestive and insightful essay. In true Derridean style Hartman intersects the poem with other texts, speaking first for this tradition and then for that tradition, for this poem and that poem, in an interpretive act far removed from abyssmal rhetorical gamesmanship. As we read Hartman on Keats we hear many articulate voices expressing a complex and profound sense of time and place, deeply felt experiences of the problematical world, of belonging to a particular, nineteenth-century, European, English culture. Superficially, the same technique is used in Hartman's theoretical essays on Derrida's *Glas*. There we can see the implications of de Man's expansion of literary criticism to the rhetorical analysis of any text whatever, even philosophical texts. I do not want to be misunderstood on this point, this expansion has much to recommend it, but there is no reason for Hartman to leave behind the depth of historical meaningfulness found in his analysis of Keats when he turns his attention to Derrida. Yet this is precisely what he has done with *Glas*; a different set of rules seems to preside; a different goal is in sight. Wilfully repressed here is that rich sense of time and place, human experience, which would put us in contact with Derrida, the philosopher of our era. I will allow one rather long passage to stand as an example, a passage partially quoted by Lentricchia for very similar analysis. Note Hartman's fascination with verbal play at the expense of meaningfulness.

> Derrida's style is not unique, though its extravagance (to use Thoreau's word) confronts the reader from an English text-milieu with as much of a problem as the heavier Heidegger.
>
> * * *
>
> The problem, on the surface at least, is the persistence, the seriousness, with which an intelligence of this order employs devices that may seem to be at best witty and at worst trivial. Yet . . . how do we take all those verbal tricks, so productive yet so easy to parody? So functional in foregrounding language, in making us aware of it as the only subject, compared to which ego and author are episodic notions discarded by an interminable demonstration?
>
> Indeed, it is not the devices themselves but the interminable character of the analysis they impose which may tire us into antagonism. The . . . boa-deconstructor aspects of Derrida's systematic play, his *serio ludere,* is the real issue. To call it "freeplay" seems understated even if we remember that the term is adapted from the world of machines. For a machine with this much play in it is either a surrealist, erotic, morphological fantasy, like Marcel Duchamp's *Le Grand Verre,* or a language game with so many trick-possibilities that to say there are seven types of ambiguity is suddenly of the same order of truth as that there are four humours or seven cardinal sins.
>
> * * *

> Derrida tells literary people only what they have always known and repressed. Repressed too much, perhaps. The fullness of equivocation in literary structures should now be thought about to the point where Joyce's wordplay seems normal and Empson's *Seven Types* archaic. A 1001 nights of literary analysis lie before a Scheherazade to keep an emperor awake beyond his intentions.

Caught between "fantasy" and "game," Hartman's analysis of Derrida comes dangerously near the fallacy of imitative form. It is a "fullness of equivocation" that condemns one to always fall back on what "seems" to be, and, however problematical, the Real has a more solid claim to the orders of truth than seems possible in witty, trivial wordplay. It is my contention, of course, bolstered by Lacan's theory, that the freeplay rhetoricians are the ones who "repress"–perhaps, too much. The mistake is the same one made by Addie Bundren (under Faulkner's guidance), the forgetting of the Real in a 1001 nights of verbal foreplay. It is not a mistake made by Faulkner. The rude decentering of Addie, her easy replacement both on the level of rhetorical play and on the level of real human relationships, jars us out of the world of verbal contemplation back into the world of real-politics, what R. D. Laing called "family politics." Addie cannot close off the family, not merely because her logocentric joke suffers a Derridean deconstruction, but also because desire, that is, producing and consuming, builds on the foundation of a substantial, a material, world. The decomposition of Addie's body in *As I Lay Dying* is perfectly matched by the decomposition of the family unit: the loss of wagon and mules, of Jewel's horse, the fracture of Cash's leg, the institutionalizing of Darl, and the seemingly unpreventable coming of Dewey Dell's baby. Loss leads to need, to scarcity, to the denial of stasis, and, consequently, to the need to continually re-articulate our verbal systems to real experience. Faulkner teaches us that there are two extremes to be avoided in the interpretation of the problematical overlay of the Symbolic on the Imaginary, Lacan's Real: (1) the poststructuralist fallacy of logocentricity which results from the power play of a cruel rhetorician like Addie, and (2) the fallacy of absolute freeplay which, as Darl's madness represents, is not an adequate counter to logocentricity insofar as it rests on a repression of the problematical Real.

Oedipal Problematics

Once in this problematics, however, interpretation has just begun. For example, we are still confronted by the ambiguity of Addie's character, which leaves us puzzled by the question of Faulkner's attitude toward her. In part, the answer is trivial. Faulkner is trapped within the masculine fantasy/nightmare of the Oedipal Age, a cultural myth that forces women into the role of replaceable commodities. The violence of Faulkner's chauvinism is familiar to his readers, and particularly to readers of Meta Carpenter's book on her love affair with him. But more interesting, perhaps, are the cultural attitudes which project this myth of ambiguous desire and fear toward women as castrated and castrating. The Freudian myth is dominated by the Ideal of wholeness, of the perfect wife/mother/sister who stands for postponed gratification, forbidden pleasure, and economic exchange. Such an Ideal is necessarily repressed, but the absence of the whole sets in motion that desiring production that characterizes the Oedipal family and the Oedipal society.

This myth is exposed in Lacan's definition of the Symbolic, since the Ideal whole is not a biological but a social, a linguistic fact. It is metaphor: the Romantic icon of unity and fulfillment which, if impossible to achieve, at least keeps us going, trying out one part-object after another, or, in Anse's case, one woman after another, in a futile longing for the Utopian dream. Thus the Oedipal myth which binds Faulkner extends itself, via the metaphorical Ideal, to include the nineteenth-century dream of progress, as well as the poet's mystical faith in the One, and the modern world's love affair with anxiety, overwork, overproduction, and environmental waste. These are, in part, the social and historical conditions within which we should read Faulkner.

Even Lacan is caught in this schema; he marks the accession to Language, entry into the Symbolic Order, by what he describes as a metaphorical eruption, by a crossing of the bar of repression, that socially-placed bar which protects the ego from its unconscious desires. To some extent this argues that the very basis of Language is in metaphor, in the Ideal of wholeness—negatively, because it is forever forbidden, but necessarily, because it is the vital focus of desire, the driving force of society. Again, we sense a lingering Romanticism in Lacan's theory. This is the basis for Derrida's challenge to Lacan in that now famous Poe-reading contest made available to us in *Yale French*

Studies. The prominence of metaphor is what underlies Derrida's accusation that Lacan's theory is logocentric. The metaphoric foundation of the Symbolic Order is a phallic mythology in disguise; the metaphor is a privileged center for language's freeplay, centering that freeplay yet itself repressed in order that freeplay can be set in motion. Lacan's theory, Derrida argues, is phallogocentric, a point well taken, I believe, and one not lost on several feminist readers of Lacan. Derrida's charge, of course, delights the Yale Derrideans; it is occasion for a further decrying of the logocentric fallacy, and for the continued repression of the phallogocentric Real. The extremity of the attack by Derrida may even have deflected Lacan from his original purposes.

I have no desire to defend Lacan on this matter; on the contrary, I want to point out that it is the attempt to repress the Imaginary, the refusal to confront the problematical Real, that results in a heightening of phallogocentrism, in the privileging of metaphor. This is true of Derrida as well as of Lacan. The driving force of the Symbolic Order, as we have seen, is desire for a wholeness that is wholly illusory. This is the discourse of the Other which speaks for and to us in Lacan's system. However, unless we see this force in contact with real people, real social situations, it becomes merely an abstraction. And only then does the Symbolic Order become truly, hopelessly, phallogocentric—become a system of *particular* uses and abuses of language centered about an Ideally abstract, universal, and absent symbol. To repress the problematical Real does not actually free metonymic substitution; rather it evokes the intimacy of synechdoche, the desire for that Idealized part-object that will integrate the whole. To repress the problematical Real castrates the Symbolic Order, leaving a substantial gap in the fabric of language. It also puts rhetorical play into the hands of the phallic power seekers, the exploiters of need, lack, and scarcity who owe allegiance only to an Ideal that they seem to deny, but secretly long for.

It is Addie's phallic pun, however, which makes it difficult to forget the Real. Her graphic repression of the phallic word and image is too deeply personal, experiential, substantial to be abstracted into mere verbal wit. We feel the power of a cultural myth coming to rest on her personal dilemma. In a similar way the graphic image haunts Lacan, especially in his "graphs of desire." These drawings, nothing more than energy flow charts, make sensible the reality his Symbolic Order tends to forget. The charts grow from page to page in his essays only to be repeatedly crossed, cut, castrated by lines that represent particular speech acts. Hence, they insistently re-present the Imaginary; they "image" the experiential realm of real social exchange. They are phallic images; they are castrated and yet remain whole. As such they are sexuality unsexed, neither masculine plenty nor feminine lacking. The presence of the graphic images demystifies the mysterious masculine Ideal by exposing it for what it is: a problematical image of the Real, a myth. Once that mystery dissipates we can stop the obsessive search for the phallogocentric and the excessive Idealization of freeplay which has its phallogocentrism in disguise, conveniently forgotten. Lacan's theory can escape this Idealism through the insistent return of the Imaginary which particularizes rather than mystifies. That is not to say that Lacan is always true to his own principles; he is not, but the irrespressible Real will not allow him to stray too far.

The point is, finally, to return poststructuralism to concrete human circumstances, to the recognition of the Real, historical, even material, conditions of production, including the production of both literary and philosophical texts. Absolute freeplay is an invitation to abuse, as Faulkner's Idealization of the metaphoric wife/mother/sister allows him to harass his more earthly female characters. Such Idealization is typically masculine; the Ideal woman is a logocentric principle of social order, but she is thereby removed from real experience. It is a form of masculine self-indulgence: men are allowed experiences, but women must remain pure. In *As I Lay Dying,* as he must in all his writing, Faulkner represses the Ideal by projecting it outside of the text, and this leaves us with Addie as a corrupted particular case. Again, this is Addie's appeal, her "fascination," but also it is a form of stereotyping. When Addie becomes too real, too much of a presence even in her absence, she is punished by being summarily replaced. What we learn from Faulkner and Lacan in this instance—perhaps learn negatively—is that we must persistently particularize as we work out of Idealizing myths. It is a difficult task, and I suspect we cannot fully accomplish such a goal, one of a truer freedom than that of poststructuralist freeplay, until we pass beyond the Oedipal Age.

LITERATURE AS ASSERTIONS

Gerald Graff

Nobody denies that literary works contain propositions about various real-life subjects. But literary theorists for some time have disagreed about whether these propositions are to be viewed as genuine *statements*. A distinguished line of theorists—going back to Kant—argues that literature (and more generally, art) invests its propositions with a kind of immunity, that propositions stated or implied in literary works, even those which appear to make general claims about human experience, are not meant to be taken as serious assertions. Literary propositions do not make the kind of truth-claims, it is said, for which they might be liable if they occurred in non-literary forms of discourse. According to this view, the statements in literary works are pretended or fictive statements, and therefore the question of their truth or adequacy to life should not arise. One distinguished theorist, for example, Richard Ohmann, says that "there is a perfectly clean cognitive break between literature—poems, plays, novels, jokes, fairy tales, fantasies, etc.—and discourses that are not literature. Literary works are discourses with the usual illocutionary rules suspended. If you like, they are acts without consequences of the usual sort, sayings liberated from the usual burdens of social bond and responsibility."[1] A second theorist, Barbara Herrnstein Smith, concedes that a poem (or other literary work) *can* often be used to make a genuine statement, as for instance when one selects a greeting card because the sentiments expressed by its verses happen really to convey what one wishes to say. But Smith goes on to argue that "insofar as they are offered and recognized as statements in a poem," that is, insofar as they are treated *as literature*, such sentiments must be seen as fictive or pretended rather

1. Richard Ohmann, "Speech, Literature, and the Space Between," *New Literary History*, IV, no. 1 (Autumn 1972), p. 53.

than real assertions.[2] In a third instance, Martin Steinmann and Robert Brown argue that "if we know the rules constituting" fictional discourse, we recognize that an utterance in a literary work "is not a commitment but a pretense of one."[3]

On the other hand, a number of recent theorists (myself among them) dissent from this anti-assertionist view, as it may be called.[4] John Searle maintains that "serious illocutionary intentions" can "be conveyed by the pretended illocutions of literary fictions." Conceding that many of the propositions in literary works are pretended illocutionary acts, Searle holds that such pretended acts may themselves be used to make serious statements: "serious (i.e., non-fictional) speech acts can be conveyed by fictional texts, even though the conveyed speech act is not represented in the text. Almost any important work of fiction conveys a 'message' or 'messages' which are conveyed *by* the text but are not *in* the text."[5] On the other hand, such non-fictional messages

2. Barbara Herrnstein Smith, "Poetry as Fiction," *New Literary History*, II, no. 2 (Winter 1971), p. 271.

3. Robert L. Brown, Jr. and Martin Steinmann, Jr., "Native Readers of Fiction: A Speech-Act and Genre-Rule Approach to Defining Literature," *What Is Literature?* Paul Hernadi, ed. (Bloomington: Indiana University Press, 1978), p. 149. Brown and Steinmann add: "Briefly, to take a discourse as fictional is, as other writers have observed, to take it as an utterance act that pretends to be, but is not, a propositional act and an illocutionary act as well. In performing an utterance act, the speaker or writer pretends to refer to things, to predicate properties or relations of them, and to perform an illocutionary act, but he does not really do so. And *pretend* is the key word" (p. 148).

4. *In Poetic Statement and Critical Dogma* (Evanston: Northwestern University Press, 1970), I used the term "antipropositional" to describe this kind of theory. But "anti-assertionist" is technically more precise. Some theorists, however, are fairly described as antipropositional as well as anti-assertionist. See below, pp. 152 ff.

5. John R. Searle, "The Logical Status of Fictional Discourse," *New Literary History*, VI, no. 2 (Winter 1975), p. 332. For Searle, the "essential rule" is that "the maker of an assertion commits himself to the truth of the expressed proposition" (p. 322). In arguing that "serious speech acts" are conveyed by literature, Searle does not restrict the range of these acts to assertions alone but includes others such as warnings, pleadings, scoldings, and so forth. Presumably, he would agree with J. L. Austin's point that though such speech acts do not themselves constitute assertions ("constatives" in Austin's vocabulary), they nevertheless *imply* or *presuppose* assertions. (See Austin, *How to Do Things with Words*, ed. J. O. Urmson [New York: Oxford University Press, 1965], p. 100.) Ohmann, Smith, and others who use speech act theory in literary criticism have neglected the implications of this point: from the fact that an utterance *does* something, we should not infer that it does not also *say* something.

sometimes do appear *in* the text, as in the case of the opening sentence of *Anna Karenina*, which seriously asserts that "All happy families resemble one another, but each unhappy family is unhappy in its own way."[6] E. D. Hirsch makes the point even more succinctly: "Fiction has value beyond the pleasure it gives only because it presents something that is not fiction."[7]

The anti-assertionists argue that because literature is a species of fictional discourse, any commitments that may appear to be made in it are necessarily pretended rather than serious. They concede that utterances in literary works may be *used* to make serious commitments, but only by taking them out of the work and thus divorcing them from their literary use. When we read a text as literature we necessarily treat its propositions as pretended, fictive, hypothetical, and thus without liability for claims of truth. The assertionists, in countering this view, do not deny that literature often makes use of fictive discourse, but they go on to hold that one important use of such discourse is to assert "messages" which ask to be taken seriously as statements about real states of affairs. The point at issue, then, is how far the principle of fictionality is to be taken. Consider the following passage from Céline's *Journey to the End of the Night*: "It's no good the rest of us striving: we slip, stumble, over-balance into the alcohol which preserves both the living and the dead, we get nowhere. It's been proved."[8] The anti-assertionist presumably would argue that the sentiments expressed here have the same fictive status as do propositions in Céline's novel about characters, settings, and actions. He might point out that these sentiments are spoken by a character—the first-person narrator of the novel—but he would hold that even were they spoken by an authorial narrator they would still have the status of fictive statements. Even if it could be shown that Céline endorsed the view of life expressed by these statements, the fact that they appear in a work of literature obliges us to suspend their normal illocutionary force. For the assertionist, by contrast, there is nothing in the nature of literature that

6. Searle, "The Logical Status of Fictional Discourse," p. 332.

7. E. D. Hirsch, *The Aims of Interpretation* (Chicago: University of Chicago Press, 1976), p. 157.

8. Louis-Ferdinand Céline, *Journey to the End of the Night*, trans. John H. P. Marks (New York: New Directions, 1960), p. 330.

obliges us to treat Céline's propositions as non-assertions. Of course if it could be shown that other elements of the novel call into question the adequacy of these propositions—as might be the case if scenes could be adduced which seem to suggest that there *is* some point, after all, in "the rest of us striving"—then the assertionist could concede that the original propositions should not be accepted at face value. But he would argue that in such a case, the message of the work would simply be more complex: it would be a message implied *by* the text, arising dialectically out of a clash of different messages, and would not appear *in* the text. Insofar as the text is a "serious" work of literature (an important stipulation, to which we will return), such messages ask to be received as genuine statements. The reader, that is, is asked to *believe* in their truth, or at least to *take them seriously* as statements which might be true. Their adequacy or applicability to real life, whether as historical descriptions, moral judgments, or philosophical generalizations, is not a question to be waived merely because they appear in a work of literature.

The question arises whether it might be possible to reconcile these opposing theories. One could argue that they are actually concerned with different aspects of literature and therefore are not really in disagreement. The anti-assertional view, one could hold, is concerned primarily with what we have come to call the "intrinsic" aspect of a literary work, its internal coherence as a self-contained universe of discourse which can be enjoyed or studied without posing the question of its adequacy as a representation of something external—just as sentences can be looked at in terms of their grammatical and syntactical well-formedness without respect to whether they happen to be true or false. The assertional view, it may be said, is concerned with the "extrinsic" question of how the literary work relates to the worlds of morality, society, and history. Both kinds of critical attention are justifiable and thus complementary; each has its eye on a different object, so that any quarrel thought to exist between the two is a pseudo-quarrel.

Much though there is to be said for this kind of attempted accommodation, it works only up to a point. For finally these two views are not concerned with different aspects of literature. They are concerned with the single question of how readers are supposed to take those statements, or ostensible statements, which both parties concede are present at some level in literary works, and they offer conflicting and incompatible answers to this question. Confronted by the same literary work, these two views propose entirely different models of proper response. The one maintains that the beliefs and values reflected by the work must be taken as pretended commitments, the other that these beliefs and values (assuming agreement by the two sides on what they are) make genuine truth claims and thus demand to be taken seriously by the reader. The problem is not merely hypothetical: we read Milton, Lawrence, or Céline, and wonder how seriously we must take the author's view of life in order to appreciate his work. Are we to suspend this sort of interest as a non-esthetic irrelevance, or is such suspension merely patronizing? We encounter students who think they detect racism or sexism in literary works; do we accept such criticisms as relevant to literature or not? The question need not of course be settled in an either-or way, either by flatly rejecting or accepting the work on ideological grounds alone. The question is not whether the statements made by the work are the *only* things that matter but whether they are at least *among* the things that matter. If one view holds they are and the other denies it, both views can't be right.

To this last point it may be objected that no one way of responding to a work of literature, after all, is "right." Yet we do normally expect responses to literary works by qualified readers to share some degree of common ground. We assume there are minimal conditions which everybody's experience of a given work will fulfill, and when these are not fulfilled we are reluctant to concede that the work has successfully been "read" at all. If a student came away from *Moby-Dick* convinced that Starbuck is the author's norm because he gives Ahab sound commercial advice, one would be obliged to tell him that he had—as we say—missed the point of the book. We assume that in this respect literary works are like jokes, having a "point" (or points) that can be "got" or "missed" to a greater or lesser degree. We are not dissuaded from this assumption by knowing that the point or points of a literary work are seldom easy to summarize in so many words (but neither, for that matter, is the point of a good many jokes) and that what the point actually is may be highly debatable. The proponents of the opposing views I have been summarizing could easily agree that the student just mentioned above had missed the point of *Moby-Dick,* and there is no reason why they might not also agree on what that point is, or how it could be more successfully formulated. Where they would begin to disagree would be over the question of what sort of thing that "point" is, how it is to be taken. And this brings us back to the difficulty with which we started.

The difficulty is, how do we *know* how the point of a literary work is to be taken? By what process does one determine that the usual illocutionary rules are suspended, or not suspended, when it comes to dealing with literature? Literary theory is more abundant in strongly worded pronouncements[9] deciding the matter one way or the other than in examinations of the grounds on which any pronouncements can be based. Common sense may seem to dictate that we need only *look* at specific literary works, confident that pure induction will yield the answers we want about how these works mean. But this procedure is not much help, since the problem to be solved is precisely what it is we mean by "looking" in this context, which is to say, how are literary works to be looked at? Since no anti-assertionist theorist denies that propositions having the ostensible *form* of assertions do often appear in literary works, simply to adduce the presence of a number of such propositions in specific works does nothing to refute the theoretical claim that literature as such makes no assertions. One could adduce any number of seemingly asserted propositions from literary works, but the anti-assertionist will be unperturbed by this "evidence," which for him begs the question. For he is not denying that ostensibly asserted propositions occur in literary works, but rather that these propositions are genuinely asserted.

Adopting another strategy (one I myself have used frequently), one could point out that the anti-assertionist position often derives from an extraliterary ethical or political belief about the nature of assertion. That is, his resistance to permitting literary works to be read as making assertions comes not from any notion that it is not *possible* for such works to be read that way—he concedes, in fact, that many people do read them this way; it comes rather from the conviction that literary works *ought* not be read as making assertions, that if they are read that way we give encouragement to a philistine or reactionary view of

9. For example, in *Poetic Statement and Critical Dogma,* I find myself claiming that "the poet, regardless of what type of poet he is, . . . cannot help saying something about the human situation in general, cannot avoid incurring the risks of assertion" (p. 25). Perhaps so, but how did I *know* that? On what grounds could such a claim be defended? I would no longer hold that a poet "cannot avoid" making assertions, though I would question the likely importance and value of a poem that avoided making them.

culture. In other words, what is often at issue for the anti-assertionist is the fear that literature will be degraded to the purely utilitarian level to which a practical and commercial society reduces all objects. (It is no accident that anti-assertionism arose historically at the moment when the practical-commercial society triumphed.) By defining literature as immune to assertions, anti-assertionist theory both protects literature from instrumentalism and even puts it forth as an antidote to instrumentalism, the latter strategy being one of the most common ways in which anti-assertionist theory recovers and redefines a moral and political purpose for literature. To the degree to which anti-assertionist theory is animated by some such ethical or political logic as I have just described, we can see that it has shifted the focus of the debate from the nature of literature as such to the way the nature of literature will have to be conceived if certain bad cultural consequences are to be avoided. This move is vulnerable to criticism, then, on the ground that (1) it has not been clearly demonstrated that attributing assertions to literature really does necessarily promote the kind of bad instrumentalism that worries the anti-assertionist; and (2) even if it could be shown that attributing assertions to literature does necessarily promote bad instrumentalism, that would not be a compelling reason for denying that literary works make assertions. The fact that a practice may have bad consequences is not a reason for denying that the practice occurs, or supposing that we can prevent it.

To attack the arbitrariness, or wrongness, or irrelevance of the ethical or political assumptions that often underly the anti-assertionist theory does not, however, take us very far toward answering the original question: how do we know how propositional elements in literary works are to be taken? A promising beginning, I think, is afforded by approaches such as structuralism, speech act theory, and "institutional" theory of art, approaches which consider the problem to be one of *convention*. Communication between writers and readers is seen by these approaches to depend on tacit contracts, the understanding of which is entailed in the acquisition of linguistic and literary competence. Such a view helps to demystify questions about literary meaning by viewing meaning not as a mysterious essence but as a function of human institutional behavior, behavior theoretically open to empirical investigation. The anti-assertionist arguments I quoted above are in each case grounded in an appeal to convention:[10] they hold that literary convention calls for the suspension of the usual illocutionary rules governing assertions. The assertionist counterargument appeals equally to convention but conceives it differently. How can one decide which view presents the convention accurately—which is not the same as asking which proposed convention is morally or culturally preferable?

It may be useful to look at non-literary occasions in which the usual illocutionary rules governing assertions *are* suspended and enquire how it is we are able to tell the suspension is in force. Speech act theory suggests that we determine whether an illocutionary act counts as seriously performed or not by noting whether certain conventionally established "felicity conditions" have been fulfilled. A person cannot be said to have performed the illocutionary act of promising if it is well known that he has no power to carry out his promise. The sentence "I now pronounce you man and wife" sounds like an act of marrying somebody, but it counts as such only if spoken under special circumstances by an accredited official. In other words, the semantic properties of an utterance are *in themselves* not sufficient to tell the hearer or reader whether the utterance has been used to perform an illocutionary act. We need to know what an utterance is being used to do in a particular situation in order to understand in any adequate way what it means.

Suppose, for example, I am on different occasions called an insulting name, once by a personal enemy, once by a close friend. In the first instance, I have reason to suspect the insult is seriously meant, that an illocutionary act of "insulting" has taken place. In the second instance, I take the remark as a pretended insult which actually "performs" a gesture of affection. Since both the words and even the intonation in the two cases may be identical, the difference in illocutionary force can only be inferred from the situation. Knowledge of analogous situations in which epithets have functioned either as insults or as badinage provides a set of precedents for guessing what is intended in such cases. But it is easy to imagine a third situation (being called the name by somebody one does not know, or by a friend with a reputation for irascibility, or a friend one has recently offended) in which it would be

10. Smith, for example, writes that "when we read the text of a poem or hear it read aloud, our response to it as a linguistic structure is governed by quite special conventions, and it is the understanding that these conventions are operating that distinguishes the poem as a verbal artwork from natural discourse" ("Poetry as Fiction," p. 267).

difficult to decide for sure whether the insult were intended seriously or not.[11] The relevant point here is that utterances do not acquire functionally determinate meanings until they are used to *do* something in specific situations; being seriously meant or pretended are instances of such use. Thus propositions do not become *assertions* until used by somebody, under appropriate conditions, for the purpose of asserting that such-and-such is the case.

To say that literature is a discourse with the usual illocutionary rules suspended, then, is to imply that utterances in literature are rather like mock-insulting epithets spoken by a friend. We are not to take them as doing the work, bearing the freight of serious assertion, that they could and do perform under real life circumstances. Presumably, the propositions in literature have other uses besides assertion—to exhibit turns of consciousness, to move the emotions, to try out ways of viewing the world to which neither writer nor reader need be absolutely committed. Just as my understanding of the conventions of friendly badinage prevented me from taking my friend's epithet as the performance of a serious insult, so (it is implicitly claimed) a comparable convention prevents competent readers of literature from taking literary propositions as genuinely asserted. This, at any rate, I take to be the implicit logic of theories which argue that literary propositions are protected from the responsibility of real assertions. But there are problems with this view.

It is true that we have conventions for distinguishing between pretended and seriously committed illocutionary acts. But in everyday situations, we do not know *in advance* which convention may be actualized. That is, in these situations, we have to have *reasons* for deciding whether a given act is probably pretended or serious: So-and-so

11. The utterer of the epithet might *himself* be unsure whether or to what degree he intends it as a serious insult, or he might half-intend it as such while half-intending it as a mere gesture. Theorists of intention have not, so far as I know, devoted much attention to the problems posed by blurred or ambivalent kinds of intentions—kinds which are increasingly important in a fluid social world where the proprieties are not clearly defined. Jacques Derrida exploits this difficulty in his critique of Searle's implicitly intentionalist view of meaning (see his essay, "Limited Inc abc. . . ," trans. Samuel Weber, *Glyph*, 2 [1977], pp. 215-16). But Derrida is content to revel in the presumed duplicity and indeterminacy of all intentions rather than make the careful distinctions that seem to me to be needed.

is a habitual kidder and sometimes goes too far; or, So-and-so dislikes Such-and-such's habit of insulting people and thus must want me to see he is parodying it. Now to say that in literature the usual illocutionary rules are suspended is to say that in literature we do not need such reasons for inferring pretense or seriousness, since literary convention decrees that we have no choice. Again, it is important to recall that this view aims to cover not merely narrative propositions about, say, settings or characters' actions, but also any larger general claims ("messages") which may be stated or implied as exemplified by the narrative. There is according to anti-assertionist theory no breaking out of the limited liability imposed by the convention that deems literature to be fiction; presumably (to follow out the apparent logic of this view), even if a writer sets out deliberately to violate this convention by actually *saying* something in a literary work, he cannot succeed. Either he succeeds in creating a work of literature, in which case his work (as literature) can make no statement, or he succeeds in making a statement, in which case his work is not literature.

This strong view might be supported if it could be shown that competent readers of literature *do* operate according to the convention put forward. But one of the better recent treatments of literary convention, Jonathan Culler's in *Structuralist Poetics*, suggests they do not. Culler's testimony is all the more pertinent, since he himself seems to endorse what he takes to be the structuralist view "that literature is something other than a statement about the world,"[12] and he thinks of his account of literary convention as confirming this view. That it may not actually confirm it, however, is suggested by Culler's discussion of the convention or "rule of significance," which dictates that to read a work as literature is to read it "as expressing a significant attitude to some problem concerning man and/or his relation to the universe."[13] "Reading a poem," Culler says (and his observation would seem to hold for other genres as well) "is a process of finding ways to grant it significance and importance, and in that process we call upon a variety of operations which have come to form part of the institution of

12. Jonathan Culler, *Structuralist Poetics: Structuralism, Linguistics, and the Study of Literature* (Ithaca: Cornell University Press, 1975), p. 130. For the argument of this section, as for much else in this paper, I am indebted to my colleague Martha Woodmansee. See her forthcoming critique of literary-critical uses of speech act theory in *Centrum*.

13. *Ibid.*, p. 115.

poetry."[14] If reading a text as literature is, among other things, a process of finding ways to grant it "significance and importance," "a significant attitude to some problem concerning man and/or his relation to the universe," does this not call into question the view that to read literature as literature we have to refrain from attributing any statements to it? What after all is a "significant attitude" to problems of man and his relation to the universe if not at the very least a statement that there are such problems? That "significance" for Culler himself can equal some kind of statement is seen, for example, in his observation that "if all else failed, we could read a sequence of words with no apparent order as signifying absurdity or chaos and then, by giving it an allegorical relation to the world, take it as a statement about the incoherence and absurdity of our own languages."[15] What Culler means, however, is that such statements in literature function merely as organizing principles ("myths"), and not as theories about the world, as they would be if uttered as part of a "communicative project."[16] Why, though, would such an organizing principle need to be "significant and important" unless readers were supposed to take it seriously as a statement about the world? If it were merely a matter of furnishing an arbitrary conceptual scaffolding on which to build the work, why would not trivial propositions ("Human beings drink water") do the job? As I point out elsewhere,[17] Culler despite himself grants serious theoretical status to a literary view of life when dealing with Flaubert's work.

In an intriguing application of the convention of significance, Culler takes up the problems posed by so-called "found poetry." It seems that almost any verbal expression can be made to count as poetry if presented in such a manner as to invite readers to apply specifically poetic

14. *Ibid.*, p. 175.

15. *Ibid.*, p. 138. See also his comment that "if a poem seems utterly banal it is possible to take banality of statement as a statement about banality and hence to derive a suggestion that poetry can go no further than language. . ." (p. 177). Culler is here talking about the convention "that poems are significant if they can be read as reflections on or explorations of the problems of poetry itself." For a poem to say, in effect, "This poem is about its own language," or "This poem cannot be about anything outside language" is to make a statement.

16. *Ibid.*, p. 146.

17. *Literature Against Itself: Literary Ideas in Modern Society* (Chicago: University of Chicago Press, 1979), pp. 159ff.

conventions to it.[18] Thus the most banal news item presented in the right format (in a book of verse, or arranged typographically to resemble verse) will be recognized as a poem, though not necessarily a good or great poem. Such a news item will acquire significances in the transformation it had not seemed to possess before, by virtue of the convention of significance. The more banal the item, in fact, the more readily will it lend itself to being read in terms of one kind of significance, appearing as an allegory of the banality of modern life. To those familiar with modernist art, nothing is easier than converting seeming nonsense into statements about the modern world.

What is especially worth noting here is that the process of converting the news item into literature in this case involves us in *adding* the element of statement, not in subtracting it. Literary theorists have been so intent on distinguishing literary from nonliterary discourse by proving that it possesses a special freedom from assertion that they have hardly considered the possibility that the reverse is true: that literature differentiates itself from other modes not by refraining from assertion but by making a stronger, more universalizable kind of assertion, that it is *hyper*-assertive rather than *non*-assertive. We do not attribute "significance" in Culler's sense to "natural" utterances. When we overhear the neighboring couple quarreling on the backstairs, for example, we "read" their remarks very differently from the way we would if we encountered their dialogue in a serious novel, where we would look for thematic links between this episode and the rest of the novel and implications relevant to the world of experience.[19] We might, of course, regard the real-life quarrel as "significant" in a *symptomatic* way of many things, e.g., the imminent likelihood of a divorce, the deterioration of the nuclear family, the need for better apartment insulation, and so forth. But this kind of interpreting differs from the kind we do in construing literary significance, for our object in the latter case is the discovery of an author's rhetorical purpose. Real-life conversations differ from novelistic ones in that they are not arranged by any author for any rhetorical purpose; they are free to be random and pointless in a way novelistic conversations are not. Literary conversations are expected to illustrate some point, and when a work comes along in which they fail to do so (e.g., *Tristram Shandy* or Ionesco's *The Bald Soprano*),

18. Culler, *Structuralist Poetics*, pp. 161-62.

19. I am indebted for this illustration to an unpublished paper by Marilyn Cooper of the University of Minnesota.

we begin to look for the point of their not illustrating a point. Real-life talk does not convey a message the way literary talk does, though individual speeches convey messages. The messages conveyed by real-life speeches do not exemplify any larger illustrative message, as do the speeches in a literary work. Thus to say that a real-life quarrel exemplifies the breakdown of human communication is different from interpreting a quarrel in a literary work in this fashion. Only in the second instance could one claim to describe a meaning communicated by another person.

The potential of a text to be read thematically (as exemplifying an intended general point or message) may finally, then, have more to do with determining whether we read it as a literary work than the presence in it of fictionality. Such a view would explain why non-fictional works such as *The Gulag Archipelago* are accorded literary status in a way that fully fictional works like the James Bond novels are not. It would also explain why it is often difficult to determine whether or not certain works of history and sociology (Gibbon's *Decline and Fall of the Roman Empire*; Oscar Lewis' *The Children of Sanchez*) should be classed as literature. Many works of literature contain no fiction whatsoever, and much fictional narrative is not literature, as has been pointed out by Mary Louise Pratt, who draws on William Labov's studies of "natural narrative," in *Toward a Speech Act Theory of Literary Discourse*. On the other hand, it is also true that certain literary genres—didactic lyrics, most notably—cannot be said to invite a thematic reading, since their messages are directly asserted and not exemplified by any action.[20] Thus one cannot go so far as to argue

20. Some (not all) anti-assertionists argue that even didactic works like Pope's *Essay on Man* and *Essay on Criticism* must be read as spoken not by the poet but by a *persona* distinct from him. This view is probably less widespread today than it was in the heyday of the New Criticism, but it still resurfaces from time to time, especially in the classroom. The problem with this view is that it rests on nothing but an *a priori* assertion about the nature of poetry or literature. If, as in the case of Pope, there appears to be no evident discrepancy between the views and attitudes advanced directly by the speaker of the poem and the author, it is difficult to see what is gained by insisting that these views and attitudes be ascribed to the speaker, not the poet. There are many poems, of course, in which there does appear to be such a discrepancy, and in these cases the distinction between poet and *persona* is necessary. But erected into a general rule alleged to cover *all* poetry, the doctrine that it is always a *persona* who speaks, never the poet, is transparently a last-ditch strategy designed to avoid having to treat poetry as a form of statement.

that thematic exemplification (through application of the convention of significance) is *the* defining principle of literature. Didactic lyrics differentiate themselves from non-literary discourse by other means, by the use of verse, for example, or certain rhetorical figures. But of course these works too are not immune from assertions.

How is a text's "potential to be read thematically" to be assessed, especially if virtually any text, when presented in a format conventionally recognized as literary (e.g. in verse), seems to have this potential? Consider once more the case of the news item. A trained reader guesses that such an item set up typographically as verse is meant to be read as literature, hence as thematically significant, since his training enables him to see that kind of typographical arrangement as a clue to the presence of that kind of authorial purpose. It does not follow that any text can be turned into literature by the mere fact that somebody looks at it that way, however. Suppose you were to publish a complicated thematic interpretation of, say, a daily gossip column. Most readers would assume you intended a parody of pretentious or over-ingenious literary analysis. Successful critical parodies, which are based on such works as *Winnie-the-Pooh,* "Thirty Days Hath September," and *The Chicago Telephone Directory,*[21] exploit the fact that the convention of significance cannot be applied to all texts. Parodists, that is, take for granted their readers' secure confidence that nobody could be serious in ascribing to such texts any profound thematic purposes, though each of these texts has plenty of presuppositions.

On the other hand, distinctions between "serious" and other genres are far from fixed or clear-cut. Contemporary experimental writers have persistently reminded us of that fact by making a systematic project of conquering the latent resistance of certain kinds of linguistic raw material (e.g., slang, obscurity, dialect, jargon, scientific and technical argot, and so forth) to be used for literary purposes. Nobody today is surprised when poets violate what was once considered proper "poetic diction" by incorporating prosaic styles into poetry. In another kind of genre-shift, critics have recently begun taking detective fiction more

21. My references are, successively, to Fredrick Crews, *The Pooh-Perplex* (New York: E. P. Dutton & Co., 1963); Theodore Spenser, "How to Criticize a Poem (In the Manner of Certain Contemporary Critics)," *Inquiry & Expression: A College Reader,* ed. Harold C. Martin and Richard Ohmann (New York: Holt, Rinehart & Winston, 1961), pp. 489-92; W. B. Scott, "The Problem of Tragedy," *Chicago Letter and Other Parodies* (Ann Arbor: Ardis Publishers, 1978), pp. 13-16.

seriously as literature, often by reading it as a form of epistemological inquiry. It is possible to imagine an analysis of the James Bond novels as deep statements about the amorality of modern life that would not be taken as a parody, though it might not convince anybody either. Whatever the case, such genre-reclassifications reinforce my point: in order for a text to make the crossover from the "pure entertainment" category to that of "serious literature," it is necessary that readers begin to exploit whatever potential these texts may have to be thematized as significant statements.

I have mentioned that all texts (or all events, for that matter) have a kind of *symptomatic* potential, as it may be called, to be seen as significant, but that this potential has nothing to do with our reading them as literature, since what we are thematizing in a literary work is something which has already been thematized by the purposive decision of the author. But cases arise frequently in which it is difficult or impossible to tell whether a text's significance is symptomatic or purposive, which is to say, whether the deep thematic meanings we apprehend in the text are part of its rhetorical purpose or not. Some critics of intentionalism have argued that it is irrelevant whether the meanings we apprehend are intended by the author or not, but this view does not seem to me to square with the actual behavior of readers, who in fact worry a good deal about whether or not they are connecting with the author's purposes. If we were to learn that an apparent hieroglyphic found on a rock had actually been created by natural erosion, we would stop treating it as a hieroglyphic.[22] It would no longer be seen as a text or as readable at all. Though "extrinsic" information drawn from biography, social history, and interviews with the author is never conclusive evidence for an interpretation, we are unsettled when such information contradicts or fails to confirm our hunches.

Texts which harbor any large degree of unconscious meaning pose the most acute problems in this respect, both of classification and evaluation. Are Poe's tales, for example, profound explorations of the depths of the psyche or are they lightweight thrillers which happen to be rich hunting-ground for psychoanalysts? There is room for disagreement, but one's view of Poe's status may turn on the degree to which the

22. Michael Hancher makes this point in "Sermons in Stones," *Centrum,* II, no. 1 (Spring 1974), pp. 79-86.

depth-meanings attributed to his work are intended, if unconsciously.[23] That it may not ever be possible to say whether they are shows that it is not only difficult to pin down the meaning of a literary work–a fact well enough known–but that it may be difficult even to determine the relevance of looking for meaning. We cannot always be sure that a particular text invites the kind of thematization called for by the convention of significance. But the fact that we do not always know whether the convention applies to a text does not make it any less authoritative.

To see what these generalizations may mean in practice, let us try to apply them to Joyce's *Ulysses*. Richard Ellmann takes the central theme of *Ulysses* to be that "casual kindness overcomes unconscionable power. Stephen's charge against Mulligan is that Mulligan is brutal and cruel; Molly's complaint against Boylan is again on the score of brutality, of animal sensuality without feeling. Bloom is allowed to formulate the theme of the book, though in comic circumstances, when he defends love to the Cyclops, and defines it meekly but deftly as 'the opposite of hatred.' It is opposite also to chauvinism and force."[24] Note that Ellmann's formulation–which is not unlike what could be found in countless critical essays–commits Joyce to a number of beliefs and values. If one argued that all commitments in a literary work are by convention only pretended, these beliefs and values would have to be pretended commitments. But this argument, as I hope is by now clear, is arbitrary. There is no evidence that readers actually observe such a convention; Ellmann, who surely qualifies as a competent reader, does not observe it. He assumes that Joyce is expressing a certain view of the world and that this view matters both to Joyce and to his reader.

How far must the reader, then, commit himself to the commitments of the author? Or, to put it another way, to what degree will the reader's inability to accept the commitments of the author affect his judgment of the work? Such a question cannot be answered with a simple formula, since readers are capable of imaginative appreciation of widely divergent, perhaps even mutually contradictory, views of the world. But this capacity operates within certain limits. Few readers would not find their response of *Ulysses* tempered or at least altered if

23. See above, n. 11.

24. Richard Ellmann, *James Joyce* (New York: Oxford University Press, 1959), p. 390.

Joyce had made it his point to show unconscionable power, brutality, and cruelty *justly* triumphing over love and kindness. The reader of *Ulysses* is asked to believe in a vast number of propositions about the real world in order to read the book sympathetically, beliefs not only about morality but about history and psychology as well. Many of these beliefs are so universally taken for granted that doing without them is practically inconceivable, and therefore it is difficult to recognize that in accepting them we are trafficking in "beliefs" at all. Yet to imagine a situation in which we learned these beliefs were false is to discover how important it is to assume them. Suppose that we were somehow to learn that no such place as Dublin really ever existed, or that the type of society Joyce depicts there—which includes such things as modern transportation and communication systems, modern political and economic organizations, and a diverse group of social and national types—never existed in anything like the fashion in which Joyce presents them. Suppose too that we were to learn that human beings have never acted according to the patterns of thought and motive Joyce presents, that is to say, out of lust, greed, pride, curiosity, and so forth. Though Joyce, like any novelist, takes liberties with historical, social, and psychological truth, he does not assume that the reader's sense of this truth can be suspended.

Many of the beliefs we need to entertain in order to read *Ulysses* are *presupposed* rather than asserted explicitly. They "go without saying," so to speak, as do perhaps most of the beliefs to which authors and readers commit themselves. The specific content of what can be left to go without saying, what can be taken for granted as already understood and accepted by readers and thus need not be asserted explicitly, varies from period to period and culture to culture. Thus the degree to which literary artists may need to make their commitments explicit varies with the period and the culture, and the conventions of expression in different periods and cultures will be affected by this variation in the degree to which explicit foregrounding of assumptions is necessary. These conventions will also be affected by the prevailing attitudes in a culture toward explicit or implicit communication. In the modern period, an interesting contradiction has arisen, for while on the one hand the diminished supply of the cultural givens that create a consensus between readers and writers forces writers to become more "ideological" and aggressively schematic, on the other hand a strongly suspicious attitude toward aggressively ideological, schematic expression encourages writers to conceal or mute their commitments. I have argued elsewhere that contrary to a popular view, modern literature tends to be more rather than less didactic than earlier literature, in part because the beliefs which earlier writers could assume they could presuppose as cultural givens in their readers now have to be made explicit. But at the same time, these beliefs cannot be made too explicit lest the work be found guilty of serving as instrumental discourse. One response to this dilemma is to make one's meanings so complex that they cannot easily be formulated in terms of any simple message.

The very complexity of the thematic meaning of a work like *Ulysses* inspires scepticism about the possibility and the propriety of thematic readings. What this scepticism ignores is that when thematic assertions become complex, ambiguous, contradictory, plural, and even indeterminate, they do not cease to be assertions. One may argue—with some justice—that *Ulysses* dramatizes the un-thematizable irrationality of experience. But to dramatize the un-thematizable irrationality of experience is still to thematize that experience in terms of assertions. I am aware that no self-respecting New Critic—to say nothing of a post-structuralist—will allow me to get away with this last claim. "No," it will be objected, "here is where any assertional view of literature must break down: for 'dramatizing' experience, which is what literature specializes in doing, is not at all the same as making statements 'about' experience. The enormous difference between abstractly generalizing about experience and *presenting* it is what your view ignores." With this objection, however, the anti-assertionist strategy has changed its ground. Up to now, its key argument has been that literary propositions are pretended assertions, utterances in which the usual illocutionary rules are suspended. This argument implicitly conceded that the unit-meanings, as we may term them, of a literary work are propositions. The objection I have just mentioned goes further, arguing that it is incorrect to talk about literary meanings as an affair of propositions at all.

Again, a good way to counter this objection is to look at the way actual readers behave, and in this case we can consult relevant studies of the reading process. It is true that not much information about specifically literary reading exists, the bulk of the data being about the dynamics of reading in general. Though one may seem to be begging the question to apply this information to literary experience, it is worth while examining it to see where it may lead. Fortunately for my purpose, E. D. Hirsch, in *The Philosophy of Composition,* has summarized much of the available research on the reading process. According to Hirsch's abstract of this research, the reader of a text must project a sense of the whole even as he experiences the text part by part. One perceives the work "all at once" at the same time as one encounters it as a linear sequence. "In order to perceive something all at once," Hirsch observes, "though it passes through our attention system bit by bit, we need to have a consolidating function that supplements our attention-monitor. We need a perceptual depository able to store perceived but not yet organized items and to keep them available on demand."[25] Psycholinguists call this depository "long-term" (as opposed to short-term) memory. Long-term memory receives what has already faded from the reader's immediate conscious awareness and must be fished up, in William James's figure (as quoted by Hirsch) "from a reservoir in which, with countless other objects, it lay buried and lost from view."[26] Its counterpart, short-term memory, stores impressions of which we are still immediately aware. For example, my reference to William James' fishing metaphor will still at this moment be present to my reader's immediate awareness (short-term memory), since he encountered it in the previous sentence. But a page or two hence, it will have faded into his long-term memory of my essay, where it will repose (one hopes) available to be recalled if I should later on need to refer back to it (as it happens, I will not). There is a well known short story by Jorge Luis Borges entitled "Funes the Memorious," whose protagonist has so capacious a short-term memory that he is virtually incapable of abstract thought. We would all be so incapacitated if our long-term memory did not relieve us of the burden of the immediate experience flowing in on us and permit us to stop thinking of it.

What is significant for my purposes here is the finding that the nature of what is processed by the reader of a text is modified as it passes from short-term to long-term memory. In order to understand a discourse, it seems we must be able to forget a good deal of it, to forget selectively. What we recollect of what we have read is not particular details so much as that schematic sense of the whole we projected in

25. E. D. Hirsch, *The Philosophy of Composition* (Chicago: University of Chicago Press, 1977), p. 110.

26. *Ibid.*

order to make sense of the details. Experiments repeatedly prove that readers recall meanings much more successfully than they recall the specific lexical and syntactic forms in which the meanings were expressed, which is to say that our recollection of abstract content exceeds our recollection of the formal means by which that content is conveyed. Hirsch relates the 1894 findings of Binet and Henri, who reported that "when children were asked to recall short, eleven word passages, they *could* remember the syntactic and lexical form of the utterances; but, when asked to read longer passages of sixty to eighty-six words, they remembered the meaning accurately but not the form."[27] In the light of later confirmations of these results, it may be reasonable to conclude that "after a linguistic clause has been processed [i.e., after it has passed from short-term to long-term memory], it is stored in a nonlinguistic, nonsequential form," which is to say, as a conceptual schema.[28] According to Johnson-Laird, "all forms of syntactic structure are normally lost to memory within a few seconds. . . . No one knows how meaning is represented within memory, but there is no evidence to show that any form of syntactic structure is directly involved."[29]

If I understand these findings correctly, they challenge some of the cherished assumptions of literary theorists and teachers. If it is true that we tend to detach meanings from syntax when we store them in our memory, then the sacred doctrine that form and content are inseparable in literature would seem to need qualification. And the so-called "heresy of paraphrase," which several generations now of critics have been seeking to expunge, begins to appear not as a heresy but as a normal and unavoidable aspect of the reading process. Of course it may be objected that what holds in general for the reading process does not necessarily hold for the reading of literature, and it can be argued that literature is a special case in which meaning cannot be detached from syntax, content from form, without serious impoverishment. For some literary texts perhaps, if not for all, these arguments would be reasonable. In *The Aims of Interpretation,* where Hirsch argues that meaning may be independent of surface structure, he exempts some literary works, whose meaning seems to be

27. *Ibid.*, p. 122.
28. *Ibid.*
29. *Ibid.*, pp. 122-23.

language-constituted.[30] It need not follow from psycholinguistic research that surface linguistic features are never effective in the experience of reading literature, much less that it makes no difference how literary meanings are conveyed as long as the writer's message gets across. Nevertheless, one need not go to the extreme of holding that nothing but the message matters in order to argue that literary theorists have overemphasized the degree to which messages are tied to the forms in which they are embodied and have underrated the importance of abstract schematization in the process of making sense of literature.

One theorist who has studied the literary reading process seems to me to give support to this view. Teun A. Van Dijk, writing on "Cognitive Processing of Literary Discourse," states that "a hearer or reader . . . gradually constructs a *conceptual representation* of the text in memory. Thus the variety of 'surface structural,' e.g., morphological and syntactic information in the text is 'translated' or 'transformed' into meanings which are cognitively represented in terms of 'concepts.' "[31] I do not take Van Dijk to be saying that readers of literature simply substitute abstract schemas for literary scenes or poetic stanzas, as if to say that we read novels and poems by translating them into essays. He implies rather that though thematic concepts to some degree displace the more concrete level of literary detail, they also help us store and retrieve this level of detail, for we tend to store in long-term memory those details which are particularly relevant to the concepts we have formed. In this respect, abstract concepts are not in *competition* with the scenes, actions, stanzas, and the syntactic and structural forms of a

30. E. D. Hirsch, *The Aims of Interpretation*, p. 51: "The issue is not whether the forms of the mother tongue sometimes constrain forms of thought, but whether they always necessarily do so." Hirsch argues (in the essay "Stylistics and Synonymity") against the latter view.

31. Teun A. Van Dijk, "Cognitive Processing of Literary Discourse," *Poetics Today*, I, no. 1 (Autumn 1979), p. 145. Van Dijk, however, seems to espouse the "anti-assertional" view when he says "the poem is produced, read and understood as a speech act which need not have the usual 'practical' pragmatic functions, such as [real] assertion, question, threat, or promise in our everyday conversation, but may have only or primarily a *ritual* function" (p. 151). He does not elaborate, except to add that "this specific pragmatic function of literature as a kind of ritual speech act is further specified by the socio-cultural context. . ." p. 152). But what evidence is there that in our specific "socio-cultural context" literature *has* been accorded a "ritual" rather than an assertive function?

literary work, for they assist the reader in retaining these things. Thus an answer becomes possible to those who object that propositional views of literature ignore literature's "dramatic" nature: one can reply that it is through propositional understanding that the dramatic materials of literary works are retained in memory and are made intelligible. We should not be asked to choose between the propositional and the presentational.

Van Dijk would seem to be moving in the direction of such a view when he observes that "in literary processing more than in other kinds of communication, cognitive comprehension, storage, rehearsal, and memory (and reproduction, i.e., telling about it), is geared toward the assignment of *relevance* of *salient* detail."[32] This is not to suggest that readers recall nothing except what they can appropriate conceptually, for to widely varying degrees, readers recall conceptually "irrelevant" materials. Van Dijk terms this kind of recall "incidental memory."[33] But as a rule, readers retain best what they have been able to process conceptually. It is not a question of the reader's translating the concreteness of scenes and actions into an abstract idea, but of making use of the idea to retain a sense of the scenes and actions themselves in their interconnection.

I submit the above arguments are confirmed more than discredited by the most extensive account of the experience of reading literature that has so far been provided, that by Wolfgang Iser in his two books, *The Implied Reader* and *The Act of Reading*. At first sight this claim may seem improbable, since Iser repeatedly insists in these works on the discrepancy between the reader's grasp of abstract concepts and his experience of the dynamic process of the literary text unfolding in time. Rather like the early Stanley Fish of the theory of "affective stylistics," Iser tends to view the temporal flow of the text as resistant to and subversive of all efforts to conceptualize the text by means of abstract ideas. Indeed, this very resistance of the process of temporality to abstract conceptualization is for Iser central to the meaning of literary works such as *Tom Jones*, which he reads as exemplifying the "gulf between the rigid confines of principle and the endless fluidity of human experience." One might object, however, that to experience the temporal flow of *Tom Jones* as an instance of the gulf between abstract

32. *Ibid.*, p. 157.
33. *Ibid.*

principle and the fluidity of experience is itself to experience the work as an idea as well as a temporal process—or, more precisely, it is to experience the temporal process of the work *as itself implicated in a set of ideas.* Iser's model of the reading experience, then, depends more heavily on the application of thematic ideas to the text than Iser allows. John Reichert has acutely pointed out this dependence in his review of *The Act of Reading*:

> A peculiar feature of *The Act of Reading,* given its stress on the discovery of the meanings of novels, is its initial exposé of the "traditional expository style of interpretation" whereby the work is "reduced" to a "single 'hidden' meaning" (p. 10). Iser makes use of James's "The Figure in the Carpet" to discredit such reductions, but proceeds to enunciate the story's meaning: "that meaning is no longer an object to be defined, but is an effect to be experienced" (p. 10). Indeed, Iser tells us the "hidden meaning" of every text he discusses, and he may be read not as having discredited traditional interpretation but as having lent it theoretical substance. While he insists on the difference between "image" and "discourse," the fact remains that we must fall into discourse when we start to discuss a work. Like Iser, we come up with general propositions to account for the fictional "world" we have discovered and assume them to represent the novelist's ideas about the world we live in.[34]

I would add only two things to this excellent statement: first, that one need not subscribe to the view that literary works can be reduced to "a single hidden meaning" in order to defend "the traditional expository style of interpretation" as I have been doing here and as Reichert does above. There are, after all, no countable *units* of meaning; hence the notion of a "single" meaning is meaningless on the face of it. An interpreter who expounds a set of meanings in a text does not pretend to exhaust all its meanings; he simply claims that those he is expounding are there and presumably are important. Second, I would argue that "we must fall into discourse" not only when we "start to discuss a work," but even before that, when we start to read it.

34. John Reichert, review of Wolfgang Iser, *The Act of Reading: A Theory of Aesthetic Response, Philosophy and Literature,* 4, no. 1 (Spring 1980), p. 132. The above quotation from *The Act of Reading* is taken from Reichert's review.

Reading any complex literary work is rather like a filing operation in which one must find conceptual "filing drawers" for an immense stream of detail. Ellmann's paraphrase, quoted a moment ago, may stand for a mental "drawer" labelled "kindness vs. power." It is but one of the many such drawers the reader must be able to open up in order to assimilate successive events in *Ulysses* effectively. Usually, a formulation like Ellmann's takes shape only gradually, after many revisions, readjustments, and corrections. Thus the contrast between kindness and power is instanced as early as the opening encounter between Stephen and Mulligan, but the relevance of this scene to that contrast is likely to occur to the reader only in retrospect, and he may be forced to discard an earlier thematic construction of the scene. When one construction fails to fit—fails to help process further detail—we discard it or set it aside temporarily and try out others. There may be whole episodes for which a reader cannot be sure he has found the correct conceptual drawer—or *a* correct one, since there may be several. We can lose the thread for long stretches without total breakdown as long as we recover it within a reasonable time. The average critical paraphrase gives little sense of this step-by-step process of reading in all its unruliness, and of course it should not be expected to give such a sense. But this mistaken expectation may be at the root of much of the resistance against recognizing the importance of conceptualization in the process. If we mistakenly expect a paraphrase to be equivalent to the meaning it partially abstracts, we will naturally end up rejecting the possibility of paraphrasing meanings.

If the foregoing arguments have any merit, they ought to have relevance to the teaching of literature. Many students who have no difficulty comprehending literary works on the level of action and story are unable to perform the operations required to make conceptual sense of action and story. This failure to process literature conceptually leads to impoverishment of emotional response as well. All but the most receptive students of literature have difficulty performing the thematizing operations that come so easily to the practiced teacher and critic. If the problem of the degree of belief required by a work of its reader arises only intermittently in the classroom, this is because many students fail to arrive at the stage of conceptualization that would enable the question of their engagement with the author's outlook to become an issue. The student whose papers are repeatedly marked down for failing to go beyond plot-summary has usually not learned to produce the conceptual propositions that organize the dramatic materials. Not only do his grades suffer, his response to literature are constricted.

Nobody wants to deprive readers of the pleasures of reading *Gulliver's Travels* or *Moby-Dick* as pure adventure yarns. And one can concede that the use of literature as an object of classroom analysis runs the risk of placing too much emphasis on thematic reading and on the ability to verbalize it in a highly conscious way. As the university and the school become practically the only places where literature is taken seriously, various diffuse resentments against overintellectualization—resentments long present in our culture—are turned against classroom procedures. One can frequently sympathize with the student who feels oppressed by what looks to him like an arbitrary and pedantic demand that he discover Hidden Meaning and Symbolism in every work, who finally concludes that critical analysis is a kind of game, the goal of which is to "read into" the work meanings that are not there. Other students learn to play this game all too well and become either enthusiasts or cynics before their time. The psychology of student revulsion against overinterpretation seems to me to have more than a little in common with that of sophisticated efforts to theorize the propositional element out of literary experience. Both hostile reactions arise from exposure to the wrong kind of thematic reading, which is either far-fetched and wrong or else fails to acknowledge sufficiently that there is more to any literary work than its thematic message. Such reactions are understandable enough, but they create a false dilemma, putting thematic reading into an unnecessary competition with appreciation and experience. The student (or layman) conceives of reading for pleasure and reading for meaning as incompatible activities. The literary theorist conceives experiencing literature as incompatible with entertaining conceptual statements. Ideally, learning how to thematize a literary work should enhance the experiential pleasure, not compete with it.

Everybody who has learned to read literature successfully has acquired the trick of thematization and knows how to use it to enhance rather than limit experiential pleasure. Perhaps if this trick came as easily to most students as it does to professional critics and teachers, there would be more to be said for efforts to discourage the "message hunting" mode of reading. But it is questionable tactics to warn a student against the abuses of message hunting if locating any kind of message in a literary work is precisely what he has not learned how to do. Perhaps at one time, students had to be cured of the habit of making glib appropriations of literature; this is no longer the case—most students are uncertain what to say or think about literature at all. The critic or teacher who warns his students not to hunt for messages is a bit like a millionaire who warns poor people not to be overly concerned about material prosperity. The real challenge of literature teaching is not to get students to stop hunting for messages, but to show them how to hunt for messages in a fashion that is not simply coarse and crude. To argue as if the choice in dealing with literature were between messages or no messages, instead of between crude and complex messages, contradicts what is known about the experience of reading and makes the teacher's job harder.

To be sure, "what is known about the experience of reading" is as yet not much, especially as regards these problems of belief in literature. Furthermore, even if a great deal more were known, and empirical evidence supporting my argument were conclusive, there would still be plenty of ground for objection. One could always object that even though it may be true that readers obey the convention of significance by thematizing literary works, they *ought* not to do so. One could go on to try to modify the convention, to install a new convention according to which literary works would be read as immune from any liability to assertion. In a sense, recent literary theories which would have us believe that this latter convention is already in effect, and perhaps always has been, may be seen either as wishful thinking or as attempts at "behavior modification." In any case, the grounds of this theoretical impulse are often ethical, springing from the deep-seated feeling that there is something demeaning about propositional modes of discourse and therefore that literary communication is degraded insofar as it is associated with these modes.

I have discussed elsewhere some of the reasons for this feeling and shall not go into them here, except to say that the moral opposition to assertion would not have become so influential in literary criticism had it not been reinforced (one might even say, inspired) by an impressive body of literature which itself sets out to frustrate efforts to reduce it to an assertion. Assertion, conceptual appropriation of any kind, is identified with the predatory utilitarianisms of commercial effort, technological domination, advertising and propaganda, abstract moralism, and the processing and consumption of commodities. Assertion-making is viewed as a kind of "packaging" of thought and feeling, as the rhetorical complement of the acquisitive spirit. But these efforts have not succeeded in making literature less propositional and assertive, and it is hard to see how they could succeed without cancelling both their own seriousness and their critical thrust. If anything, such literature has had to become *more* propositional and assertive than its predecessors, for exposing the corruptions of packaged discourse and its cultural correlatives requires making assertions, even though these assertions may be directed against the making of assertions. The anti-assertionist stance is despite itself a means of asserting, and therefore one must not take its theoretical claims literally. Whether writing and reading literary works as discourses with something to say is a form of behavior that could be altered is difficult to judge. But it is what we have long done and what we continue to do.

To summarize, then, there are two arguments for rejecting the anti-assertionist view and accepting the claim that literary works make assertions. Briefly put, the arguments are that authors intend assertions and readers can scarcely help looking for them. Authors intend to make assertions whenever they set out to write "serious" works. Even when an author attempts to undermine or negate all assertions—as frequently is the case with modern authors—that very enterprise involves him in making or presupposing assertions to which he commits himself. Readers, for their part, can scarcely help formulating assertions, in the form of thematic propositions, in making sense of literary works, and in practice readers are balked when these thematic propositions are greatly at variance with their own beliefs about the world. There is a third argument, which I have emphasized elsewhere more strongly than in this essay: the link between literary works and the real world is through the assertions advanced or presupposed in the work. If literary works make no assertions, then they are trivial, and it is difficult to understand why so much time, effort, and attention has been expended on them.

NARRATIVE VERSIONS, NARRATIVE THEORIES*

Barbara Herrnstein Smith

Contemporary narrative theory is, in many respects, a quite sophisticated area of study: it is international and interdisciplinary in its origins, scope, and pursuits and, in many of its achievements, both subtle and rigorous. It also appears to be afflicted, however, with a number of dualistic concepts and models, the continuous generation of which betrays a lingering strain of naive Platonism and the continued appeal to which is both logically dubious and methodologically distracting.

The sort of dualism to which I refer is conspicuous in the title of Seymour Chatman's recently published study, *Story and Discourse.* That doubling (that is, story *and* discourse) alludes specifically to a two-leveled model of narrative that seems to be both the central hypothesis and the central assumption of a number of narratological theories which Chatman offers to set forth and synthesize. The dualism recurs throughout his study in several other sets of doublet terms: "deep structure" and "surface manifestation," "content plane" and "expression plane," "*histoire*" and "*récit,*" "*fabula*" and "*sjužet,*" and "signified" and "signifier"–all of which, according to Chatman, may be regarded as more or less equivalent distinctions: "Structuralist theory argues that each narrative has two parts: a story *(histoire)* [that is,] the content . . . and a discourse *(discours),* that is, the expression, the means by which the content is communicated."[1]

Chatman outlines various arguments that have been presented by various narrative theorists to support this model, one of which originates

*Reprinted with minor revisions from "Narrative Versions, Narrative Theories" by Barbara Herrnstein Smith, *Critical Inquiry* 7 (Autumn 1980), 213-326, copyright © by The University of Chicago.

1. Seymour Chatman, *Story and Discourse: Narrative Structure in Fiction and Film* (Ithaca, N.Y. and London, 1978), p. 19.

in the observation that the same story may exist in many different versions and, indeed, in many different modes and media. Thus, in a subsequent essay, he notes that *Cinderella* may be manifested "as verbal tale, as ballet, as opera, as film, as comic strip, as pantomime, and so on"[2] and, in *Story and Discourse,* elaborates Claude Bremond's claim that every narrative contains

> a layer of autonomous significance, endowed with a structure that can be isolated from the whole of the message. . . . [This basic and autonomous structure] may be transposed from one to another medium without losing its essential properties. . . . [Thus,] the subject of a story may serve as argument for a ballet, that of a novel can be transposed to stage or screen, one can recount in words a film to someone who has not seen it.[3]

"This transposability of the story," remarks Chatman, "is the strongest reason for arguing that narratives are indeed structures independent of any medium" (p. 20). Among the other related reasons are (1) that there is a difference between "discourse-time" and "story-time," that is, between the length of time it takes to read (or hear) a narrative and the length of time occupied by the events referred to in it, and (2) that a set of events that occurred in one order can be narrated in another order or in what is called "nonlinear sequence." These facts and phenomena, it is claimed, require us to posit the existence of two independent levels of narrative structure: the first or basement level, underlying every narrative, is its "deep structure" or "basic story"; the second or upper level is the *narrative discourse* itself, where the basic story is "actualized," "realized," "expressed," or "manifested" in some form—or in many different forms, modes, media, and thus, *versions* (pp. 22-28).

There are many grounds, logical and empirical, on which one could take issue with this set of claims and arguments, and I shall not attempt

2. "What Novels Can Do That Films Can't (and Vice Versa)," *Critical Inquiry* 7 (Autumn 1980), 122.

3. Claude Bremont, "Le Message narratif," *Communications* 4 (1964), 4; translated by Chatman and cited in *Story and Discourse,* p. 20; all further references to *Story and Discourse* will be cited in the text.

to stake them all out here.[4] I shall attempt to demonstrate, however, that the set of narrative "properties" or "phenomena" frequently invoked by Chatman and other narratologists in connection with the two-leveled model of narrative structure neither requires nor supports that model but, on the contrary, reveals its major logical flaws and methodological limitations. In the first section I shall examine the related concepts of narrative versions and basic stories and, in the second, what narratologists refer to as "anachrony" or the various disparities between "the dual time orders" of narrative structure. I shall be concerned, in both sections, not merely to indicate certain weaknesses of the structuralist model but to suggest alternate ways of formulating the problems and explaining the phenomena in question. And, in the concluding section, I shall outline an alternative conception of narrative discourse which, when developed further, would, I believe, permit us to construct richer and more coherent accounts of the nature of narratives generally.

1. *Versions and Variants*

There are a number of senses in which narratives are commonly said to *be* versions and, conversely, to *have* versions. To recall some of the most familiar: we speak of the King James version of Genesis, Shakespeare's version of Plutarch's *Life of Antony*, an abridged version of *Clarissa*, an expurgated version of *Lady Chatterley's Lover*, a movie version of *Barry Lyndon*, the star witness' version of the shooting, and my teenaged daughter's version of what happened in the girls' bathroom at school on Monday. Most of these versions seem to involve some sort of translated, transformed, or otherwise modified retelling of a particular prior narrative text; the last two seem to involve a narrative account from a particular perspective or from a perspective that is rather pointedly understood to be but one among many (actual or possible). These

4. I have taken issue with a number of them elsewhere; see "Surfacing from the Deep," *PTL: A Journal for Descriptive Poetics and Theory* 2 (1977), 151-82 (rpt. in *On the Margins of Discourse: The Relation of Literature to Language* [Chicago, 1978], pp. 157-201), for a general critique of the use of models and concepts drawn from transformational-generative linguistics in literary criticism and theory.

two major senses of narrative "versions"—that is, as *retellings* of other narratives and as accounts told from a particular or partial *perspective*—will concern us throughout this discussion. I should like to turn now, however, to a specific example to which Chatman alludes, namely, *Cinderella,* and ask to what extent the existence of its many versions, in many modes and media, either supports or illustrates the two-leveled model of narrative.

We may consider, first, the claim that in any narrative the two levels are "autonomous": that is, the repeated reference to a basic story that is independent of any of its versions, independent of any surface manifestations or expression in any material form, mode, or medium—and thus presumably also independent of any teller or occasion of telling and therefore of any human purposes, perceptions, actions, or interactions. As this description suggests, the narratologist's own versionless version of *Cinderella*—that is, its hypothetical basic story—bears an unmistakable resemblance to a Platonic ideal form: unembodied and unexpressed, unpictured, unwritten and untold, this altogether unsullied *Cinderella* appears to be a story that occupies a highly privileged ontological realm of pure Being within which it unfolds immutably and eternally. If this is what is meant by the basic story of *Cinderella,* it is clearly unknowable—and, indeed, literally unimaginable—by any mortal being.

The narratologist might observe, at this point, that although the basic story of *Cinderella* is indeed "an abstraction," its features are not at all difficult to imagine, for it is simply the underlying plot of the fairy tale or what all the versions have in common. This basic story or deep-plot structure is revealed, he might say, whenever we construct a plot summary of any—or all—of the versions. Indeed, he might add, it is the fact that each of us would construct the *same* plot summary of *Cinderella* that demonstrates our intuitive apprehension of its basic story.

It will be instructive, however, to take note of the five hundred-page volume, published in 1893 by the British Folk-lore Society, entitled *Cinderella; three hundred and forty-five variants . . . abstracted and tabulated; with a discussion of mediaeval analogues and notes,* by Marian Roalfe Cox.[5] This volume does not include the cartoon version or the musical version, but it does include the familiar Grimm brothers'

5. Cox, *Cinderella* (London, 1893).

version, the earlier version by Charle Perrault, and abstracts of hundreds of other versions from all over Europe, North Africa, India, and the Middle East. In most of them, we find an initially ill-treated or otherwise unfortunate heroine, though sometimes her name is not Cinderella but Cencienta or Aschenputtel, Echenfettle, Fette-Mette or Tan Chan; and sometimes she isn't the youngest stepchild but the oldest daughter; and sometimes she is not a heroine but a hero; and usually the fairy godmother is a cat, a cow, or a tree; and the glass slipper is often a gold ring. Moreover, the turns of plot in many of these tales are likely to be disturbing or intriguing to someone who knows only one set of versions of the Grimm brothers' version. There is, for example, an Icelandic tale, collected in 1866, in which after Cinderella (who is named Mjadveig) marries the prince (who is the captain of a ship), the married couple invite the wicked stepmother to a feast on board the ship at which they serve her salted meat from twelve barrels which contain the remains of the ugly stepsisters, whom Mjadveig and her husband have previously murdered.[6]

I shall return to Cox and some other folklorists but, for the moment, I should like to draw a few morals from the 345 versions of *Cinderella*. The first, which I shall not belabor, is simply that all of us–critics, teachers and students of literature, and narratologists–tend to forget how relatively homogeneous a group we are, how relatively limited and similar are our experiences of verbal art, and how relatively confined and similar are the conditions under which we pursue the study of literature. It is likely that if each reader of this article were asked to give a plot summary of *Cinderella*, the individual summaries would indeed resemble each other fairly closely. The shape of the data is not in dispute; the question is how best to explain it, and I do not believe that we need invoke a two-leveled model to do it. For what the similarities would reveal, I think, is not the uniformity of the intuitively apprehended deep-plot structure of all the versions of *Cinderella* but rather (1) the similarity of our individual prior experiences of particular individual tellings designated *Cinderella*; (2) the similarity of the particular ways in which almost all of us have learned to talk about stories generally; and (3) the fact that all of us, in attempting to construct a plot summary in this particular context and in connection with these particular issues, would be responding to similar conditions and constraints.

6. Abstracted by Cox, pp. 144-45.

Because we are so accustomed to performing certain kinds of abstraction, abbreviation, and simplification in the name of "giving plot summaries," those operations come to seem natural, obvious, and nonarbitrary to us. The inclination and ability to perform precisely those operations are, however, by no means innate; they must be learned, and they may be learned differently—or not at all—and therefore performed differently, or not at all.

There is a second point here with even broader implications for narrative theory. Not only will different summaries of the same narrative be produced by people with different conventions, habits, and models of summarizing, but even given the *same* conventions, their summaries will be different if the motives and purposes of their summarizing are different. Thus, one would present a different plot summary of a given novel if one's motive were to advertise it to potential buyers or to deplore its sexism to a friend and still different if one were summarizing the novel in the course of presenting a new interpretation of it or of writing a critical biography of its author. Each of these summaries would simplify the narrative at a different level of abstraction, and each of them would preserve, omit, link, isolate, and foreground different features or sets of features in accord with the particular occasion and purposes of the summarizing. It is evident, moreover, that each of these summaries would, in effect, be another *version* of the novel; an abridged and simplified version, to be sure, but, in that respect, like the one-volume version of *Clarissa* constructed for busy or impatient readers or like the abridged and simplified *Gulliver's Travels* constructed for the amusement of children. My point here is that what narratologists refer to as the basic stories or deep-plot structures of narratives are often not abstract, disembodied, or subsumed entities but quite manifest, material, and particular retellings—and thus versions—of those narratives, constructed, as *all* versions are, by someone in particular, on some occasion, for some purpose, and in accord with some relevant set of principles.

This point will be given further concreteness if we return to Cox's study of *Cinderella* and to its rather touching preface. Clearly the task of collecting, transcribing, classifying, and abstracting those 345 variants was an arduous one. Nevertheless, she wrote, she would "in no wise begrudge the time which that labor has absorbed" if it helped to settle certain difficult questions, "especially [the question] of the origins, independent or otherwise, of stories similar in their incident and widespread in their distribution"[7]; that is, whether all the French, Spanish, German, and Italian Cinderellas, Aschenputtels, and Fette-Mettes were translations or transmissions, migrations or distortions, elaborations or degenerations of some single original story and, if so, whether that archetype or ur-story originated in Europe, or came from India by way of North Africa, or from Iceland by way of Norway, and so forth. Those questions were not, of course, settled by Cox's labors. Nor were they settled by the labors of her successor, Anna Birgitta Rooth, although the latter's study (*The Cinderella Cycle,* published in Lund in 1951) took into account several hundred additional variants and was conducted in accord with a considerably more sophisticated folkloristic methodology. Nor were the questions quite settled in 1974 by the Chinese folklorist Nai Tung-Ting who, after concluding from his examination of eighteen newly discovered Far Eastern variants that "the earliest complete version of Cinderella on record seems to have arisen in North Vietnam," nevertheless ends his book as follows:

> Finally, this writer is not maintaining that Cinderella *certainly* originated in this region. He is merely pointing out that, with our limited knowledge, such a possibility cannot be ruled out. . . . This writer hopes that his humble study has added a little to our knowledge; he hopes as earnestly that he has also shown how much there is still to learn. [Italics mine][8]

In short, the origin of "*the* story of Cinderella" has not yet been determined. Moreover, in the view of most modern folklorists, it cannot be determined: not because the evidence is so meager—or so overwhelming—but rather because it becomes increasingly clear that to ask the question in that form is already to beg it.

By now, folklorists around the world have collected about a thousand variants of *Cinderella.* All of these stories are in some respects similar and in some respects dissimilar. The incidence, nature, and degrees of resemblance and disparity are so diverse, however, that they allow of just about every conceivable type of causal relation among the

7. Cox, pp. lxxi-lxxii.

8. Nai Tung-Ting, *The Cinderella Cycle in China and Indo-China* (Helsinki, 1974), p. 40.

stories, including none at all. Cox left no record of her own more desperate speculations, but I think she began to suspect not only that the original version of the Cinderella story could not in the nature of things be tracked down but that the very concept of "the story of Cinderella" might be an artifact of folkloristic assumptions and methodology. In any case, we might now say that the basic Cinderella who was sought by the early folklorists was neither before, behind, nor beneath the 345 variants but was, rather, *comprised* of them—and, more generally, that what *anyone* could mean by "the story of Cinderella" would have to be some set of particular tellings that he or she determined (or agreed) were covariants of each other in accord with some particular, but arbitrary, set of relational criteria.

I emphasized a bit earlier that no narrative version can be independent of a particular teller and occasion of telling and, therefore, that we may assume that every narrative version has been constructed in accord with some set of purposes or interests. The significance of this point for the concept of basic stories will be clearer if we recognize the potential range and variability of such purposes and interests. It will be useful, then, to take brief note of certain types of narratives which Cox did not include in her catalog of variants but which we would nevertheless have good reason to speak of as "versions" of *Cinderella*.

There are, to begin with, such narratives as one might read in popular magazines about the careers of those movie stars and rock musicians who seem to rise recurrently from poverty and obscurity to exalted status in the glittering world of Hollywood or New York. One such magazine advertises on its cover: "Read the Real-Life Cinderella-Story of Sylvester Stallone"; and it is clear that the story within *is* a version of *Cinderella* and that both are "basically the same story"—rags-to-riches, as we sometimes put it, in a neat three-word plot summary (and version) of *Cinderella*.

There are also such retellings of the tale as the one that appears in Julius E. Heuscher's volume, *A Psychiatric Study of Myths and Fairy Tales: Their Origin, Meaning and Usefulness.* Heuscher offers a reading of *Cinderella* as basically a story of psycho-sexual development. The three visits to the prince's ball, he suggests, are occasions for erotic arousal from which the young girl flees, trying to evade sexual maturity. "Eventually," however, Heuscher tells us, "Cinderella is able to confront her lover, and painlessly she lets the foot slip into the slipper."[9] This reading is, of course, an "interpretation" of *Cinderella*. It is also a retelling and thus a version of the tale; indeed, it also represents an attempt to identify the basic story of *Cinderella*, though it is certainly not the *same* basic story that might be identified by a folklorist or narratologist.

A supplementary catalog of *Cinderella*-variants might include other readings produced by other types of literary scholars—such as critics, biographers, and historians—who have had occasion to discover and/or construct versions of *Cinderella*. I recall, for example, a colleague who was able to demonstrate that all of Charles Dickens' novels are basically versions of *Cinderella*. Since this scholar did not claim that Dickens intended his novels as adaptations of or allusions to the fairy tale, it would be hard to say whether his own readings of *David Copperfield*, *Oliver Twist*, and *Great Expectations* as Cinderella-stories actually made those novels into versions of *Cinderella* or only discovered that they were versions. When we reconsider the work of Cox, Heuscher, and the magazine writer, we see that a troubling question arises here, namely, who is responsible for a version *being* a version? Can it be only someone who, like Rossini and Walt Disney, *designs and intends* a narrative as such? Or can it also be someone who, like Cox and the other folklorists, *identifies and classifies* it as such? And, in that case, can it not also, apparently, be someone who, like the Dickens scholar, *perceives and interprets* it as such?

Before attempting to solve that puzzle, I should mention a theological-minded friend who, when I revealed my interest in *Cinderella*, revealed to me in turn that the story is, basically, an allegory of Christian redemption: Cinderella is the soul, he said; her initial consignment to a place in the ashes represents the soul's initial confinement to the flesh; the fairy godmother is Grace, the transformation of the pumpkin is transubstantiation, and the prince. . . . I stopped him at that point, just as he was warming to the subject and beginning to explain how Cinderella is thus basically the same story as *The Divine Comedy*, *Pilgrim's Progress*, *King Lear*, and the *Aeneid*. I thought once more of Cox and the 345 variants, one of which is, in fact, what she called "the King Lear branch" of the story.[10] I thought especially of her uneasy

9. Julius E. Heuscher, *A Psychiatric Study of Myths and Fairy Tales* (Springfield, Ill., 1974), p. 225.

10. Cox, pp. lxvii *et passim*.

feeling, as she intimated it in the preface, that if she had continued her labors long enough, all stories would have turned out to be versions of *Cinderella*—and of my own increasing suspicion, as my friend spoke, that *Cinderella* would turn out to be basically all stories.

It has not been my intention here to display a chaos of paradoxes and infinite regresses. It has been, rather, to suggest how a consideration of the phenomenon of narrative versions leads repeatedly to certain conclusions that challenge either the validity or the necessity of the two-leveled model of narrative structure. I alluded earlier, in connection with the Platonic version of *Cinderella* projected by that model (disembodied, untold, unheard, and so forth), to the evident absence from that version of any tellers or occasions of telling and thus the absence of any human purposes, perceptions, actions, or interactions. I was not indulging there in the familiar humanistic pieties commonly directed against structuralist theories. My point was, rather, that *to the extent that contemporary narrative theory omits consideration of such variables, it drastically constricts its own explanatory resources.* I shall return to those variables in the second and third sections. Here, however, I should like to review and summarize the preceding general points:

1. For any particular narrative, there is no single *basically* basic story subsisting beneath it but, rather, an unlimited number of other narratives that can be *constructed in response* to it or *perceived as related* to it.

2. Among the narratives that can be constructed in response to a given narrative are not only those that we commonly refer to as "versions" of it (for example, translations, adaptations, abridgements, and paraphrases) but also those retellings that we call "plot summaries," "interpretations," and, sometimes, "basic stories." None of these retellings, however, is more absolutely basic than any of the others.

3. For any given narrative, there are always *multiple* basic stories that can be constructed in response to it because basic-ness is always arrived at by the exercise of some set of operations, in accord with some set of principles, that reflect some set of interests, all of which are, by nature, variable and thus multiple. Whenever we start to cut back, peel off, strip away, lay bare, and so forth, we always do so in accord with certain assumptions and purposes which, in turn, create hierarchies of relevance and centrality; and it is in terms of these hierarchies that we will distinguish certain elements and relations as

being central or peripheral, more important or less important, and more basic or less basic.

4. The form and features of any "version" of a narrative will be a function of, among other things, the particular motives that elicited it and the particular interests and functions it was designed to serve. Some versions, such as translations and transcriptions, may be constructed in order to preserve and transmit a culturally valued verbal structure. Others, such as adaptations and abridgments, may be constructed in order to amuse or instruct a specific audience. And *some* versions, such as "interpretations," "plot summaries," and "basic stories," may be constructed in order to advance the objectives of a particular discipline, such as literary history, folklore, psychiatry—or, of course, narratology. None of these latter versions, however, is any less motivated or, accordingly, formally contingent than any of the other versions constructed to serve other interests or functions.

5. Among any array of narratives—tales or tellings—in the universe, there is an unlimited number of potentially perceptible relations. These relations may be of many different kinds and orders, including formal and thematic, synchronic and diachronic, and causal and non-causal. Whenever these potentially perceptible relations become actually perceived, it is by virtue of some set of interests on the part of the perceiver: thus different relations among narratives will be perceived by anthropologists and anthologists, theologians and folklorists, literary historians and narratologists. Since new sets of interests can emerge at any time and do emerge continuously, there can be no ultimately basic sets of relations among narratives, and thus also no "natural" genres or "essential" types, and thus also no limit to the number or nature of narratives that may sometime be seen as versions or variants of each other.

2. *Narrative Anachronies and the Legacy of Linguistic Dualism*

As indicated earlier, there are certain phenomena relating to *temporality* that are frequently invoked by theorists as evidence for the validity or necessity of the double-leveled model of narrative structure. I should like to turn now to a consideration of two of the most prominent of these:

(1) what Chatman, in *Story and Discourse,* refers to as the distinction between "discourse-time" and "story-time" and explains as the

fact that there is commonly a disparity between "the time it takes to peruse [or to "present"] the discourse" and "the duration of the purported [or "actual"] events of the narrative" (pp. 62-63) and (2) what Nelson Goodman, in his analysis of time-twisted tales, refers to as the possible "disparity between the order of telling [the incidents in a narrative] and the order of occurrence."[11]

One would not deny, of course, that the time it takes someone to read *War and Peace* may differ from the time it took the Russians to defeat Napoleon—or Pierre and Natasha to live out their lives. It is certainly also the case that a narrator may relate events in a nonchronological order, telling us, for example, about someone's funeral before telling us about his childhood, as Tolstoy does in "The Death of Ivan Ilych." The question at issue, however, is neither the existence of these possibilities nor their interest and significance in the experience of narrative. Rather, it is whether either of these temporal disparities—or both of them taken together—requires us to posit the existence of two distinct, independent time orders for every narrative or, conversely, whether they can be understood in terms that do not already *assume* a dual-leveled model of narrative structure.

With respect to the first of the temporal disparities mentioned above—that is, the possibility of a difference between the *durations* of discourse-time and story-time—we may begin by observing that it is not clear what makes this disparity especially remarkable, or especially relevant to narrative, or especially relevant to narrative time. After all, there is also a difference between the length of time occupied by the siege of Moscow and the length of time it takes me to *say* "the siege of Moscow," as well as a difference between the area of space covered by Moscow, the city, and the area covered by the inscribed word, "Moscow."[12] All of these disparities—along with those cited as "phenomena," "features," and "salient properties" of narrative time—are what we learn to take for granted as the consequences of the conventional nature of language: that is, the fact that there may be and usually

11. Nelson Goodman, "Twisted Tales," *Critical Inquiry* 7 (Autumn 1980), 104.

12. Indeed, see *Story and Discourse,* pp. 96-106, for a corresponding and equally problematic discussion of "story-space" and "discourse-space." (The disparity of area mentioned above does not, it should be noted, receive any attention from Chatman or, to my knowledge, from any other narratologist.)

are *differences* between the formal properties of a linguistic event and the set of conditions conventionally implied by the occurrence of an event of that form.

The question then becomes why, in view of their considerable sophistication concerning literary, linguistic, and semiotic conventions, narrative theorists appear to regard these temporal disparities as so phenomenal in connection with *narratives* and in need of special explanations and explanatory models. Part of the answer, I suspect, is the prominence given to such disparities in early Formalist theory—often as illustrations of, precisely, the taken-for-granted conventions of language and fiction and their possible "defamiliarization" in such novels or antinovels as *Tristram Shandy*.[13]

There may be another part to the answer, however, and it brings us closer to the issue at hand, that is, to the relation between the various phenomena of narrative time and the dualistic model of narrative structure. Specifically, I would suggest that temporal disparities or anachronies will appear especially noteworthy only to the extent that one expects them to be otherwise: only, in other words, if one expects these two time orders to be conformant, equivalent, synchronic, or otherwise *correspondent*. As Gérard Genette remarks, the narratologist, in "pinpointing and measuring these narrative *anachronies* . . . implicitly assume[s] the existence of a kind of zero degree that would be a condition of perfect temporal correspondence between narrative and story."[14] Such an expectation of conformity is encouraged and supported by a conception of discourse as consisting of sets of discrete signs which, in some way, *correspond to* (depict, encode, denote, refer to, and so forth) sets of discrete and specific ideas, objects, or events. It is precisely such a conception of discourse that dominates contemporary narrative theory, and it is the dualism at the heart of that model of *language* that provides the scaffolding for the two-leveled model of narrative. (This model of language has, of course, been the major one in Western

13. See esp. Viktor Shklovsky's classic essay, "Sterne's *Tristram Shandy*: Stylistic Commentary" (originally published in 1925), in *Russian Formalist Criticism: Four Essays*, trans. and ed. Lee T. Lemon and Marion J. Ries (Lincoln, Neb., 1965).

14. Gérard Genette, *Narrative Discourse: An Essay in Method*, trans. Jane E. Lewin (Ithaca, N.Y., 1980), pp. 35-36. Genette's immediately subsequent observation, that "this point of reference is more hypothetical than real," is discussed below in connection with nonlinear sequence.

intellectual history and, in spite of some epistemological doubts and technical modifications introduced recently by various linguists and philosophers of language, it continues to be the model that dominates not only narratology but literary studies generally.)

An alternative conception of language views utterances not as strings of discrete signifiers that represent corresponding sets of discrete signifieds but as *verbal responses*—that is, as *acts* which, like any acts, are *performed in response to various sets of conditions*. These conditions consist of all those circumstantial and psychological variables of which every utterance is a function. Although *some* of these conditions are conventionally implied by and are, accordingly, inferable from the linguistic form of an utterance, they are not confined to and cannot be reduced to specific "referents" or "signifieds." In accord with this alternative view of language, individual narratives would be described not as sets of surface-discourse-signifiers that represent (actualize, manifest, map, or express) sets of underlying-story-signifieds but as the verbal acts of particular narrators performed in response to—and thus shaped and constrained by—sets of multiple interacting conditions. For any narrative, these conditions would consist of (1) such circumstantial variables as the particular context and material setting (cultural and social, as well as strictly "physical") in which the tale is told, the particular listeners or readers addressed, and the nature of the narrator's relationship to them, and (2) such psychological variables as the narrator's motives for telling the tale and all the particular interests, desires, expectations, memories, knowledge, and prior experiences (including his knowledge of various events, of course, but also of other narratives and of various conventions and traditions of storytelling) that elicited his telling it on that occasion, to that audience, and that shaped the particular way he told it.[15] Since all the formal properties of an individual narrative would be regarded as *functions of all these multiple interacting conditions* rather than as *representations of specific, discrete objects, events, or ideas*, the expectation of a conformity or formal correspondence between any of the properties of a narrative and anything else in particular simply would not arise. I would suggest,

15. As I have stressed elsewhere, we cannot and need not draw a strict line between the "internal" and "external" or "physical" and "psychological" variables to which any act is a response; see *On the Margins of Discourse*, p. 17. On the narrator's prior "knowledge of events," see the discussion below.

moreover, that the development of this sort of alternative conception of discourse and symbolic behavior generally may help clarify why traditional assumptions and latter-day affirmations of a correspondence between "language" and "the world" are untenable and thus move us beyond the mere *denial* of such a correspondence (as in the Heideggerian and post-structuralist insistence on "discrepancies," "failures," "ruptures," and "absences")–in short, beyond the whole "problematic of language."[16]

Given this alternative view of language, much of the scaffolding of the double-leveled model disappears; but so does the need for that model, for an alternative conception of narrative accordingly becomes available.

* * *

Most of the foregoing remarks concerning narrative anachrony in the sense of the disparities between the duration of discourse-time and story-time may be extended directly to the phenomenon of nonlinear sequence, that is, to the fact that, as narrative theorists sometimes put it, the sequence of events "in a given story" can be rearranged "at the discourse-level." I shall consider nonlinear sequence separately, however, because it constitutes one of the major arguments for the two-leveled model of narrative structure and because that argument in turn raises questions of more general interest for narrative theory.

We may first note that most descriptions of nonlinear sequence imply the possibility of *linear* sequence: the possibility, once again, of there being an exact match or correspondence, here between the chronological order of some set of events and the temporal deployment

16. The conception of language and symbolic behavior to which I allude here is developed further in *On the Margins of Discourse*; see esp. pp. 15-24 and 85-104. For related discussions representing a number of disciplines and intellectual traditions, see Kenneth Burke, *The Philosophy of Literary Form: Studies in Symbolic Action* (Baton Rouge, La., 1941; New York, 1957); B. F. Skinner, *Verbal Behavior* (New York, 1957); V. N. Vološinov, *Marxism and the Philosophy of Language*, trans. Ladislav Matejka and I. R. Titunik (Leningrad, 1930; New York, 1973); Dell Hymes, *Foundations in Sociolinguistics* (Philadelphia, 1974); Erving Goffman, *Frame Analysis: An Essay in the Organization of Experience* (New York, 1974); and Morse Peckham, *Explanation and Power: The Control of Human Behavior* (New York, 1979).

of the elements of some narrative utterance. The question that is raised or begged, then, is whether—or to what extent—such a correspondence ever can or does occur. Genette, who has extensively explored the various aspects of narrative anachrony, remarks that the possibility of such a correspondence is "more hypothetical than real" but continues: "Folklore narrative habitually conforms, at least in its major articulations, to chronological order, but our (Western) literary tradition, in contrast, was inaugurated by a characteristic effect of anachrony."[17] He then goes on to describe in some detail the "beginning *in medias res*" of the *Iliad*. There is reason, however, to question the propriety of that contrast between folklore and literary tradition, especially the implication of a literary-historical progression from some presumably prehistoric naive narrative synchrony to a subsequent more sophisticated narrative anachrony. For it can be demonstrated not only that absolute chronological order is as *rare* in folkloric narratives as it is in any literary tradition but that it is virtually *impossible* for any narrator to sustain it in an utterance of more than minimal length. In other words, by virtue of the very nature of discourse, nonlinearity is the rule rather than the exception in narrative accounts. Indeed, for that reason, the literary-historical "progression" is probably closer to being the reverse of what Genette implies: that is, to the extent that *perfect* chronological order may be said to occur at all, it is likely to be found only in acutely self-conscious, "artful," or "literary" texts.

There is, however, a second and even more significant question raised when narrative theorists speak of the chronological order of "a given set of events" (or the sequence of events "in a given story" or "the succession of episodes" in the "underlying plot") as being rearranged (or "reordered," "distorted," "deformed," "twisted," or "zigzagged") in or by "the narrative." For all such statements imply that prior to and independent of the narrative in question there existed some particular determinate set of events in some particular determinate (untwisted) order or sequence. And the question here is whether, for every time-twisted narrative (which is to say, for virtually every narrative), there always is such a prior and independent set and sequence of events—and also in what sense any of those stories or sets of events are "given."

The answer to the first part of this question is, I think, *no*. There are, of course, narratives (such as chronicles, news reports, gospels, and

17. Genette, *Narrative Discourse*, p. 36.

personal anecdotes) that are the accounts of events that have presumably already occurred in some determinate chronological sequence. There are also narratives (such as latter-day versions of *Cinderella* or *The Life of Jesus*) that relate events (whether presumed to be historical or fictional) which are already known to their narrators (and probably to their audiences) from prior tellings or other sources. And, in these cases, it makes some sense to speak of the narrative in question as having rearranged the sequence of some given set of events or the events of some given story. Indeed, one suspects that these two types of narrative (that is, historical reports and twice-told tales) serve as unconscious paradigms for the narratologist, which may, in turn, help explain his need to posit underlying plot structures or basic stories to account for the sequential features of those rather different narratives that he *does* study most closely, namely, works of literary fiction. For in addition to the two types of narrative just mentioned, there are all those fictive narratives which consist neither of the reports of particular historically determinate events nor the retellings of more or less familiar tales. And, in these instances, which would include such works as "The Death of Ivan Ilych," *The Good Soldier,* and *Absalom, Absalom!*, there evidently are *no* sets and sequences of events that, already arranged in some particular way, could be spoken of as *re*arranged—unless one *posits* them in the form of subterranean plots or immaterial Platonic stories in which all the events that are "twisted," "zig-zagged," or "deformed" up above in the narrative level are, by definition, always "given" in proper chronological sequence.

It may be objected here by those who are not especially committed to the two-leveled model that novels and other works of fiction nevertheless *do* have certain prior and independent sets and sequences of events that their authors *thought of* or *imagined* prior to composing those narratives. But this objection simply begs the original question in another way. To be sure, a novelist is likely to have had images of particular incidents which, together with various more or less articulated ideas and more or less vivid recollections of actual incidents, persons, and places, formed the creative materials from which a novel was ultimately fashioned. There is, however, no reason to suppose that these images, ideas, recollections, and so forth were themselves narrative in structure—that is, no reason to suppose that they comprised plots or storylike sets of events arranged in some determinate sequence—prior to and independent of the very narrative by which their author made them manifest.

We may, in fact, extend this point back to those paradigm narratives, mentioned above, that report not imaginary events but events which presumably occurred at some particular prior time. For like our imaginings of events that never occurred, our knowledge of *past* events is usually *not* narrative in structure or given in storylike sequences: on the contrary, that knowledge is most likely to be in the form of general and imprecise recollections, scattered and possibly inconsistent pieces of verbal information, and various visual, auditory, and kinesthetic images–some of which, at any given time, will be more or less in or out of focus and all of which will be organized, integrated, and apprehended as a specific "set" of events only in and through the very act by which we narrate them as such.[18]

It appears, then, that there are very few instances in which we can sustain the notion of a set and sequence of events altogether prior to and independent of the discourse through which they are narrated. Indeed, it appears that the best way to conceive of the sets of events that narratives seem to relate is not as specific, historically determinate, or otherwise stable and given phenomena but, rather, as the variable inferences and constructs that narratives characteristically elicit from their audiences or, indeed, as the various processes and activities of inferring, construing, projecting, hypothesizing, imagining, anticipating, and so forth that constitute our characteristic cognitive *responses to* narratives.

Two points should be emphasized here. One is that the audience of a narrative may not ever have any reason or occasion to arrest, stabilize, or verbally articulate this set of responses, in which case his inferences and constructs will *remain* in a fluid and mutable state. In other words, if no one ever asks us to *tell* "what happened" in *King Lear* or in *Madame Bovary*, our sense of what happened in the play or novel will remain indeterminate and unfixed, moving from an active process of

18. On this point see also Hayden White, "The Historical Text as Literary Artifact," *Clio* 3, no. 3 (1974), rpt. in his *Tropics of Discourse* (Baltimore, 1978), pp. 81-100, and Jonathan Culler's discussion of the recurrent opposition between "the priority and determining power of events and the determination of events by structures of signification" in "Fabula and Sjuzhet in the Analysis by Narrative," *Poetics Today* 1, no. 3 (1980), 27-37. On the general movement from assumptions of "a world fixed and found" to the recognition of "a diversity of . . . versions or worlds in the making," see Nelson Goodman's *Ways of Worldmaking* (Indianapolis, 1978), p. x.

imagining and inferring to a subsequent condition of variable recollection or potential retrieval. The second point is that the degree of specificity and richness of our inferences will, in any case, always depend upon, among other things, the nature of our *interest* in that narrative. Thus, if one is a jury member attending to a witness' account of a shooting or a professor of literature preparing a lecture on *King Lear* or *Madame Bovary,* one is likely to attempt to draw maximally specific and detailed inferences, perhaps rehearsing the narrative many times over, covertly or overtly, in an effort to visualize details with maximum vividness and to arrange the sequence of events with maximum coherence. If, on the other hand, a colleague rambles on about some car accident he passed driving to work that morning, one's inferences and constructions in response to *that* narrative are likely to be relatively vague and thin, and the entire cognitive engagement that it elicits is likely to be exhausted fairly rapidly.

It is clear from the foregoing discussion that an adequate account of the phenomenon of nonlinear sequence must turn that phenomenon around: that is, what must be described and explained is not how a narrator can *re*arrange the chronology of a given set of events but rather how (and, sometimes, whether) his audience can infer from his narrative the chronology of some set of events that is *not given.* I suggested above that, as part of the total process of a listener's (reader's or viewer's) engagement with any narrative, he will usually attempt to construe some chronology of events, more or less stable or unstable, rough or precise, depending on the nature of his interest in the narrative. It may be further observed that he will always tend to do so on the basis of some combination of the following: (1) his prior knowledge or beliefs concerning the chronology of those implied events as derived from other sources, including other narratives; (2) his familiarity with the relevant conventions of the language in which that narrative is presented (verb tenses, adverbs, and adverbial clauses, and so forth, and comparable time markers in other modes and media); (3) his familiarity with the relevant conventions and traditions of the style and genre of that narrative; (4) his knowledge and beliefs, including cultural assumptions, with respect to how things in general, and the particular kinds of things with which that narrative is concerned, happen and "follow from" each other–that is, his sense of the "logic" of temporal and causal sequence; and (5) certain more or less universal perceptual and cognitive tendencies involved in his processing–apprehending and organizing–information in any form.

Narrators, literary and other, characteristically assume the potency and operation of all these tendencies in their audiences and design their tales to exploit them accordingly. Commonly, a narrator will design his tale so as to lead his audience to make certain more or less specific and stable inferences appropriate to the nature of his *own* interests in the narrative transaction. The success of his design cannot, of course, ever be insured, and it is most unlikely to be total for all present, presumed, or potential audiences. It might be noted, moreover, that (as the Formalists delighted in demonstrating and as the works of Sterne, Borges, Robbe-Grillet, and Barth, among others, exemplify) the narrator always has the option of subverting the conventions and thwarting the operation of any or all of the cognitive tendencies listed above. The result may be a tale that provides for its audience an increased measure of cognitive interest at the expense of a smooth and efficient access to information. And, at the extremes noted above, it may offer, if that much less of the profit and pleasure provided by *un récit bien fait,* then that much more of the gratification one derives from observing (and perhaps having the occasion to exhibit) the twist and play of one's own mind in its engagement with a well-made narrative toy.[19] Contemporary narrative theorists have certainly recognized the existence of conventional linguistic and generic time markers and of the various cognitive tendencies outlined above. Indeed, a number of narratologists, including Genette and Chatman, have made them the focus of very substantial attention. What they apparently fail to appreciate, however, is the extent to which a consistent recognition of the operation of these conventions and tendencies would eliminate the need for such concepts and entities as dual time orders and underlying plot structures in describing and explaining the phenomena of narrative temporality.

3. *Narrative Acts and Transactions*

In the preceding two sections, I have suggested that descriptions and accounts based on a dualistic model of narrative discourse are not only empirically questionable and logically frail but also methodologically distracting, preventing us from formulating the problems of narrative

19. On the relation between art and "cognitive play," see *On the Margins of Discourse,* pp. 116-24.

theory in ways that would permit us to explore them more fruitfully in connection with whatever else we know about language, behavior, and culture. As already indicated, an alternative to the current narratological model would be one in which narratives were regarded not only as *structures* but also as *acts*, the features of which—like the features of all other acts—are functions of the variable sets of conditions in response to which they are performed. Accordingly, we might conceive of narrative discourse most minimally and most generally as verbal acts consisting of *someone telling someone else that something happened.* Among the advantages of such a conception is that it makes explicit the relation of narrative discourse to other forms of discourse and, thereby, to verbal, symbolic, and social behavior generally.

It is certainly the case that a narrative action may be accomplished, as Chatman and Bremond observe, through gestures, the display of pictures, and various other nonlinguistic modes and media. It is important to recognize, however, that, even in the narrow linguistic sense, narrative discourse may be composed of quite brief, bare, and banal utterances as well as such extensive and extraordinary tellings as might occupy 1,001 nights or pages. It is also important to recognize that narrative discourse is not necessarily—or even usually—marked off or segregated from other discourse. Almost any verbal utterance will be laced with more or less minimal narratives, ranging from fragmentary reports and abortive anecdotes to those more distinctly framed and conventionally marked tellings that we are inclined to call "tales" or "stories." Indeed, narrative discourse is, at one extreme, hardly distinguishable from description or simply assertion. That is, "telling someone that something happened" can, under certain circumstances, be so close to "saying that something is (or was) the case" that it is questionable if we can draw any logically rigorous distinction between them or, more generally, if any absolute distinction can be drawn between narrative discourse and any other form of verbal behavior.

To be sure, the common opposition of such terms as "report" versus "describe" and our ability to teach children to discriminate between such phrases as "telling a story" and "having a conversation" attest to the *functional* integrity and clarity of such categories and distinctions. Also, narratologists themselves may, in accord with their particular interests and purposes, always establish technically useful distinctions and demarcation points: stipulating, for example (as they sometimes do), that a telling counts as a hardcore narrative only if it describes a transition from one state to an antithetical state or only if the something-that-happened comprises at least two temporally sequential and causally related events. Nevertheless, it is also useful to be mindful of the continuities of narrative with all other discourse and of the extent to which these definitions and distinctions are drawn, not discovered, by narratologists.

A second, related advantage of conceiving of narrative this way—which is to say, as part of a *social transaction*—is that it encourages us to notice and explore certain aspects of narrative that tend to remain obscure or elusive when we conceive of it primarily as a kind of text or structure or any other form of detached and decontextualized entity.[20] For it suggests not only that every telling is produced and experienced under certain social conditions and constraints and that it always involves two parties, an audience as well as a narrator, but also that, as in any social transaction, each party must be individually motivated to participate in it: in other words, that each party must have some *interest* in telling or listening to that narrative.

In view of the fact that things are always happening, it may be reasonably asked why, in any given instance of narrative discourse, someone has chosen (or agreed) to tell someone else that something happened and why the latter has chosen (or agreed) to listen. The general answer to this question is that participation in the narrative transaction is sufficiently in the interest of each party to win out over all currently competing activities for both of them.[21] To make this answer useful, however, we must emphasize that the *nature* of the interests involved on both sides may vary greatly from one transaction to another as may the total *structure of motivation,* that is, the dynamics of the interaction between the narrator's interests and those of his audience. The significance of this emphasis for narrative theory is that it suggests why, in seeking to account for either the forms and features of individual narratives or the similarities and differences among sets of narratives,

20. For comparable reasons, a comparable conception of narrative is urged upon folklorists by Robert A. Georges in "Toward an Understanding of Story-Telling Events," *Journal of American Folklore* 82 (1969), 313-29.

21. This is an application to narrative discourse of a law that holds for all discourse, namely: *The fact that something is true is never a sufficient reason for saying it.* The law, some of its implications, and some other related aspects of the economics of verbal transactions are discussed in *On the Margins of Discourse,* pp. 16-17 and 85-106.

we might profitably direct our attention to the major variables involved in those transactions: that is, to the *particular* motives and interests of narrators and audiences and to the *particular* social and circumstantial conditions that elicit and constrain the behavior of each of them.

It is clear, for example, that quite *different* sets of interests, motives, and constraints would be involved in each of the following situations: (1) two junior executives in the club car of a commuter train pass the time by exchanging office anecdotes and off-color stories; (2) a radio broadcaster, during the evening news, reports to an audience of several hundred thousand Americans the events surrounding a military coup in central Asia; (3) a political prisoner, under torture, recounts to his interrogators the events leading to the formation of an underground organization; (4) an eminent scholar, whose previously published works have come under attack by revisionist historians, is typing out the final draft of his monumental new history of the antebellum South. It is also clear, I think, that the nature of the particular tale that got told in each of these situations would be a function of the sorts of conditions I have been emphasizing: the social and circumstantial context of the narrative and the structure of motivation that sustained the narrative transaction between the teller and his audience.

This last point can be elaborated just a bit. Any narrator's behavior will be constrained in part by various assumptions he will have made concerning his present or presumed audience's motives for listening to him. Although these assumptions will usually be formed on the basis of the narrator's prior knowledge of that audience, they may also be *re*-formed on the basis of feedback from the listener during the transaction itself. The efforts and ability of listeners to shape the tales they hear are evident from the sort of proddings and promptings that are familiar in face-to-face narrative transactions: "And then what happened? But what did he look like? Weren't you frightened? Why don't you just summarize that part? Yes, but what's the point?" I would emphasize, however, that face-to-face transactions are not exceptional in this respect. For we all inevitably learn to anticipate and re-create such reactions: this is, we learn in effect to impersonate our own audiences in advance, and, therefore, this sort of feedback controls the structure of our tales even when our audience is silent or absent—as when we compose narrative texts.

Of course, human motives and interests are always to some extent unpredictable or unknowable, even in face-to-face transactions. Moreover, individual narrators may vary greatly in their ability to gauge accurately their audience's interests and in their sensitivity and responsiveness to feedback. In any case, we know that not every story is "a good story." What may be added is that the conception of narrative discourse outlined here would permit us to describe the necessarily contingent *value* of a narrative in terms of how successfully it accommodates the interests of the parties involved in any of the particular transactions in which, at any time, it figures.

Pursuing this point, we might observe that under certain sets of constraints–for example, during a "prime-time" newscast–the interests of all the parties involved in the transaction will be served best by a narrative of utmost concision, while in other kinds of situations–for example, while attempting to "kill" or "pass" time on the commuter train–the total structure of motivation will accommodate and elicit the most highly elaborated development and extensive digression in the stories that are narrated. The general point suggested here is that the features of *individual* narratives, including literary and fictional works, can be described and accounted for as functions of certain variables that control the features of *all* narratives, including nonliterary and nonfictional ones, and, as a corollary, that similarities and differences among *sets* of narratives can be explored and explained on the basis of similarities and differences in the specific conditions that elicit and constrain them.

Two further methodological implications of the view of narrative outlined here may be briefly noted. One is that, in seeking to account for the distinctive nature, value, and effects of *fictional* narratives, we may take a less travelled road by observing that *the extent to which* a narrator takes or claims responsibility for the veridicality of his tale will serve different interests and, accordingly, have a different sort of value for himself and his audience depending on the nature and constraints of the transaction between them and, conversely, that different situations and structures of motivation will elicit and reward different *kinds and degrees* of truth claims. It is evident, for example, that claims and assumptions of veridicality will have a different significance for each of the parties in the transactions between the prisoner and his interrogators and between the historian and his readers. It is also evident that, under *some* conditions, as when we exchange narrative jokes or present certain other kinds of fictive tellings, such as fables and folktales, the interest and value of an account-of-something-that-happened may be altogether independent of the extent to which veridicality might be claimed for or attributed to it.[22] What these observations suggest is that a number of key problems of narrative theory that are commonly posed and analyzed in philosophic terms—for example, as questions of the "truth value" of fictional "propositions"—would be profitably reformulated in terms of the variable constraints, conventions, and dynamics of verbal transactions and explored accordingly. There is, in fact, no good reason to give logical priority or methodological sovereignty to the traditional preoccupations and procedures of philosophy when, as narrative theorists, we undertake to explore such problems.

Similarly, in seeking to identify the *functions* of storytelling for the individual narrator or his community, a recognition of the variety of possible narrative transactions and the range of interests that they may thereby serve should encourage us to acknowledge and explore the *multiplicity* of functions that may be performed by narratives generally and by any narrative in particular. We would, accordingly, be less likely to expect to find (or to claim to have identified) any single fundamental social purpose or psychological effect of narratives, whether it be to reflect reality or to supplement it, to reinforce ruling ideologies or to subvert them, to console us for our mortality or to give us intimations of our immortality.

I have offered here only a partial survey of how narratives might be explored from the alternative perspective outlined above, and that perspectives is itself only a partial one. My general purpose here, however, has not been to launch an altogether new or preemptive theory of narrative but to suggest that to the extent that our current theories remain tied to dualistic models of language and confined to the examination of decontextualized structures, they are deficient in descriptive subtlety and explanatory force—and, conversely, that our accounts of narrative, literary and other, will be richer, sturdier, and more coherent when they are developed as part of a *comprehensive* theory of narrative which reflects a better appreciation of the nature of verbal transactions and the dynamics of social behavior generally. In short, our current versions of narrative are not the whole story or the only story.

22. For a further discussion of the relation of fictive narratives to narrative discourse generally, see *On the Margins of Discourse*, pp. 127-31 and 194-97.